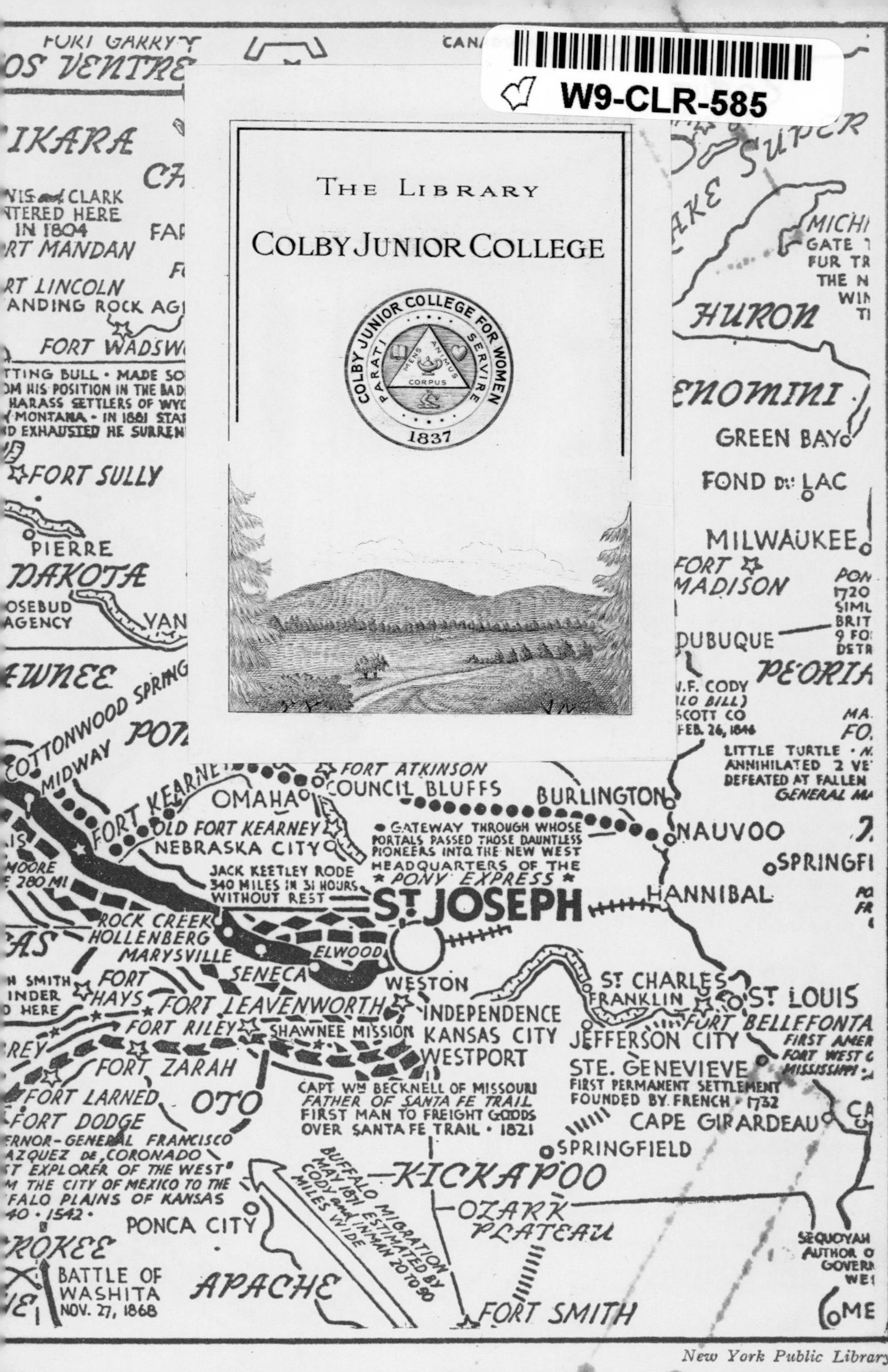

New York Public Library

BUFFALO BILL: King of the Old West

BUFFALO BILL:

by ELIZABETH JANE LEONARD
and JULIA CODY GOODMAN

edited by JAMES WILLIAMS HOFFMAN

King of the Old West

Biography of William F. Cody -

Pony Express Rider · Buffalo Hunter ·

Plains Scout & Guide · Master Showman

LIBRARY PUBLISHERS

New York

8 West 40th Street, New York 18, N. Y.
Library of Congress Catalog Card Number 55-10309

This is the first complete and authoritative biography of William F. Cody. It bears the full endorsement of the CODY FAMILY ORGANIZATION.
All illustrations without credits were given to Dr. E. J. Leonard by Julia Cody Goodman.
This book has been set in various sizes of Linotype Baskerville and P. T. Barnum display type faces.
It was designed by Myrtle Powell, and printed and bound by The Haddon Craftsmen, Inc., at Scranton, Penna.

This true history of the
Isaac and Mary B. Cody family—
especially of my brother
William Fredrick Cody, "Buffalo Bill"—
is affectionately dedicated to
my beloved children.

JULIA CODY GOODMAN

Culver Service

William F. Cody (Buffalo Bill)
photographed in 1878

Contents

Illustrations

Introduction

As the last survivor of the Isaac and Mary B. Cody family it gives me great pleasure to present to the public the first true history of our family, especially the life story of my famous brother, Colonel William F. Cody, Buffalo Bill.

As joint author of the book, *Buffalo Bill—King of the Old West* (*The Biography of William F. Cody*), I unhesitatingly chose Elizabeth Jane Leonard, a true Westerner, raised on the prairies not far from Scout's Rest Ranch, North Platte, Nebraska, and a novelist who is thoroughly conversant with every phase of Western life.

All of the so-called authentic life stories of Buffalo Bill have come short of the truth, some pathetically so.

For many years I have kept an accurate family history and Providence seems to have spared me, who am now past my three score years and ten, to give this history to the world. In submitting this offering, it is my desire that those who scan its pages may come to know the great scout as I knew him.

I want the world to become acquainted with the Buffalo Bill who loved and revered his mother and his mother's God; the boy who each month brought his earnings and laid them in his mother's lap.

I want the world to know the Buffalo Bill who said, "Julia, I love the mountains where I can be alone with God and commune with Him." I ask the reader to become acquainted with the grief-stricken father as he prayed that God might spare the life of his only son, Kit Carson Cody.

They lionized Colonel Cody as he rode his white charger gallantly through the throngs of New York, London and Paris. He was feted and praised by royalty, visited by kings and presidents, received by queens and princesses. Yet he was plain Buffalo Bill to his old friends the plainsmen; and whether at Buckingham Palace or home at Scout's Rest Ranch, he was the same modest, kind, cheerful man.

I want the world to know that with all his great heart he loved the red man, and although he had been forced to do his duty in battle or in self-defense it was always with reluctance. To the Indians he was their beloved long-haired chief *Pahaska*.

Lastly, I want the children to know that my brother loved children. He took great delight in relating to them some of his many thrilling experiences. Nor was he unmindful of less fortunate youngsters; many times he hired carriages to bring hundreds of children from orphan homes and institutions for the crippled and defective, that they too might enjoy the spectacle of the Wild West show.

JULIA CODY GOODMAN

Foreword

It has been my privilege to revise and rearrange for publication the manuscript, *Buffalo Bill—King of the Old West (The Biography of William F. Cody)*, by Julia Cody Goodman, eldest sister of William Frederick Cody, "Buffalo Bill." My one regret is that Mrs. Goodman is not alive to share in the pleasure of seeing the true and complete story of Colonel Cody and the Cody family made available to the American reading public.

The active collaboration between Julia Cody Goodman and myself, in the preparation of this manuscript, occurred over a period of more than a year, in person and by correspondence, until her death in Honolulu, Hawaii, on November 2, 1928. (She had gone to Hawaii to visit her son, Walter Goodman, and his family). Funeral services were held for her at the First Presbyterian Church, North Platte, Nebraska, on November 15, 1928, and she was buried at the North Platte cemetery. (I attended the last services.)

In the years that have followed Julia Cody Goodman's death I have checked and re-checked the details of the life of William F. Cody. But this research has merely been the frosting on the cake. The substance of this biography is rooted in the recollections of Mrs. Goodman, upon her phenomenal memory that re-created with minute exactness the feeling and the flavor of years gone by. In her conversations with me and letters to me about her brother, she remembered with ease specific dates of happenings on the frontier which had transpired 40 and 50 years before—dates which my own subsequent research with other source materials have completely verified. After I had completed the initial draft of the biography, Mrs. Goodman answered fully and vividly hundreds of questions that I put to her—answers that cleared up many minor points.

Buffalo Bill—King of the Old West represents, I believe, a vital part of the spiritual legacy that Julia Cody Goodman bequeathed to her children: daughters—Elizabeth Goodman Williamson and Josephine Goodman Thurston; sons—Edward R., Finley A., George C., Henry J., Captain Walter and Dr. William A. Goodman.

We are indebted to the following persons and organizations for the cooperation and information they provided:

Mr. J. G. Masters, principal of Central High School, Omaha, Nebraska; regional director of Oregon Trail Memorial Association; author of *Blazing the Trail.*

Mr. L. H. (Lute) North, captain of Pawnee Indian scouts; honorary member, Oregon Trail Memorial Association.

Mr. Gordon W. Lillie ("Pawnee Bill"), partner of William F. Cody in "Buffalo Bill's Wild West and Pawnie Bill's Far East."

Mr. A. W. Wilson, Le Claire, Iowa.

Mr. J. P. Hulet, Le Claire, Iowa.

Mr. Frank H. Sloan, Osage, Minnesota.

Mr. Paxton Cody, president of Cody Family Organization.

Mr. Luther M. Cody, secretary of Cody Family Organization.

Rev. W. O. Harper, first pastor of Presbyterian church, Cody, Wyoming.

Mrs. Josephine Goodman Thurston, daughter of Julia Cody Goodman.

Mrs. Frank Frederici, sister-in-law of William F. Cody.

Mrs. Irma Frederici Wienbarg, niece of Mrs. William F. Cody.

Mrs. Julia Nelson Goings, daughter of John Y. Nelson, famous squaw man.

Miss Doris Minney, writer for the *Omaha World-Herald.*

State Historical Societies of Colorado and Kansas.

The Academy of Sciences, Davenport, Iowa.

The United States War Department.

Outdoor Life Magazine.

It was thrilling to hear the matchless story of Buffalo Bill from the lips of his eldest sister. When she finished, I had the same feeling the audience used to experience at the close of a Wild West performance, when Colonel Cody—the hero of the vanishing frontier—gave a last salute from his white charger and backed out of the arena. At that moment something which had to do with romance, with dauntless courage, with youth and chivalry, left the scene, disappearing from our hearts and from our lives forever.

ELIZABETH JANE LEONARD

Editor's Note

Julia Cody Goodman played a unique role in the life of her famous brother, William F. Cody. She was his confidante, the one person he trusted above all others, the sympathetic sister who always stood by him in the many peaks and valleys of his bizarre career. As children they were close; as adults, however, they were often separated for years by continents and oceans, but it was to Julia that Buffalo Bill wrote constantly, telling her of the changing fortunes of the Wild West show, and it was from her that he received the welcome news of his family in the States, and of his various enterprises in Nebraska and Wyoming. Throughout his life, whenever he was able to take a vacation from hunting, scouting, soldiering, express riding, acting, guiding and starring in the Wild West, he headed home first to Julia.

From him, Mrs. Goodman was able to get an off-the-cuff, honest, immediate account of his adventures, his feelings, his defeats and his triumphs—before they were exaggerated by press agents or distorted by his detractors. These confidences from brother to sister form the backbone of the present biography. Julia Cody Goodman had an amazing memory, and in her conversations and correspondence with Elizabeth Jane Leonard was able to recall and recapture a great number of incidents and events in which she participated with her brother, or of which he had informed her shortly after they had occurred; numerous anecdotes appear here for the first time. In addition, she preserved many of the letters her brother had sent her through the years and rendered these available to Dr. Leonard. Contemporary attestation of Julia Cody Goodman's faculty for recalling events and facts in her brother's life is provided by Chauncey Thomas in his last interview with Buffalo Bill shortly before the great plainsman's death. Thomas wrote: "When he was lacking for a date or some childhood incident, it was supplied by the sister who raised him, Mrs. Goodman. . . . And right here I want to pay what tribute words will pay to this woman of the frontier. Her kind, like that of her noted brother, is almost gone, and will never be seen again, for that splendid type of womanhood was bred on the frontier, and nowhere else. And much that Buffalo Bill was, he owed to this sister-mother, Julia Cody."

As editor, I collated and arranged, after research and authentication, the material which Julia Cody Goodman had furnished and which Elizabeth Jane Leonard had written so well. My personal gratitude goes to all who gave me help and advice: to James, Robert and William Reich (Junior and Senior) for their special efforts during the summer of 1954; to Irene Reich for her aid in preparing and typing the final copy; to Claire Williams for putting certain special material pertaining to Cody on tape; to Martin L. Wolf, editor-in-chief of Library Publishers, for his kindness and cooperation; and to Jae Lyle for her work, encouragement and understanding.

JAMES WILLIAMS HOFFMAN

PROLOGUE

The Duel With Yellow Hand

YELLOW HAND, the great chief of the Cheyennes, cantered back and forth on the hill in front of his men. From left to right, and then back again he rode, resplendent in the brilliant ornaments reserved for a chieftain, bedecked in ceremonial robes and bedaubed with bright war paint.

Behind him, 800 of his braves waited to do battle. Shrieking bloodcurdling taunts and threats, the Indians glared at the enemy, 500 soldiers of the U. S. Army's Fifth Cavalry, drawn up in battle formation on the opposite hill. Impatiently they awaited Yellow Hand's signal to charge.

Suddenly the chief raised his hand, but not to beckon his forces forward. It was a completely different gesture, a quieting motion, bidding them be silent.

Stillness settled over the hills and over the valley. Only the occasional snorting of a horse—sometimes an Indian's pony, sometimes a trooper's mount—disturbed the tranquility.

Then Yellow Hand's voice rang out and his words lashed across the valley, reached the cavalrymen on the hill beyond, and then ricocheted back again, thrilling the Cheyennes with their audacity.

"I know you, *Pahaska.* I know you well. Come and fight with me! Sitting Bull has killed Custer. Now, I will kill you."

All of the troopers heard the chief's words, but few of them understood the Indian tongue. One of them caught the complete meaning, for the challenge was directed at him. He was *Pahaska,* Long-Yellow-Hair. To the soldiers of the regiment, to the thousands of men building the Kansas Pacific railroad who had depended upon his hunting prowess for fresh buffalo meat, and to the people of America who had followed his career as hunter, pony express rider, scout, stage driver, guide, Indian fighter and actor in their newspapers, magazines and dime novels, he was known formally as William F. Cody, affectionately as Buffalo Bill.

Slowly *Pahaska* urged his horse forward, carefully threading his way through his comrades. Cody sported a beaded buckskin suit and a bright crimson shirt, while the troopers wore variegated costumes, some corduroy, others buckskin, a few flannel.

No one can say for certain what Buffalo Bill was thinking as he moved toward Yellow Hand. But one thing is sure: he had responded violently to a word in the chief's challenge—the word "Custer." For etched in the scout's memory—as it was in every soldier of the regiment—was the fact that just three weeks previously the gallant, the brave and intrepid General Custer and practically his entire force had been massacred by Sitting Bull and his Sioux hordes at the battle of the Little Big Horn. The news of this decimation had been a terrible and profound shock to the entire nation, and especially to the soldiers of the Fifth Cavalry.

The victory over Custer by the Sioux had been a spark igniting the Indians to further rebellion against the whites. Dormant for years, suffering sullenly under the abuses, real and imagined, of their oppressors, the red men had suddenly revived their hopes of stopping the westward progress of the white men.

Sitting Bull had become the symbol for and spearhead of this redskin renaissance. Like a magnet of revolt he was attracting dissatisfied Indians into his orbit. To his camp in the Big Horn country were journeying entire tribes as well as solitary braves, all seeking to make common cause with the chief who had wiped out Custer.

It was to nip this revolt in the bud that Brevet-General Wesley Merritt and his 500 soldiers of the Fifth Cavalry had made a forced march to War Bonnet Creek to intercept the 800 Cheyenne warriors before they could join Sitting Bull.

On July 17, 1876 Buffalo Bill, scouting ahead of Merritt's troops, had located the Cheyennes. Yellow Hand then issued his challenge to Buffalo Bill to engage in a personal duel, and Buffalo Bill had agreed to fight.

The Indian chief and the cavalry scout urged their steeds forward. Both horses broke into a gallop. The two antagonists sped across the valley toward each other. When they were just thirty yards apart, both raised their rifles at the same moment and fired simultaneously. Yellow Hand's horse fell dead beneath him and the warrior rolled clear of the carcass. A second later Cody's horse stepped into a gopher hole and pitched the scout over his head.

The two men scrambled to their feet and grabbed their rifles. Again two shots rang out as one. Yellow Hand's bullet whistled harmlessly over Buffalo Bill's head. The scout's shot sped directly to its mark, piercing the chief's chest.

The Indian reeled and fell. Cody ran forward and stabbed him through the heart with his long knife. He then removed the chief's war bonnet and scalped him.

Infuriated at the death of their beloved chief, the Cheyenne braves charged down the hill, intent upon cutting off Buffalo Bill from the rest of the command. General Merritt ordered Colonel Mason and Company K to the rescue. As the soldiers approached, Buffalo Bill swung Yellow Hand's topknot and bonnet in the air and shouted, "The first scalp for Custer!"

The Indians broke and ran. For thirty-five miles the troopers followed hard at their heels, driving them into the Red Cloud Agency. Thousands of redskins had gathered here planning to push on to Sitting Bull's camp but the sight of the fleeing Cheyennes suddenly in their midst seemed to discourage them. The soldiers of the Fifth Cavalry, inspired by the heroism of Buffalo Bill, had by this one action broken the back of the Indian rebellion and avenged the massacre of General Custer and his soldiers.

The heart of the nation which had despaired at the death of Custer, soared in response to the triumph of Buffalo Bill and the Fifth Cavalry. Cody's name was on everyone's lips. Where previously he had been admired and praised, he now was idolized. Buffalo Bill was the hero of the hour.

The public wanted to know everything about him: his parentage, his childhood, his education, his Civil War service, his scouting adventures, his buffalo hunting record, his pony express experiences, his Indian fights, his show business triumphs, his present activities and his future plans.

The press agents and pulp writers, the hacks and historians, the myth makers and maligners, the sugar-coaters and scandalmongers all wrote press handouts and dime novels, magazine pieces and learned articles, panegyrics and diatribes, whitewashes and scurrilous attacks in which Buffalo Bill was presented as god or devil, superhero or charlatan.

Among all the millions of words written then and since about Cody, it is most difficult to find the complete picture of a man—not all white or all black, but containing the shadings, gradations, contradictions and confusions which characterize the life and career of any public figure. The question that the public asked in the mid-eighties still remains to be answered: what is the real and full story of frontier scout William F. Cody, the man called Buffalo Bill?

CHAPTER 1

The First Years

IN THE EARLY summer of 1839 a beautiful, young, eighteen-year-old girl, Mary Bunting Laycock, was journeying slowly down the Ohio River in an excursion boat. This was a wonderful vacation for Mary. As the steamer chugged along and she watched the murky waters of the Ohio churning out behind in the wake of the vessel, it seemed to her as if all the worries and troubles of her early years were also being washed away into the past. Ahead lay clear, open water; new hope and new life were just around the bend.

Mary's mother had died when her daughter was very young. After his wife's death the father soon remarried. A seaman, he was drowned in the Atlantic during a terrible storm, when Mary was just fifteen. After his death, the stepmother ignored Mary and lavished all of her love upon another daughter, Eliza. She soon packed Mary off to live with an aunt. The rejected girl was shuttled off again, this time to her brother William Laycock, a Cincinnati stock dealer.

For the next three years she lived in her brother's house. He tried his best to give her affection, but he was a very busy man and the young girl was extremely lonely. To cheer her up—and when he could find the time—her brother would tell stories about their ancestors. Her mother, whose maiden name was Bunting, had been descended from the prominent Bunting family of Derbyshire, England, whose members were among the colonists sent to the New World by William Penn in the years between 1680 and 1690. He would repeat the account, passed on from generation to generation, of how Josiah Bunting had witnessed the famous treaty Penn had made with the Indians. And most often he would regale her with tales of her father's adventures on all the Seven Seas. This brave mariner had ridden out the severe winds and stood up against the violent storms until the most treacherous of seas, the Atlantic, had rebelled against his mastery and had sent him to his death.

No matter how vividly William Laycock brought the past to life, it remained the past and Mary was eager for life itself.

Life for her at the moment represented the excitement and conviviality of the excursion steamboat. In a brief time she had made many new friends. A distant relative, a married woman who had gone with her on the trip, was proving to be a pleasant surprise indeed, much more companion than chaperon. In fact it was this woman who for a lark had suggested that they visit a fortuneteller at the next stop. Shortly after the boat pulled up to the landing at Louisville, Kentucky, the two ladies hurried ashore and sought out a Gypsy seeress who had been recommended to them by their fellow passengers. Just before they entered her parlor they agreed to confuse her by saying that Mary was married and that the relative was not.

No sooner did they actually make these statements than the prophetress saw through their deception. "Leave my house," she cried. "You try to fool me. You tell me lies."

The visitors soothed her by opening their pocketbooks and pressing money into her hand. First, she told the older woman's fortune. Mary was so excited at the prospect of having her own future disclosed that she hardly heard a word that was said. Now, it was her turn. The fortuneteller shuffled the cards, turned them face up on the table and then looked searchingly into the young girl's eyes.

"You are going to meet a man on this trip," she said. "A fine man. A kind man. He will love you. You will love him. You will be married. Together, you will go far away to lands that lie beyond the setting sun. You will be a good wife and a good mother. Your first child will be a son. You must help him to spread the word of God. Your next child will be a girl. Your third child will be a boy. You should give him to the world. He will be famous. His name will be known to all—young and old, rich and poor. People will love and praise him. He may even be president of the United States."

The two ladies left the fortuneteller and returned to the boat. Each assured the other that she "really didn't believe what the Gypsy said," but secretly Mary hoped and prayed that the words of prophecy would come true.

A day or two later Mary was introduced to Isaac Cody, who with his brother Elijah was en route to Missouri from Cincinnati, where Elijah planned to settle and build a new home. Mary and Isaac soon were inseparable. Loneliness gave way to love.

Reluctantly, they parted—Isaac to accompany his brother, Mary to return to her own brother's house in

Ohio. Letters went back and forth between the two, letters that made the late summer, the long autumn and the endless winter seem shorter. In the spring of 1840 Isaac Cody returned to Cincinnati and he and Mary Bunting Laycock were married. And like thousands of other Americans they prepared to head westward to carve out a new life for themselves in yet unsettled land.

Isaac's brother had asked them to join him in Missouri, but the newly-weds preferred to strike out on their own. They sailed down the Ohio to the Mississippi and then up the Mississippi to the Iowa Territory. They were overwhelmed by what they saw there: verdant forests which had yet to be ribboned by the farmer's plow. Rich land, fertile land—guarded on its eastern and western limits by rugged bluffs which served as ramparts against the mighty Mississippi and its turbulent tributary, the Missouri.

For a short time they lived at Davenport, where Isaac eked out a precarious existence trading with the Indians. But neither Isaac nor Mary was happy. Both wanted something permanent and substantial. Finally they found what they desired, a beautiful plot of land in Scott County, Iowa, two miles west of the town of Le Claire. Isaac immediately staked claim to this piece of land. Here he built a comfortable log cabin and here Mary Cody, the mature woman, found that complete happiness which had been denied her as a girl.

In 1841 a son was born to Isaac and Mary Cody, whom they named Samuel. A second child, a daughter, was born in 1843. They called her Julia Melvina. And on February 26, 1846 a second son, William Frederick, came into the world.

Thus, "Napsinekee Place," the name by which the Cody homestead was known, became the birthplace of the boy who was destined to be one of frontier America's most famous heroes, Buffalo Bill.

When Billy was just a few months old, Mrs. Cody entertained some of her friends from Le Claire by taking them rowing. The little boy and his sister Julia were permitted to go along. Somehow the small boat capsized and the whole party was dumped into the water. Julia snatched up her little brother and held him safely over her head until help arrived.

In 1847 Isaac Cody contracted to survey and to oversee a 600-acre tract of land twelve miles west of Le Claire, on the Wapsi River, for Senator Breckenridge, of Kentucky. He was also to erect a large stone house on the premises for the use of himself and his family.

Breckenridge Place was a typical western farm. As soon as young Billy was old enough to toddle around, he followed his father everywhere as he went about the business of managing farm activities. Early in the morning he would dog his father's heels, as he visited the fields to supervise the planting. To break the land, 25 separate plows were used, each drawn by a yoke of oxen, one driver to each team. Other men followed, dropping seed corn into the fresh furrows. And behind both crews rode Mr. Cody, with Billy perched on the saddle horn, watching the long line of ox teams creep slowly across the field—turning 25 ribbons of green earth downward. As the boy and his father rode back and forth, up and down, they could hear other men, all strong, sturdy, dependable German laborers, working in the quarry, getting stone for the new house. Late in the afternoon the tall man and the small boy would go to the big barn. There they waited until some of the farm hands would drive the cows in from the lower pasture. Then, as twilight settled over fields and pastures and house and barn, they would stand by as the men milked the cows—milk for the Cody family, milk for the farm workers, milk to be sold to the people in surrounding communities.

Billy Cody's wilderness kindergarten lay even beyond these cultivated, domesticated limits. The farm itself stretched from the river to the bluffs. The hills were heavily timbered and full of bears, wild hogs, deer, wildcats and other animals. Often the young boy would gaze wide-eyed, with his sister Julia and his brother Samuel, as wild deer raced down from the bluffs and skipped effortlessly over the fences which Isaac Cody had built around the farm. Occasionally little Billy disappeared and a frantic Julia or Samuel would intercept him as he determinedly headed for the hills intent upon visiting the home of the wild deer.

As many times as they would hasten after their errant brother, just as many times would he tag after them. Julia would start out to school in the morning and Billy would follow her. She didn't have the heart to force him to return home. So off they would go, the enrolled student and her small shadow, until they reached the one-room schoolhouse. No sooner were they seated in the classroom than the little boy fell asleep. Waking with a start, he would listen quietly to the proceedings for a few minutes. Soon bored, he would dip his fingers into the inkstand and start to finger-paint on the rough-hewn, homemade benches.

The first few times this happened, the schoolmistress tried to stop him, but she soon found that the youngster had unlimited resources for mischief. Thereafter, she fought a rear guard action, attempting only to minimize the damage.

Her forbearance could be explained in part by the fact that Isaac Cody paid the greater part of her wages. Few of the other parents were interested in spending money to give their children an education. Further than this, Mary Cody, whose education was far above average, had been unofficially designated by the local school board to examine all applicants for the position of teacher. Under these circumstances, it was little wonder that the teacher handled Billy with kid gloves.

In 1849 the Cody family pulled up stakes once again and moved back to the village of Le Claire. They occupied the same home which Isaac had built for them a few years before.

As he bridged the difficult years from infancy to boyhood, Billy Cody's interests and activities began to include much more than his immediate home and family. He found the town of Le Claire a fascinating one. It was an important river port, a key point on the Mississippi, at the head of the Rock Island Rapids.

Billy and his cronies in the barefoot boy brigade made their headquarters in the branches of a stately elm which overarched a large plot of ground a few rods upstream from the river landing place. From this vantage point they watched the comings and goings of steamboats on the river as they stopped at Le Claire for a while before bucking the rapids or after having traversed them. The river men hurried ashore from these boats and gathered under the tree. So popular a rendezvous did the old elm become that the river hands dubbed it the "Green Tree Hotel."

The little Tom Sawyers and Huck Finns, hidden in the tree above the heads of the congregators, listened in amazement to the stories, boasts and tales of adventure told by the men below.

Tiring of this, they pretended they were pirates on a renegade ship, and that the treetop was a crow's-nest. The steamboats on the river were the vessels of the enemy. The heavy stone walls which followed the river or bordered the rude slab walks that mounted the steep bluffs were the ramparts of the town itself, which the pirates planned to sack once they had boarded the "navy's ships." The business houses and dwellings in the village, many constructed of iron-stained Niagara limestone from the nearby quarries, loomed like ancient castles, fair prey for marauding buccaneers.

Mark Twain, in his book *Life on the Mississippi,* immortalized ante-bellum life in Le Claire. Young Billy Cody was also to be honored in later years because of his youthful association with the village of Le Claire. For the old green elm still stands today, and under it there is a granite monument, erected by another of the youngsters who played in its branches in those faraway days. The little fellow's nickname was in those early days "the runt." The inscription on the granite slab reads:

Dedicated to
Col. Wm. F. Cody,
"Buffalo Bill"
By his friend and
boyhood playmate,
Joe Barnes.
Erected in 1924.[1]

Thus did Joe Barnes, chronicler of the early history of the Mississippi Valley, and one of Buffalo Bill's first and closest friends, pay tribute to the youth with whom he had played in the green tree.

In the year 1848 a fever erupted in California, a peculiar fever not named or catalogued in medical books, which was transmitted from man to man not by germs, not by viruses, not by any means known to science, but by the spoken word. In one year's time the disease spread to all sections of the United States. During the summer of 1849 alone it is estimated that 80,000 men succumbed to this epidemic.

This mass malady—more malignant than the bubonic plague—which afflicted the nation, was gold fever. A fever, because the excitement engendered by the California Gold Rush was completely disproportionate to the actual amount of yellow dust available. The grocer told the butcher, "I hear they struck gold in California"; the butcher told the baker, "There's gold all over the state, all ya gotta do is stake your claim and start diggin' "; the baker told the grocer, "Gold dust is everywhere, coverin' the roads, and the farms and the woods. Just scoop it up and it's yours"; and the grocer told the barber, "The nuggets are as big as tomatoes, and they're easier to pick." And all of these men, and their customers too, left the shops, deserted the factories and fled the farms to join the Argonauts, long trains of white-sailed wagons, going west to gather the golden fleece.

Isaac Cody was not immune to the fever. In 1849 he too decided to go to the California gold fields and arranged to cast his lot with a party of twenty men from the Le Claire district. He bought a complete new wagon and all the necessary gear and awaited the arrival of his neighbors' wagons. In the interim he took ill. His friends delayed their departure for several days but Isaac did not improve and upon his physician's advice he reluctantly abandoned the project. The Le Claire contingent finally started out without him.

They became part of a seemingly endless caravan pushing its way towards the West Coast. From every state, every territory and every section of the nation individual wagons, groups of wagons and fleets of wagons funneled into the mainstream of traffic. By April 1, 20,000 people had gathered along the banks of the Missouri River ready to take the overland trail, 1,000 miles of which was a trackless waste inhabited by tribes of hostile Indians. The 20,000 gold seekers were mobilized to begin the journey as soon as the spring grass would make its appearance to sustain the mules and oxen.[2]

About 2,850 wagons had crossed the river at just one point, St. Joseph, Missouri, by May 18. More than 4,000 wagons had passed Fort Kearney on the south side of the river by June 1. All in all, from 8,000 to 10,000 wagons traversed the trail that year.[3]

A dread scourge of the body, Asiatic cholera, attacked those who were already suffering from the disease of the mind, gold fever. Poorly prepared and ill-outfitted in their eagerness to snatch the pot of gold at the end of the trail, vast hordes of emigrants fell victims of this killer. Once cholera had struck, entire wagon trains were decimated. Freshly dug graves soon lined both sides of the great roadway. On the flat prairie just east of Old Fort Laramie the bodies of the dead piled up along the trailway while the volunteer gravediggers worked double shifts through the night to give them a decent burial. At least 5,000 people,[4] and probably many more, died as a result of the ravages of cholera.

From time to time Isaac Cody received news of the La Claire wagoners. They had fought off a number of Indian attacks. Some of their group had been wracked with cholera. A few of them had met death from this plague in the desert wastes along the Platte River. The remaining members of the party finally fell in with a company of Mormons and spent the winter in Salt Lake City, Utah, as the trail across the mountains was blocked by the heavy snows. Only six of the original twenty who had left Le Claire in the early part of 1849 finally reached California in the spring of 1850.

All this commotion about gold sifted through to the children. But little Billy's attitude was more skeptical than the other kids' and a whole lot saner than most adults'.

He "borrowed" an old franc from his mother, a prized possession, when she wasn't around. Then he went down to the river where the barefoot brigade was playing. Soon he was leading the gang in a game of follow-the-leader. Led them he did, out on a long plank which extended a few feet over the water.

He stopped at the end, stooped over suddenly as if he had lost something, and then announced, "Fellows, I've dropped mother's coin in the water. It's worth a terrible lot."

The entire crew took off shoes and plunged in. Billy remained perched on the plank, directing the diving operation. "Think it's over there," he yelled. "Might be over here. Stay down longer, Jim. Don't let Runt beat you to it, Bob."

For an hour he hollered commands and suggestions. For

an hour the boys dived until they were shivering like sheared beavers. Finally they called a halt to the search when darkness made it impossible to see.

Just as they were putting on their shoes to go home, Mrs. Cody, alerted by Samuel, arrived at the scene. "Willy," she asked, "did you drop my franc in the river?"

The boy smiled but didn't answer.

"Willy Cody, come here at once!" she said. "Stealing is bad. Making your friends work for you while you stand by idly is worse. Not answering your mother when she asks you a question is the most terrible thing of all."

The boy obeyed and Mrs. Cody took off her slipper to give him a good tanning. Just as she was about to deliver the first blow, he pulled the coin from his pocket and said, "Here it is, mother. I was only teaching the boys how to hunt gold in California."

Mary Cody, who had been secretly very happy that her husband hadn't been able to join the other men from Le Claire on their Hegira to the West, laughed and slipped the shoe back on her foot.

After recovering from the illness that had forced him to cancel his trip to the Coast, Isaac swapped his covered wagon for a stagecoach and contracted to carry the U.S. mail from Davenport, Iowa, to Chicago, Illinois. Once a week he returned to the village, and the children looked forward to the arrival of the brightly-colored coach, pulled by four magnificent horses, which meant that father was home again. Mr. Cody operated the stage line successfully until 1850, when he was elected to the Iowa legislature (Iowa had been admitted to the Union in 1846).

The harsh reality of school finally intruded itself into Billy Cody's happy existence. Now that he had to attend officially, he didn't like school. Being confined indoors didn't make sense when there were enemy ships to be sunk and quails to be trapped. Billy's three-legged dog Skip agreed with his master. Daily he followed the boy to school as previously Billy himself had toddled after his sister Julia. Once inside the schoolroom the dog became extremely fidgety. He had a disconcerting habit of climbing up on one of the writing tables and gazing soulfully out of the window. This habit was catching. Soon dog and pupils were all looking out at the tempting woods and fields which bordered the classroom.

This had to be stopped. The teacher couldn't keep Skip out of the building—he would climb in one of the windows if she barred the door—and when she closed all the entrances, he pawed at the door and scratched at the windows and whined for his master trapped inside. In desperation she would send Billy out to quiet the animal. The only way he could effectively do this was to take Skip away from the school. Which was what Skip wanted, and what Billy wanted too.

Three-legged Skip died and was replaced by four-legged Turk, a large, strong dog. Mrs. Cody was glad that the children had such a powerful pet, for in 1852 the family had moved again to another large farm, the Walnut Grove, six miles west of Breckenridge Place, and south of the Wapsi River. The children needed a protector, because the woods here abounded in wild hogs. She felt that the children were safe as long as Turk was with them.

Julia Cody Goodman recalls this period vividly. Her father again employed only German labor and the farm was known as the German Village. An American-born foreman, Mr. Agerman, served as interpreter between the working crew and the Cody family. Mr. Agerman taught Julia enough German so that she could order the meals and supervise the other household chores. Samuel and Julia were kept busy helping their mother with the innumerable tasks necessary to keep a house in order.

In the beginning Billy was also given a few simple duties. But just as in the schoolroom when he had constantly peered out of the windows at the wilderness world beyond, in this instance too he went about his work ritualistically, fumbling with his hands while his thoughts and his heart were elsewhere—in the forest outside. Though no precise words were ever spoken, the Codys released him from four-walled bondage, and he spent his days roaming the fields and woods. Julia remembers that he would hunt snakes, rabbits, squirrels and other small game, and that Turk would kill the animals and the two would bring home what they had bagged. It was the family's unvoiced opinion that Billy Cody was a genuine child of nature and that his personality grew and found its fullest expression where life was at its wildest and freest.

In addition to Billy, Samuel and Julia, the Cody children now also included Martha, Eliza Alice, Helen (Laura Ella), and Mary Hanna (May). Although Martha was Isaac's daughter by a former marriage, she was loved dearly by everyone in the family. Julia knew her as a sweet child, a blessing to Mary Cody and a most affectionate sister.

Tragedy struck the Cody family in the month of September, 1853, when the eldest son Samuel died in his twelfth year of life.

Mr. Cody was away from home attending an old-line Whig convention at a crossroads tavern known as "Sherman's" so that Willy and Samuel were given the task, usually reserved for Mr. Cody, of going out on horseback to round up the cows. Samuel's mount was a vicious mare which his mother had warned him against riding. The horse had thrown many men, but Samuel loved to ride the animal.

The boys reached the schoolhouse just as the children were being dismissed for the day. The high-spirited horse, frightened at the noise made by the scurrying kids, reared and plunged but failed to unseat its rider.

"You can't do it, Betsey," Samuel yelled. "You thought you could throw me but you can't."

These were Samuel Cody's last words, for the mare reared up again and fell back upon him.

His family and friends were notified immediately. Samuel was taken to a nearby house where doctors worked over him all night. He never regained consciousness and died the following morning.

The heartbroken family laid his body to rest in Long Grove Cemetery, Scott County, Iowa. Although only a lad, Willy Cody was grief-stricken by his brother's death. After the funeral he and Julia slipped off to the old swing in the orchard and together talked and cried about their absent brother. The tragedy brought Julia and Willy even closer together.

Many years later William F. Cody, known far and wide as Buffalo Bill, arranged that a monument be erected on Samuel Cody's grave.

Her eldest son's death was a terrible shock to Mary Cody. So shaken was she by his passing that doctors advised a change of scene. Isaac Cody was immediately agreeable and once again the Cody family looked westward towards a new life.

In his occasional role of politician Isaac had made many influential friends in Washington. These men informed him that a bill was pending which would open up the territories of Kansas and Nebraska for settlement. This vast area was still Indian country but the inexorable expansion of the white man was once again threatening to drive the red men from their lands and push them farther westward. These new territories, so the rumor went, would be open and available, free of charge, to whomever had the initiative to stake a claim.

At first the Codys favored Nebraska, but their decision was reversed when they received a letter from Elijah Cody, Isaac's brother, who was living in Weston, Missouri—a thriving border town on the Missouri River just across from Fort Leavenworth, Kansas. Elijah, who was becoming wealthy selling supplies and dealing in hemp, wrote in glowing terms about the Indian country of Kansas, territory he knew well because he maintained a trading post there, where he traded with the Potawatamis.

This letter was the clincher. Kansas it was to be. Isaac sold his land,[5] disposed of his business interests, visited his friends and neighbors, especially Joe Barnes and his family, for a fond farewell.

Then the entire Cody family engaged in a hectic flurry of packing, crating, purchasing and preparing. On the final day before their departure Willy Cody climbed up into the branches of the green tree for the last time. He looked out at the boats on the river, but try as he might he was unable to transform them into pirate ships. He gazed for a moment in the general direction of the graveyard where Samuel was buried, but he couldn't focus and his eyes brimmed with tears. Then he scrambled down from the tree and headed for home.

As he neared the farm a great excitement welled up in his body, and his heart beat so hard that he was certain everyone in the town could hear it. Tomorrow was the day. Tomorrow he was going to Kansas. Tomorrow the great journey was to begin that would end in the wild country to the west where the red men lived; fierce Indians and savage Indians who could scare even the bravest pirate.

CHAPTER 2

Bleeding Kansas

IT WAS on a beautiful spring day in April, 1854, that Isaac Cody and his family set out for Kansas. The Codys were traveling in style. If they hadn't seen their old neighbor Isaac Cody at the reins, the good people of Le Claire might well have mistaken the entire procession for the equipage and attendant wagons of a royal party.

The lead carriage, Isaac's pride and joy, had been specially made in the East. Elegantly upholstered, polished so that it glittered in the sunlight, this coach was drawn by a team of thoroughbred horses whose silver-mounted trappings jangled merrily as they moved along. Ensconced within were Mary Cody and her daughters.

Stringing out behind were two prairie schooners, one lighter vehicle, and one very heavy wagon pulled by four horses, containing the trunks, baggage and luggage.

Billy Cody had been appointed official "scout" for the journey. Proudly he rode his pony at the head of the procession, with Turk, the German mastiff, trotting at his side.

In keeping with the impressiveness of their carriage the Codys didn't deign to camp by the side of the road, which was the usual custom, but spent the nights at hotels and wayside taverns. This was fine for the ladies, but Billy would have preferred to rough it in the open air.

The family stopped at Keokuk, Iowa, for a brief rest. When they were ready to start up again, neither Willy nor Turk could be found. The local police finally located them. The boy and his dog were in the middle of a circle of admiring youngsters, and the boy was telling them how he was on his way to Kansas to hunt big game and fight Indians.

The first halt in Missouri was made at a farmhouse which had many small buildings in the rear. A servant who greeted them said he was certain that the mistress of the house would not allow overnight guests.

Isaac insisted upon speaking to this lady. When informed that he was the brother of Elijah Cody of Weston, whom she knew well, she invited the entire family to stay the night.

All of the servants were Negro slaves. They were the first people with black skins that the Cody children had ever seen. What impressed Willy was not their different color, but the abject way in which they did the bidding of their mistress, responding quickly—but with heads down—to her every order.

The next night was spent with a much poorer family. The evening meal of corn bread and fat pork did not satisfy the children's appetites, and Isaac walked to a nearby country store and bought food which the Codys then divided with their hosts.

Towards dusk of the following day Willy was sent on ahead to find a suitable lodging place. When the main party caught up to him, he was standing at the doorway of a large farmhouse conversing with a lady. She informed Isaac Cody that she wasn't in the habit of accommodating guests, but since he had such a bright and persuasive son, she could not refuse.

Mrs. Burns, for this was her name, also knew Elijah Cody—in fact she knew him very well. Her husband, before his death, had been for many years Elijah's partner in the mercantile business, and her sons still maintained this partnership with Isaac's brother.

Early the next morning the Cody family, accompanied by their kind hostess, drove the last 20 miles of the journey to Elijah's home at Weston. The brothers had not seen each other for 15 years and there was great rejoicing at the reunion. Elijah insisted that his visitors remain as his guests until the Kansas-Nebraska Bill, opening up the territory for settlement, was officially passed.

Isaac and Elijah sat up far into the night talking. Mostly they discussed the challenge of Kansas, and the opportunities to be found there. It was virgin country, unsullied by settlers, yet unprotected by civilization and order. "Law and morality never crossed the Missouri River. So it was said in the 'Fifties."[1] Only 800 white men, of the thousands of pioneers who had forded the river, had stopped in Kansas and these were mainly squatters who had no legal right there, as well as agents and missionaries.

In their conversation the two men touched many times on the fact that the new region which was to be opened up for settlement had been given to the exiled Eastern Indian tribes years before by Federal officials who had promised that the Kansas-Nebraska strip was to be theirs, and theirs alone, forever. The legal invasion of this territory by the white man, the brothers knew, was bound to bring trouble.

With the coming of morning, Willy and his sisters set about exploring the house and grounds. They familiarized themselves with every room, from cellar to attic, but the one thing they could not become accustomed to—and here they were undoubtedly echoing the free spirit of their father—was that Elijah owned slaves, and that they were waited on hand and foot by colored servants.

Willy soon knew the roads and river landings of Weston as well as he had known those in Le Claire. It was a very busy town, he found out, where most of the up-river traffic halted, where overland caravans were outfitted, and from which cross-river ferries shuttled regularly to the Kansas side.

The Cody brothers and their wives decided to take a trip to the Kansas country, where Isaac was to make a preliminary examination of the area, preparatory to staking out his claim, and incidentally to trade with the Indians from his wagon. The children were to stay home but at the last minute Willy wangled an invitation to go along.

Their first stop was at Fort Leavenworth, home base of a regiment of cavalry under the command of General Harney. Young Willy was tremendously thrilled when his father pointed to the blockhouse and said, "Son, you now see a military fort for the first time in your life."[2] And a real fort it certainly was. The dragoons were holding mounted drill, their sabers flashing as they galloped. Infantrymen marched back and forth in close-order formation. Caissons drawn by six-mule teams wheeled across the parade ground. Westerners in slouch hats and buckskin shirts and breeches, and Indians—Choctaws, Delawares, Kickapoos and others—lounged around watching the soldiers and the visitors.

And the visitors themselves were something to see. Like Willy, they were all amazed by the hustle and bustle of the fort. Many of them were crowded into large commercial omnibuses with which some far-sighted entrepreneur made regular trips at so much per head to the military installation. Others rode to every corner of the outpost in private carriages. The whole gathering was in a gay holiday mood.

For the soldiers, however, these drills represented more than pomp and circumstance and play and ceremony. They were rehearsals for the real thing.

To the west, 1,000 miles away in Utah, the Mormons were a growing menace. Brigham Young was defying Uncle Sam and a showdown between his followers and Government troops appeared imminent.

The rumblings of distant Indian war chariots could be heard to the north and west. Embittered by the broken promises of the white man, the redskins had decided to make a stand against further encroachments on their hunting grounds.

Free-soilers and pro-slavers poised on the Kansas-Nebraska border, both groups eager to dominate the politics of the new territory. The struggle between these factions threatened to be a long and bloody one.

At any moment the troops at the fort might be called upon to hurry to any of the potential theaters of conflict.

It was a reluctant Willy Cody who was almost forcibly pulled away from the excitement of Fort Leavenworth. Everyone in the party returned to Weston, except father and son who continued on their tour of inspection. After climbing a steep hill, Isaac and Willy came upon a vista wondrous to behold. In Willy's own words, "We looked down upon the most beautiful valley I have ever seen. It was about twelve miles long and five miles wide. The different tributaries of Salt Creek came down from the range of hills at the southwest, and at the foot of the valley another small river, Plum Creek, followed. The bluffs fringed with trees, clad in their full foliage, added greatly to the picturesqueness of the scene."[3]

Moving across the face of the valley like landlocked sailboats were white-covered prairie schooners from which flushed young faces peeped out beneath the canvas.[4] Gaudy-colored stagecoaches veered by. Huge bull-trains rattled along. Eight heavily-armed men rode on every stagecoach, each carrying a 136-shot repeating rifle to insure the safety of the carriage, its passengers, and the six Missouri mules that pulled it along.

Travelers, land seekers, soldiers, trappers, hunters, guides, visiting dignitaries, belated gold prospectors, politicos, gamblers—respectable people and riffraff—all used Fort Leavenworth as their last port of call before entering Salt Creek Valley from which they headed out across the great plains to distant frontier posts and outlying territories.

Isaac and Billy Cody fell in love with the valley at first sight and this great gateway to the West was to become their permanent home.

They spent the night camping in the valley, and the following day Isaac began trading with the Kickapoos, Potawatamis, Delawares, Choctaws, and other Indians in the area. One of the first trades he made was for two ponies, immediately named Prince and Dolly, which were given to Willy. They were wild creatures that snorted and ran away as soon as the boy approached. Finally two lariats were thrown deftly over their necks and they were dragged back to camp.

As the Codys approached their campfire, a herd of three or four hundred horses suddenly appeared on the California trail, coming in from the west. Three mounted men urged the herd forward. One of the riders broke away from the rest and rode towards the Codys, while the others corralled the horses and prepared to make camp for the night.

The stranger, a tall, well-built, pleasant-faced youth sporting a California sombrero and a full suit of beaded buckskin, slipped gracefully from his mount, and walked over to the man and the boy.

Grinning, he said, "I think your ponies are a trifle wild."

"They certainly are," answered Willy, "and I'm afraid no one will ever put a saddle on that one," pointing to Prince.

"I'd like to try riding him," the stranger said.

Given the youngster's consent, he approached Prince, and making a half hitch with his lariat, threw the rope over the animal's nose. Then he jumped onto his back.

The pony reared and pitched, scuttled sideways like a crab, tried to rub the rider off against a tree, but to no avail. The stranger just wrapped his long legs tighter around Prince's belly and rolled with every motion. Little by little the horse's jerky movements lessened. After not many minutes had passed, the pony slowed down to a walk, as docile as Turk after he had gulped down a big meal, and the stranger slid from his back and handed the lariat to Willy.

"He's all yours, boy, now anyone can ride him."

Isaac was very interested in the young man and questioned him at some length. He learned that he had run away from home while still a boy, had sailed all over the world, and had traveled with a circus as a featured bareback rider. In California he had signed on as a rider to help bring a herd of wild horses from the West Coast to the Eastern states. This cross-country trip was just what he wanted, he said, as it gave him the chance to visit his folks in Cleveland for the first time since he had left home years before. He also planned to drop in on his uncle in Weston.

Further inquiry revealed a fantastic coincidence: the young man's uncle was Elijah Cody.

"If Elijah Cody is your uncle, I am too," said Isaac. "You must be the long-lost Horace Billings."[5]

The two men embraced joyfully and tears appeared in Mr. Cody's eyes. For Horace was like a young Lazarus come back from the dead. The entire family had been convinced that he was lost at sea, and had long since mourned his death.

The next day the Codys and their unexpected guest returned to Weston. Billings was mounted on a fine California steed with a silver-studded saddle and bridle. "I envied his appearance," said Willy Cody, "and my ambition just then was to become as skillful a horseman as he was."[6]

For the following few days Julia and Willy would not allow their newly found cousin a minute to himself. They were enthralled by the stories of his adventures. They prevailed upon him not to continue eastward with the herd, but to stay with them and help Isaac Cody erect a log cabin on the Salt Creek Valley site, where he planned to stake his claim. Seven-year-old Willy never strayed from his hero's side and insisted on sharing some of the building tasks to prove that he too was strong.

One evening Horace Billings again demonstrated his consummate skill as a rider. Isaac had purchased a race horse, while the family was in transit to Missouri, but whenever someone mounted him he refused to obey and ran away. Horace climbed on his back, using just a rope to keep him under control, and stood erect while the horse galloped over the prairie. When the horse was going at top speed, Billings jumped to the ground, allowed the steed to run to the end of the guide rope until the lariat was taut, and then jerked the line with a mighty tug. The horse, suddenly at the end of his rope, turned a complete somersault in the air and landed heavily. Many years later, on recalling this incident, William F. Cody said, "The exhibition given by Billings on this occasion was really wonderful, and the most skillful and daring feat of the kind that I ever witnessed."[7]

A herd of Government horses had stampeded from Fort Leavenworth the previous year and was still running wild over the Kansas prairie. A reward of $10 per head had been offered. Billings leaped at the opportunity of catching runaways, for he had become very bored with log-splitting. He borrowed Little Gray, the somersaulting race horse, and set out after the strays.

Billy went along with his cousin. His mother was reluctant to have the boy involved in such dangerous work. The night he departed for his first hunt she cried. But she never refused him permission to go and at least had the consolation that he was in the company of an expert horseman.

In a short period of time Billings had thrown, saddled,

bridled and ridden to the fort twenty-five of the outlaws. The $250 he received as reward amounted to a small fortune in those days. Horace gave a little money to his sidekick who was overjoyed at receiving it, but happier yet that he had learned to throw a lasso, ride a wild horse, and that he had taken part in a glorious hunt.

Shortly afterwards Horace gave in to his wanderlust once again and hired on as a driver for a Mormon wagon train headed for Salt Lake City. The last Willy saw of his mentor was just before the lead wagon disappeared over the hill. Horace Billings rose in the driver's seat and flicked his long whip across the haunches of the six yoke of oxen. Then he cracked the whip crisply in the air as a final farewell salute.

On June 10, 1854 Isaac received word from his Washington friends that the Kansas-Nebraska Bill had been passed. In anticipation of the official word the family had been packed and waiting to move for days. They hurried to the crude log cabin on the 160-acre plot which they had chosen for their home. Isaac went immediately to the land office and the Codys had the honor of being the first to file for a homestead in the entire Kansas Territory. (This first land patent, signed by President Buchanan himself, is now in the possession of the Goodman family.)

Many of the initial settlers were honest and respectable people like the Codys. Others were the hirelings of political leaders, prepared to cast their ballots according to the dictates of these political bosses in the coming territorial voting to ascertain whether Kansas would be pro-slavery or free. In reality the settlement of Kansas was not necessitated by an urgent need for expansion. Actually, the huge land masses of Kansas and Nebraska were tiny pawns in the endless maneuvering for favorable political position indulged in by both North and South.

The first wavering moves in this contest had resulted in the Missouri Compromise under which the Indian territory had been equally divided into two sections, one slave and one free. The master strategist of the South, Stephen A. Douglas, pushed through the repeal of this Compromise and sponsored in its stead the Kansas-Nebraska Act which established two separate territories, Kansas and Nebraska, each of which was to decide for itself the issue of slavery or freedom.

Both sides to the controversy paid, coerced and talked men into emigrating to the two trouble spots, knowing that a few thousand votes might settle the fate of slavery over the immense area that lay between the river and the mountains. In Missouri, dedicated firmly to the proposition that it was man's sovereign right to have and keep slaves, secret societies subsidized the invasion of the new land by pro-slavery squatters to uphold the economic and social structure of the South. In far-off New England the no less dedicated Emigrant Aid Society, military and financial wing of the abolitionist movement, sent a party of recruits westward to help swing the vote in favor of nonslavery. As they left Boston on July 17, they sang a song John Greenleaf Whittier composed especially for the occasion:

We cross the prairies as of old
The pilgrims crossed the sea.
To make the West, as they the East,
The homestead of the free![8]

The Codys had been in their cabin but a few days when hundreds of these newcomers poured in from every direction to file claims. Within a fortnight, Leavenworth was organized as a town a few miles from the fort whose name it borrowed. Leavenworth's central building, as in most every other community that mushroomed overnight, was the saloon. The drifters crowded in, stood six deep at the bar, and drank "double-rectified, copper-distilled, trigger-lightning, sod-corn juice."[9]

Weeks passed, but new contingent followed new contingent into Kansas. Some came in style in carriages, others arrived in crowded covered wagons, a few appeared in pony carts, and a surprising number limped in on foot with packs on their backs. Eager, desperate, hungry, ambitious men, desiring only to squat on their own piece of land.

It was of extreme importance in the midst of all the intense factional feeling and squabbling that the section lines dividing one claim from another be clearly demarcated. Isaac, an experienced surveyor, was sought out by many squatters, both pro and antislavery advocates, to do this work. The unanimity with which both sides sought his services—although the slavery men knew that Isaac Cody was an ardent advocate of abolitionism—attested to his complete honesty and integrity, standards from which he refused to waver despite his own strongly partisan feelings.

In addition to surveying, he continued to expand his trading post business. Although his neighbor two miles to the west, a Mr. M. P. Rively, had been an established trader in the area for a much longer time, Isaac was soon giving him stiff competition. The fact that Elijah owned a general store in Weston helped a lot. A large wagon made regular trips from Weston to the trading post, bringing fresh stocks of goods which Elijah imported from the East.

A cross section of frontier America patronized Isaac's post. Among his best customers were the Indians, full-blooded members of various tribes, self-reliant, friendly, good neighbors. They were more than willing to teach Willy all the skills at which they excelled. From them he learned to shoot a bow and arrow, run foot races and even speak a few sentences in the Kickapoo tongue.

On Saturday night the squaws visited the Cody store, their ponies laden down with packs of fresh garden vegetables to trade for beads, calico, jewelry and trinkets. During the week the braves came to the post bringing furs, hides, horses and handicraft work. They left with saddles, household articles, medicine, chewing tobacco, candy and many other items, either useful or decorative, which caught their fancy.

As a gesture of friendship and a demonstration of appreciation for their patronage, Isaac played host to the Indians at a grand barbecue on Independence Day, 1854. More than 200 braves and their wives, a handful of new settlers, and a party of Westonians brought by Elijah attended the affair. The Indians roasted a steer in their own special fashion while the Codys also barbecued an entire beef, using an old family recipe.

The red men were so impressed by the succulence of the beef Mrs. Cody prepared that some of the squaws begged her to reveal the secret of how she made it. This she gladly did. First, skin, dress and thoroughly clean the steer, she said. Then fill it with strips of salt bacon. Meanwhile, sew the hide into a covering of canvas. Place the steer back into this reinforced hide and deposit it in a specially prepared oven. The oven, she explained, is made by digging a large hole in the earth and fitting it with heated prongs. The beef is rested on these tines and covered with stones. Iron rods should be set on these stones and hot coals over the rods. A brisk fire must be kept burning from twelve to sixteen hours, she concluded, depending upon the size of the animal, to insure that the finished roast possess the finest flavor and delicious taste.

To show their gratitude for the Codys' hospitality and friendliness, the Indians performed some of their traditional, ceremonial war dances. In the lands to the north and west these very rites were being danced in dead seriousness, out of hatred for the white man. At the barbecue, however, war paint and battle headdress were mere theatrical trappings, meant to thrill and not to frighten the onlookers.

During the summer Isaac added still another activity to his moneymaking projects. He contracted to supply Fort Leavenworth with 2,000 tons of hay. Willy helped in the hayfields, learned to read the surveying compass, traveled back and forth from the trading post to Weston on the supply wagon, and still found time to spend "days and nights in riding over the country with Mr. William Russell, who was engaged in the freighting business, and who seemed to take a considerable interest in me. In this way I became acquainted with many wagon-masters, hunters and teamsters, and learned a great deal about the business of handling cattle and mules . . . I acquired a great deal of practical knowledge, which afterwards I found to be of invaluable service for it was not long before I became employed by Majors & Russell. . . ."[10]

The great majority of Kansas settlers were pro-slavery men. Many of these were "border ruffians," who actually lived in Missouri, but who staked claims, voted and helped decide the political fate of Kansas. These territory shuttlers wore red flannel shirts and carried guns in their belts and bowie knives in their boots. They claimed ownership of a homestead in a simple, direct manner by marking the lines of their land with empty whiskey bottles.

Rively's trading post was the headquarters of the pro-slavers. One evening Isaac and Billy rode up to this store on their way home from Fort Leavenworth, where they had made final arrangements for delivering the hay which was already in stack. A crowd of Missourians, many of them drunk, was holding a pro-slavery meeting. They were whooping it up and shooting pistols into the air. One of the men saw the Codys and hollered to the others, "There's that abolition cuss now,"[11] and immediately the man and boy were surrounded by a gang of screaming, cursing zealots.

A tirade of insults was launched against Isaac: he was a hypocrite for favoring abolitionism when his brother owned Negroes and favored the Southern cause; he was a coward because he had never committed himself publicly on the slavery question; he was a thief because he had made numerous errors in surveying, mistakes which always were directed against the slavery advocates.

This last accusation brought a quick retort from Cody but his answer was lost in the noise of the crowd as it surged forward, dragged him from his horse, and placed him on a dry goods box in front of the store.

"Now," shouted the ringleader, "tell us whar ye stand."

"I am not ashamed of my views," he said quietly. "I am, and always have been, opposed to slavery. It is an institution that not only degrades the slave, but brutalizes the slave-holder, and I pledge you my word that I shall use my best endeavors—yes, that I shall lay down my life, if need be—to keep this curse from finding lodgment upon Kansas soil. It is enough that the fairest portions of our lands are already infected with this blight. May it spread no farther."[12]

His last few words were drowned out by a concerted chorus of boos and hisses. "Shoot him!" the border ruffians cried. "Hang the black abolitionist!"

Charlie Dunn, who ironically was an employee of Elijah Cody, jumped onto the box directly behind Isaac and stabbed him in the back. Billy's father fell forward without making a sound into the arms of his son and Mr. Hathaway, a free-soiler who was their neighbor. Saner men in the crowd restrained Dunn before he could strike again, and whisked him away.

Cody was carried into Rively's store, bleeding profusely. Mrs. Cody, informed immediately of the attack, hurried to the trading post with horse and wagon. There was no physician in the vicinity, and Isaac asked to be taken to Elijah's home. During the slow painful journey to Weston, ten-year-old Willy Cody held his father's head in his lap. Elijah did everything in his power to make his brother comfortable and to provide for his medical care. He was horrified at the vicious assault and immediately discharged Charlie Dunn from his employ. Isaac remained at Weston for a few weeks and his wound gradually healed. He was never to fully recover from the effects of this knifing—the bowie blade had pierced his lung, and Dunn's attack eventually caused his death.

Cody was the first man to shed blood in Kansas for the cause of antislavery. The path over which he was borne by wagon after the assault at Rively's is called "Cody

Bloody Trail" in early histories of Kansas. The attack on him marked the opening of undeclared war in the Territory—a war in which wanton destruction was to be thrust upon the weak and the defenseless.

Young Willy and 12-year-old sister Julia were to witness privation and suffering that would have shaken adults many years their senior. No sooner had Isaac Cody returned to his home at Salt Creek Valley than his enemies struck again. The two children were riding towards the farmhouse when they saw some men racing along the stacks of piled-up hay, applying torches to the dried grass. The children on horseback were as helpless as were their stunned parents who watched from the front stoop.

The work of months of effort went up in smoke. The Government had agreed to pay Isaac $15 a ton for the hay. Several hundred tons—representing in part the money the family desperately needed to pay Isaac's considerable medical expenses—were reduced to a handful of dust by the conflagration.

In recalling this period later Billy said, "My first real work as a scout began then for I had to keep constantly on the watch for raids by ruffians, who had now sworn that father must die."[13] In this new role as protector of his father the youngster spied a band of horsemen coming down the road a few evenings after the hay-burning. Immediately he warned his mother. Mary went to her husband, dressed him in one of her long skirts, covered the upper part of his body with a shawl and placed a pasteboard sunbonnet on his head. Carrying a water pail in one hand and gripping a revolver under his shirt with the other, he walked slowly out into the yard and entered a nearby cornfield, unchallenged by the riders.

The horsemen dismounted, asked for Cody, and were told that he wasn't at home. Nevertheless they searched the house. Then they went to the pasture, rounded up all the horses including Billy's pony Prince, and hollering back "We'll come again and get him," rode off in the direction from which they had arrived.

For the next several days strangers, sometimes singly and sometimes in groups, passed the Cody farm. Isaac remained in the cornfield and according to Billy, "There in the sod corn we made him a bed of hay and blankets and there we kept him for days, carrying food to him by nights."[14]

Isaac suffered from chills and fever during his confinement in the fields so that it was necessary, despite the danger of visits from armed marauders, for the family to spirit him back into the house one night. The very next day Billy saw a horseman mounted on Prince approaching. This man turned out to be an alcoholic, old reprobate, Judge Sharpe, who had been elected justice of the peace by pro-slavery votes. He had been one of the leaders of the group of ruffians from whom Isaac had fled to the cornfield a short time before.

Now, drunkenly, he demanded that they prepare a meal for him.

Mary, fearing for the safety of her husband upstairs, went quickly about the business of cooking dinner for Sharpe. While he waited, he slowly sharpened a large bowie knife, using his shoe as a whetstone.

Pointing towards Billy who stood close to his mother in an attitude of protection, he bellowed, "See this knife. I'm gonna make it very sharp and then I'm gonna finish the job that Charlie Dunn started."

Mrs. Cody brought food to the table and Sharpe began to wolf it down. He shoveled large pieces of meat into his mouth and then washed everything down with whiskey he had brought along.

When Sharpe was bent over his food, Mrs. Cody motioned towards the staircase and Julia and Billy slipped upstairs to join their father. He had heard everything that Sharpe had said, but was much too weak and fever-ridden to do anything about defending himself. He handed his son a double-barreled shotgun and armed Julia with an axe.

The children crouched at the head of the stairway, Billy kneeling in front, Julia standing behind him, prepared for any eventuality. But Sharpe had no sooner finished his meal then he slumped over the table, head in his plate, asleep.

For half an hour he slept and for half an hour the youngsters remained immobile on the steps. Sharpe woke up with a lurch, stumbled towards the door—seemingly having forgotten the purpose of his visit—snatched up Isaac's saddlebags from the porch, staggered over to Prince, mounted and rode away.

The following day Billy was overjoyed to see Prince come galloping into the front yard. He had slipped his halter and returned to his master.

More than 8,000 people had crowded into the Kansas Territory by September. In the early fall an election was held to ascertain whether Kansas favored slavery or free-soil policies. On election day several thousand Missourians crossed the border and rode whooping and hollering to the ballot box. The results indicated a clear pro-slavery plurality.

A trio of free-soilers, Messrs. Fraser, Jolley, and Whitney, hired Isaac Cody to locate a parcel of good land for them, and then to survey their acreage. He readily agreed. The job would mean money for the Cody family, a chance for him to get away from the trouble-spot his home had become and the opportunity to aid in the forming of a free-soil colony.

He chose a site about thirty miles west of Salt Creek Valley. There in another valley close by a river and waterfall, which Indians and trappers had named Grasshopper Falls, he laid out the village of Grasshopper. In partnership with two other men he started a grist and sawmill in the town and was kept busy sawing lumber for the many houses being erected by settlers on their claims.

During these fall and winter months Isaac Cody shuttled back and forth between his family in Salt Creek Valley and his business at Grasshopper.

In March, 1855 a second election on the slavery issue was held. Again an army of Missourians invaded Kansas and marched in force to the polling places at Lawrence. Armed with pistols, rifles and knives—and even dragging two cannons loaded with musket-balls through the streets—they stormed the booths and rolled up an even greater plurality than before for the pro-slavery faction. There were actually only 3,000 or so qualified registered voters in the Territory. Yet over 6,000 votes were cast. The legislature elected by this voting soon made it a criminal act for anyone to speak against slavery or to advocate free-soil policies in Kansas.

Isaac Cody made his own trenchant observations on the election in a letter to his old Le Claire friend, Mr. Laurel Summers. The complete letter follows:

Grasshopper Falls, Kansas Terr.
April 22, 1855.

Mr. L. Summers:—

Sir as I have spare time I would give you a short history of our election. The anti-slavers were run off the track completely by the Pukes. They came for 200 miles from the interior, formed in companies from 100 to 200, with their flags, their whiskey and their music going, there saw a famous work.

Probably 100, or a sufficient number at every precinct in the territory to force their votes, and if the judges refused they forced them off their seat, and put such men as they pleased on the seat, and men from the state of Missouri that were not citizens. The citizens of the territory did not vote, it was carried there by Missourians votes.

The candidates and judges went to the governor and demanded their papers, and many of them got theirs. They went with the determination to hang the governor or have them and I suppose the governor thought peace was best and gave some papers, and refers the whole matter to the governor general for decision.

If I should give you a correct statement of the course pursued by these outrageous fellows you would doubt, therefore you may imagine how bad a set of wild drunken fanatics could be in such a case, and even then I shall doubt whether you can make it as bad as it was.

I have always despised the name of abolitionist, but if yourself was here you would say abolitionist, or anything that would stop such outrageous acts.

Now I would say to our popular governor, gentlemen, if you do not do something to protect these unprotected territories, I shall accuse them of disloyalty.

Yours respectfully,
I. Cody.

P.S. I am building a saw mill at Grasshopper Falls some 30 miles from here. I have not seen my family for 2 weeks but heard that they are all well at Salt Creek.

Give my respects to all enquiring friends and if you please read them this.[15]

In May another son was born to the Codys whom they called Charles Whitney in honor of one of the newcomers from the East. Both the Kickapoo Indians and the Delaware tribe claimed the land around Salt Creek Valley—the Federal Government had transferred the territory from one tribe to another, and then back again, at various times—and both sent delegations to the Cody farmhouse with gifts and trinkets hailing the birth of the first white papoose on *their* land. Diplomatically, Isaac and Mary received each group of chieftains independently so that the Kickapoos and the Delawares would not fight over which tribe, by reason of ownership of the land, was legally entitled to serve as godfather to the child.

Isaac spent more and more of his time in Grasshopper Falls in the summer and early autumn of that year. During one of the short periods when he returned to Salt Creek Valley, he was instrumental in securing a new teacher, Miss Jennie Lyons, to teach at the old cabin, now transformed into a schoolhouse, which Mr. Cody had first built when he staked out his Kansas claim. For two months Miss Lyons carried on the work of the school under great hardships. Again and again pro-slavers on horseback paid visits to her classroom and informed her that they didn't intend to allow "that old abolition cuss to teach sedition to our youngsters." This pressure was finally too great and the schoolteacher returned to the East in complete disillusionment.

Most deadly of these armed pro-Southern bands were the Kickapoo Rangers. This striking-force made its headquarters at Kickapoo City, a small town seven miles from Fort Leavenworth that had become the focal point of the "extension" advocates. Unfortunately for the abolitionists the Kickapoo Rangers were not just a haphazard group of pro-slavers, but were in effect the northern division of the territorial militia of Kansas. In this official capacity they were able to wreak havoc far and wide—burning, looting, terrorizing and killing.

Late one evening, when Isaac was away at Grasshopper Falls, Mrs. Cody heard a commotion outside and discovered that the house was completely surrounded by Rangers.

"What do you want?" she called from the window.

"We're after the old man, your abolition husband. Tell him to come out on the porch with his hands up or we'll burn the house and kill you all," replied their leader.

"My husband isn't here," she answered.

"That's a lie!" the Ranger shouted. "If he's not out here in three minutes, you're all done for."

"I tell you he's not here," Mary said. "But someone else is—Jim Lane and his men. And we'll give you *two* minutes to leave this property." Outside there were a few seconds of silence. Colonel Jim Lane was the head of a little Free State army, a valiant volunteer band of abolitionists, established to defend the countryside against the raids of the night-riders. Though few in numbers, they had effectively stymied the attacks of the Rangers and other predatory gangs on a number of occasions.

Taking advantage of the brief respite, Mary told Billy, his sisters and a visiting friend to put on Isaac's boots and shoes. Then the tiny troop of children in the oversized footgear shuffled and stamped around the house, sounding like men preparing to take counteraction against the enemy. The hired man, a veteran of the Mexican War, took command. In a loud, authoritative voice he yelled orders to his imaginary troops.

The rangers began an orderly withdrawal. Mrs. Cody

fired an old musket through the window. This did it. The marauders fled in panic, certain that Jim Lane and his entire force were right at their heels.

The next morning Billy found a powder keg in the yard, from which a long fuse led to the open cellar.

In October, 1855 Isaac journeyed from Salt Creek Valley to Topeka, Kansas, where he attended the Topeka Constitutional Convention. This abolitionist political meeting adopted a constitution and set up a free-soil legislature in opposition to the "bogus legislature"[16] which the votes of the border ruffians had established at Lecompton, fifteen miles east of Topeka, in 1854. The free-soilers declared the Lecompton government illegal. The pro-slavery men, of course, refused to recognize the Topeka group. In effect two legislatures, each refusing to accept the authority of the other, and each claiming to represent the "real" sentiment of the people, were in existence after the end of October, 1855.

Isaac Cody became a member of this first free-soil legislature.

When cold weather set in, the head of the household returned home. The Cody children, now consisting of five daughters and two sons, were overjoyed at seeing their father again. The snow, ice and generally inclement weather kept their enemies away, and the entire family was extremely happy.

Trouble came again in the spring. Isaac returned to his mill in Grasshopper, but even there, among his free-soil friends, he was not safe. Two men entered the mill and asked if he was "the damned abolitionist" who wanted Kansas to enter the Union as a Free State.

When Isaac admitted his identity, one of them rushed

at him and yelled, "You will not live to see it." The attacker grabbed Mr. Cody, while his companion struck him a heavy blow over the head.

Some of the mill hands heard him fall and hastened to the scene. They found him unconscious on the floor, the assailants having made good their escape. Luckily he had suffered only a scalp wound and soon recovered.

Despite his injury Mr. Cody traveled to Topeka when the free-soil legislature was again called into session.

Shortly thereafter Mrs. Cody received word that her husband would soon be home again. Her happiness was short-lived when Mr. Hathaway, their neighbor, who had caught Isaac's falling body when he had been knifed by Dunn at Rively's, told her that the Kickapoo Rangers were stationed at various points along the road, waiting to assassinate Isaac.

Billy Cody, ill in bed with a high fever, overheard this conversation and determined to warn his father. Despite his mother's protests that he was much too ill to attempt such a hazardous mission, the boy prevailed. Julia saddled Prince. Mrs. Cody wrote a letter to her husband, which the boy hid in one of his stockings before putting on his heavy riding boots.

Billy figured that he had a 30-mile ride ahead of him before he could reach Grasshopper, where his father had headed after leaving Topeka, so he did not race his pony but kept him going at an even, steady gait. This unhurried pace had the added advantage of not attracting undue attention to the boy.

At the eight-mile point he forded Big Stranger Creek, passing a group of men who had stopped to water their horses. One of the bunch recognized Billy and yelled to the others, "There's Cody's kid now on his way to warn his father. Stop, you, and tell us where your old man is."[17]

Billy spurred Prince forward. The Rangers, for these they certainly were, saddled their mounts and chased after him. A shot rang out, but this only caused Billy's pony to gallop on with greater speed.

The young boy knew that nine miles lay between him and the house of a friendly neighbor. He reeled feverishly in the saddle, but managed somehow to hold on. Faster and faster Prince galloped. The boy was so ill that he could not see the road. But Prince knew the road well and needed no guidance. Finally a familiar landmark loomed up on the left and Billy knew that there was just one mile to go before he reached the Hewitt homestead, where he could find sanctuary.

One mile to go, the end of a tortuous ride, safety. But now Prince began to falter. He had covered twice the distance of the pursuing horses and his pace slowed perceptibly. Behind, Billy could hear the hoofbeats of the Rangers' horses. While previously the voices of the border ruffians had been just an incoherent gurgle somewhere in back, he could now make out individual words, as they closed in on him.

As quickly as Prince had slackened his speed, just as quickly did he now suddenly regain his previous form. He too seemed to know help was at hand. But another danger threatened. Billy remembered that a huge gate barred the entrance to the Hewitt acreage and that the house itself lay 300 yards beyond the roadway. He prayed that the gate would be open, for if he had to dismount and swing the huge wooden frame ajar, the Rangers would surely catch him.

He rounded the last bend. Ahead was the Hewitt farm. Yes, the gate was wide open. Through it he galloped at top speed and up the driveway to the house. The Rangers pulled up their horses in defeat and peered after the boy. They dared not enter the farmyard itself, for Hewitt was one of Jim Lane's men and the free-soilers made this place one of their headquarters.

Hewitt helped Billy into the house and Mrs. Hewitt gave him a hot bath and put him to bed. After a good night's sleep and a big breakfast, the boy, still fever-ridden and weak, continued on his way. He reached the mill at Grasshopper Falls without further incident and delivered his mother's message to his father. Isaac called Dr. Northrop—a physician from Ohio who had migrated to Kansas with his family in 1854, and who had taken care of Mr. Cody when he had been attacked at the mill—to treat his son. By the following day Billy was able to travel once again and father and son rode to Colonel Jim Lane's headquarters at Lawrence. A letter was sent to Mary Cody telling her that they were safe.

A few weeks later the two returned home. Although he was very ill, Isaac dared not remain in the house. Not a day or night went by that Billy, in his role of "scout," did not see horsemen silhouetted against the sky watching the Cody farm.

A temporary hideout was established in the same cornfield where Isaac had hidden, disguised as a woman, when marauders had sought him out before. Mr. Hathaway, who always seemed to be at the right place at the right time to aid Mr. Cody, ministered to Isaac's medical needs. Hathaway had studied medicine, but he knew that his patient required more expert care. After a few days, when Mr.

Cody showed slight improvement, he took Hathaway's advice and started for Fort Leavenworth which was four miles away.

All roads were completely blocked by the Kickapoo Rangers who were making one all-out concerted effort to capture Cody. Therefore, Isaac was forced to make his way slowly on foot towards the fort. He followed a zigzag route, full of detours. The journey took two days and two nights. Julia and Billy followed their father in a buckboard, carrying a bed and blankets to keep him comfortable and warm at night, and food to sustain him during the day.

Progress was at a snail-pace. Each step caused Mr. Cody great pain. Mostly he crept from one field of corn to the next. Every hour or so he would let the children know where he was by waving a white handkerchief above the corn. Actually only Julia would see this improvised flag. Billy, as a precautionary measure, huddled under the blankets, as they moved along, so that the Rangers would not think that anything was amiss. What could be more innocent than a pretty young girl driving a buckboard loaded only with blankets and boxes?

At last Isaac reached Fort Leavenworth and the children left him and went back home. He asked the quartermaster what the Government planned to do about Free State men. The soldier's frank reply was that nothing was going to be done, and he advised Free Staters to sit tight and mind their own business.

Mr. Cody then visited Mark Delehay, former schoolmate and intimate friend of Abraham Lincoln, who edited *The Free State Press* in Leavenworth City, the first paper in the Territory to be published in the interest of antislavery. Delehay, whose office had to be guarded twenty-four hours a day and who had recently had his presses thrown into the river by pro-slavery men, advised Isaac to leave Kansas. He gave his friend letters of introduction to Mr. Lincoln who had served as congressional representative for the central district of Illinois and had voted steadily with the antislavery bloc, and to other political leaders in the East. Mr. Cody secured passage on a steamboat to Cleveland, Ohio. There he stayed at his brother Joseph's house. Under the care of a competent physician, his condition was soon greatly improved.

Politics now engaged his interest and attention to a degree that excluded all other considerations. A new party, the Republican, commanded his allegiance and his enthusiasm.

In December, 1855 state committees of the party, representing nine states, issued a call for a founding convention at Pittsburgh, Pennsylvania, where the Republicans organized for the first time on a national basis. A nominating convention was scheduled for June, 17, 1856, at Philadelphia.

Isaac and Joseph attended this nominating conclave and officially became members of the party. Isaac was introduced to Mr. Lincoln, and shortly thereafter Mr. Cody was presented to the convention as "the man from the Kansas Territory and the New West." He addressed the delegates on the subject of "Bleeding Kansas" and stirred them with his graphic description of the ordeal of terror which the antislavery men in that area were undergoing. So impressed were the Republican leaders by this silver-tongued orator from Salt Creek Valley that they prevailed upon him to stump the country in their behalf. They also urged him to recruit antislavery men to migrate to Kansas, a request to which he also acquiesced.

Major planks in the Republican platform, a statement that Isaac helped to frame, were a declaration against the repeal of the Missouri Compromise, a blast against the extension of slavery, and a demand that Kansas be admitted to the Union as a Free State. The party nominated John C. Fremont, a free-soiler, as its candidate for the presidency, and William L. Dayton, an old Whig, as its choice for vice-president. The Republicans, putting forth the slogan, "Free Soil, Free Speech, Free Men, Fremont," campaigned vigorously, but went down to defeat.

Isaac returned to his family shortly before the election, much improved in health. He was told of the many outrages and indignities perpetrated by the border ruffians against the free-soilers during his absence, and how Billy had acted as "the man of the family," while he was gone.

Julia Cody, in recalling the winter of 1856, remembers it as a joyous time. With father home once again, Christmas was a happy occasion with extra-special gifts under the tree, sent by Joseph Cody and his family. And always there was the quiet presence of Mary Cody, the loving mother, guiding the children, helping them to solve their problems, gathering her brood together at the end of each day and reading passages from the Bible with them. Kindness, consideration, love, and the word of the Good Book—these were the things on which she based her life, these were the legacies she was to pass on to her children.

In the spring of 1857 the seeds of Isaac's speaking tour the previous year bore fruit. Hundreds of immigrant families which had heard Mr. Cody's speeches poured into the Territory. They all headed for his farm in Salt Creek Valley, from where he would help them get settled in the surrounding country. The Cody home was always crowded with men, women and children waiting to stake out their own claims. Those who were unable to squeeze into the house itself set up tents in the fields and yard.

One of the immigrant families contracted scarlet fever on the river boat en route to Leavenworth City. Once ashore and temporarily settled at the Cody homestead, four of the children of this unfortunate family died within two weeks. The Codys helped to care for the sick and bury the dead. Isaac, who had induced these people to come to Kansas, felt personally responsible for their welfare. Though worn by work and worry he labored day and night to see that the fever did not spread and to aid those who had fallen prey to the disease. He caught a severe cold which developed into pneumonia.

Physicians were called, but they told Mrs. Cody that there was no hope for her husband who had a seriously infected lung as the result of his old knife wound. The mother and her children remained constantly at his bedside. Just before he died, Julia Cody remembers, he turned to Mary and said, "Mary, you will have to do the best you can with the children. Julia and Willy have promised to be your stand-bys." Then, although Isaac had never been a churchgoer, he asked his beloved wife to read to him from the Bible and to pray to the Lord to have mercy on his soul. Just before dawn on April 21, 1857 Isaac Cody died.

His brother Elijah assisted the family with the funeral arrangements, and Isaac was buried at Pilot Knob, a cemetery near Leavenworth.

CHAPTER 3

The Destroying Angels

WILLY CODY was eleven years old at the time of his father's death. Looking back later on this tragic period he stated that he had become "the only man of the family. I made up my mind to be a breadwinner."[1] Symbolic of this change of status was his insistence that his family and friends no longer call him Willy. As the head of the household he wanted to be called Bill. A compromise was worked out: to most of his friends he was Bill, to his family—especially his mother—he was Billy.

The firm of Majors & Russell, a freight and hauling concern, was building up toward its peak period when it was to employ 8,000 men and boys, send 6,000 wagons out on TAE trails and keep 70,000 oxen busy pulling the loads. Billy heard that the company could use a willing boy and persuaded his mother to take him to the Majors & Russell department store so that he might apply for the position.

The interview with Mr. Majors was brief and to the point. The boy told him that before his father's death he had promised to support his mother and the rest of the family.

"What can you do, Billy?" asked Mr. Majors, smiling.

"I can ride as well as a man," the youngster answered. "I could drive cavayard and herd the extra cattle that follow the wagon train."

Mr. Majors was impressed by Billy's sincerity and belief in himself. After quick consultation with his partner, he hired the youngster as messenger boy between wagon trains at $25 a month plus food. Years later Majors was to recall this first job interview with young Bill Cody when he wrote:

> Nearly forty years ago in Kansas, a handsome, wiry little lad came to me accompanied by his mother, and said he had her permission to take a position under me as messenger boy. I gave him the place though it was one of peril, carrying dispatches between our wagon trains upon the march upon the plains, and little did I then suspect that I was starting out in life one who was destined to win fame and fortune. . . . Then it was simple "Little Billy Cody" the messenger, and from the first year of service he began to make his mark.[2]

Billy rode his little gray mule back and forth from wagon train to wagon train for one month's time. Each Sunday he would ride home to visit his family. When thirty days had passed, he was offered a job herding strays. He turned over his first pay to his mother and asked her permission to accept the position of cavayard rider. She refused, knowing that the work was dangerous for one so young and that it would take him far from home.

Nevertheless, he slipped out of the house one night, walked to Leavenworth and signed on as herder with a raise in pay. Mr. Russell sent Mrs. Cody a note assuring her that Billy was safe and doing well at his job.

Two months to the day after he had run away Billy returned to the Cody farm, loaded down with a sack of 100 silver half dollars. With great pride he dumped the entire contents on his mother's lap.

He told her in detail what had happened to him since he left home. She was most amused by the fact that her son, not even in his teens, had taken the oath of the wagoners which all employees were obliged to sign. This oath, which Billy signed with an *X* because he could not yet write, stated:

> We, the undersigned wagon-masters, assistants, teamsters and all other employees of the firm of Majors & Russell, do hereby pledge not to use profane language, not to get drunk, not to gamble, not to treat animals cruelly, and not to do anything else that is incompatible with the conduct of a gentleman.[3]

One fact about Billy's taking the wagoners' oath did not please Mary Cody. It was a shame, she thought, that someone as bright as her son was unable even to write his own signature. A new subscription school had opened at Salt Creek Valley, and an unwilling boy, William F. Cody by name, was enrolled as a student.

That autumn Billy worked hard at his studies and by winter's end had made good progress. But with the coming of spring came trouble. He fell in love.

His sweetheart was a pretty young girl named Mary Hyatt. Their relationship was idyllic until a villain in the form of the school bully, Steve Gobel, a boy three years Billy's senior, intruded on their happiness. Fond of Mary and jealous of Billy, Gobel interrupted the two of them during a recess period as they were building a playhouse with sticks and stones in the schoolyard. He kicked it over, a lively fight ensued in which Billy was thoroughly thrashed, and to make matters even worse both boys were soundly beaten by their teacher, although Steve had clearly been the instigator of the quarrel.

A day or two later Billy and Mary built another house. Just as the boy was gingerly placing the roof on the structure and the girl was clapping her hands in delight, Gobel struck again, pushing the building over. Billy sprang at him to do battle. They exchanged sharp quick blows. At first the younger boy held his own in the combat, making up in dexterity and swiftness what he lacked in strength. Slowly, however, Steve wore him down and finally pinned him against the wall.

In desperation Billy reached into his boot where he always kept his herder's knife, pulled it out and slashed at his antagonist's thigh. The blade barely scratched Steve's leg but blood appeared and he screamed, "I'm killed! Oh, I'm killed!"

Pandemonium broke loose. Frightened children milled around the yard, hollering, "Billy Cody murdered Steve Gobel. Steve is dead." The teacher ran out of the schoolhouse, brandishing a large stick in his hand. Billy took one look at him, then turned tail and bolted down the road. He ran and ran until he had put the scene of battle far behind.

Out of breath, exhausted, he sat down at the side of the road. A wagon train approached, and he saw that the master was an old friend, John Willis. Billy clambered up next to Willis and told him the entire story. His friend was incensed by the injustice Billy had suffered and immediately offered him the job of cavayard driver for the wagon train which was bound for Fort Kearney in the Nebraska Territory.

Billy agreed to this proposal with alacrity, requesting

only that he be allowed to tell his mother he was leaving.

Willis immediately headed one of the wagons toward the Cody homestead. A few miles from Salt Creek Valley they were overtaken by three men on horseback. Willis heard them approaching and warned Billy, who hid in the back of the wagon. The men turned out to be Steve's father and brother, and a constable. They told Willis that they had a warrant for the arrest of William F. Cody for the stabbing of Steve Gobel without cause. The wagon driver reminded the men that there were two sides to every story and denied having seen young Billy.

The men urged their horses on in the direction of the Cody farm. Willis, realizing where they were headed, drove the wagon off the main road and parked it in a field where he and Billy waited until nightfall.

Willis had guessed right. The Gobels and the officer of the law rode to Salt Creek Valley and told Mary Cody that her son was a fugitive and that they would hunt high and low to find him. Mary was frantic for she had not heard from her son since morning and had no idea where he was.

Dinner had been on the table for an hour and the food was already cold when Willis and his passenger pulled up before the house. Mrs. Cody ran out and embraced her son. He told her the entire story of his fight with Steve, and Willis supplied the additional details about the encounter with the Gobels and the constable on the road. Reluctantly Mrs. Cody gave her son permission to make the trip to Nebraska.

The canvas-covered caravan with which Billy was to travel was one of many trains carrying freight across the plains under the sponsorship of Majors & Russell. Most of these groups of wagons were hauling military stores and supplies for General Albert Sidney Johnston's army which had been ordered to Utah to quell the Mormons. Majors & Russell maintained a way station at Fort Kearney, Nebraska Territory, where Willis was to deliver his freight and from which it was to be reshipped to Johnston's troops.[4]

The trip itself was uneventful. There were no Indian raids, no run-ins with outlaws, no unusual adventures. But Billy was too busy to notice this lack. He was fascinated by the wagon train itself and the rough, good-natured men who drove it. He soon got to know personally all the thirty-one heavily-armed men who were carefully nursing twenty-five great wagons, each pulled by several yoke of oxen, through the hills and plains of Kansas and Nebraska. When proud Billy Cody on his sure-footed gray mule visited first one and then another of the men, each tried to outdo the others in spinning yarns for his benefit or in teaching him the tricks of the bullwhacking trade.

Billy lapped up the yarns and information they offered like a stray cat lapping up a big dish of milk. He learned the art of whipthrowing:[5] how to flick his wrist and follow through with his arm—after first holding the two-foot-long hickory whip handle in just the right way—so that the twelve-foot lash unleashed to its full length like a striking snake; how to perform this entire operation so accurately that he could flick the leaf off a tree with a foot-long buckskin snapper at the business end of the whip, without scarring the branch. He would "draw a bead" on his target, grasp the whip handle in his left hand, coil the lash in his right hand and the crooked forefinger of his left, whirl his hands around his head and then release the coil which would send the whiplash streaming straight out. When it had reached full length and had snapped off a leaf, he would bring the whip back with a jerk.

On the entire trip Billy never saw the bullwhackers actually use their whips on an animal. Mainly they cracked them in the air and the pistol-shot sounds urged the teams forward. The drivers also shouted encouragement to their oxen or screamed curses at them. This cacaphony of whip-cracks, yells of "wohaw," and insults miraculously kept the oxen pulling steadily together at an even pace. As a result of this trip Billy really understood for the first time why the Indians called a wagon a "goddam" and cattle "wohaw."

The wagon-master, the wagon-bosses and the drivers were all tremendously proud of their teams and all firmly convinced of the superiority of oxen over mules as wagon pullers. They grudgingly admitted that mules might be faster on very short hauls, but claimed that oxen were better and faster over long stretches, providing there was plenty of food and water along the route. Oxen were good "mudders" and could pull a wagon through a sea of mire where mules, because of their small hoofs, would have lost their footing.

The wagoners admitted that mules were less likely to stampede while oxen were easily frightened and quickly got out of hand. While the bulls were temperamental and balked at unusual noises, the mules were downright cantankerous. One stubborn mule, the bullwhackers maintained, was a darn sight more trouble than an entire yoke of stampeding oxen.

Often when the wagon train halted during the heat of the day and the entire crew crept under the wagons to sleep, while the prairie sun burned down from above,

Billy Cody would lie awake listening to the restless sounds of the animals. At these times he would think of his family at home in Salt Creek Valley. And always he wondered: Did I kill Steve Gobel?

The train averaged a dozen miles a day on the trip out when the wagons were loaded to the tops, but came back without cargo at double speed. To Billy, however, the last 100 miles was a terribly long stretch. The wagons rumbled along oh so slowly. At Osakee, a village twenty-five miles from the Cody farm, he could stand it no longer. Bidding good-by to John Willis and the other wagoners, he went home on foot.

His mother, the children, Prince and Turk were all delighted to see him. Taller, thinner, wearing the castoff clothes of some of the wagon-men, which had long since worn to shreds, filthy with the grime of the dusty trail—appearing much more a man than a boy—Billy showed he was still a youngster by bursting into tears.

A smile wiped these out when he was told that his mother and Mr. Gobel had discussed the whole matter of the fight with Steve, and that the father had admitted that Billy was not wholly to blame. Steve had fully recovered from his wound.

The time for greetings was over. Mrs. Cody rushed Billy off to the bathroom where he soon was soaking luxuriously in the warm soapy water. Then he dressed in clean fresh clothes (Julia gingerly carried the old ones to the stove and burned them) and joined the family at supper. The roast beef, vegetables, apple pie and milk constituted a magnificent feast compared to his recent steady diet of hard tack, fat pork and black coffee.

Mary Cody saved the bad news until he had eaten his fill.

Then she told him that his half-sister, the beloved Martha, had died. This time the young boy cried tears of sadness. He had been extremely fond of Martha, and her death left him grief-stricken.

A few days later Billy rode into Leavenworth and picked up his back wages. He turned over the entire amount, $100 in gold and silver, to his mother. All he kept for himself was a few dollars in tips which the wagoners had given him.

After a brief stay at the farm Billy signed on with the same firm as before—a new partner had been added and the outfit was now called Russell, Majors & Waddell[6]—and joined another train heading west with supplies for General Johnston's army. Frank McCarthy, a rough, tough, courageous wagon-master, had been selected to get the bull-train and its cargo of beef cattle through to Salt Lake City. The handful of wagons in the McCarthy train was just one group of the more than 3,000 wagons which were to carry over 16,000,000 pounds of supplies to Johnston's 5,000 troops in the Salt Lake Valley during the year 1858.

All went well until the McCarthy caravan reached Plum Creek, Nebraska. There the men stopped for luncheon and the usual midday siesta. The crew crept under the mess wagons to sleep; the cattle grazed peacefully in the fields. Only the cook and his helpers cleaning the cooking implements, and three herders lying in the grass watching the animals, were awake. Suddenly the tranquility was shattered by a volley of shots and by violent screams. The men rolled out from under the wagons to see cattle scattering in every direction, the three day-herders lying dead on the ground, and a band of Indians galloping towards the main camp.

The bullwhackers grabbed their Colt revolvers and

Mississippi Yagers and rallied around Frank McCarthy. He ordered them to hold their fire until the redskins were almost upon them. Then the command rang out, "Fire!" The Indians pulled their horses up short and retreated to reform their ranks.

McCarthy knew that his men were badly outnumbered and told them to run to the banks of the Platte and use the river banks as breastworks. They raced to the slough which was a short distance away, dragging one of their party, who had been wounded, along with them.

The banks of the muddy shallow Platte varied from five to thirty feet in height. The men crouched in the water, awaiting further instructions. McCarthy made a quick decision: he told the party to stick close together and head for the nearest place of safety, Fort Kearney.

The wagoners waded along the river for several miles, carefully keeping low behind the high banks. The slough finally funneled into the mainstream of the Platte. Here the water was deeper, up to the waists of the men and over Billy's shoulders. A raft was made from tree branches lying along the riverside, and the wounded man was placed on this and pushed along. Occasionally the water was so deep that the wagon crew had to put their weapons on the raft and swim.

The Indians trailed them as closely as they could, waiting for the chance to catch them in the open, unprotected. As night approached Billy Cody lagged behind the others, wet, tired and footsore. By ten o'clock at night he was so far in back of the others that he was unable to hear them thrashing through the water.

The moon suddenly appeared from behind a hill and like a glaring spotlight it beamed down upon him. Silhouetted against it was the plumed head of an Indian. Frightened out of his wits the boy aimed his gun and fired. The redskin screamed and tumbled over the river bank, landing kerplunk in the water in front of Billy.

McCarthy and his men came splashing back to where the youngster stood shivering from cold and fright. After a quick examination of the dead Indian, McCarthy proclaimed, "Little Billy's killed an Indian all by himself!"[7] The boy was placed on the raft next to the wounded wagoner, and the party pushed on through the night and reached the fort early in the morning without further incident.

A company of cavalry was immediately ordered out to track down the Indian marauders. The troopers found the scalped and mangled bodies of the three herders and gave them a decent burial. No trace of the Indians was discovered and only a few of the stampeded cattle were rounded up.

McCarthy and his crew were taken back to Leavenworth on a returning wagon train. Billy was at once sought out by a reporter for *The Leavenworth Times* who wrote up the youngster's heroic exploit for that paper. The newsman, John Hutchinson, called him "the youngest Indian slayer on the plains,"[8] and Billy walked around for days with his head high in the air.

Once again young Cody signed on as an "extra hand" with a Russell, Majors & Waddell ten-wagon bull-train, under the command of veteran wagon-master Lew Simpson, heading for Salt Lake City with supplies for Johnston's forces. Billy was to be paid $40 a month in gold. He requested that Mr. Russell turn over this money each month to his mother.

Mrs. Cody could make good use of the money. That summer she had sold forty acres of her land and with the proceeds built a large wayside hotel adjacent to the main road over which supply trains going west had to pass. She was in poor health. Medical bills and the cost of constructing, furnishing and painting the hotel had greatly depleted her funds. Julia, now sixteen-years-old, quit school and did most of the work of managing the inn.

With her mother ill and Billy away in the West, Julia handled as best she could the manifold problems that confronted the family. On one occasion she solved a difficult problem with a finesse and skill that pleased her mother and impressed her brother when he was told about it on his return from Utah.

Several braves from the Potowatami reservation drove into the yard one day and asked for permission to camp near the hotel until the arrival of the next boat, which was to bring Big Alec, the chief's son, and his bride, a white girl, whom he had met and married while attending Carlisle College. The Indians were in ceremonial attire so as to greet the white princess in a manner befitting her position.

When the timid young girl finally arrived and saw the welcoming delegation of full-blooded, long-haired, blanketed Indians, she was frightened and could not speak. She was unable to associate this wild-looking crew with her tall, handsome husband who had always worn white man's clothes while at school.

At the hotel, where the groom had engaged a room for his beautiful bride, the scared girl took Julia and Mrs. Cody into her confidence and told them that she could not face living with these "savages" and that she was going to desert her husband.

Mrs. Cody advised her to give the marriage a fair trial before she made a final decision.

Julia tried another tack. She spoke at length about the Indians she knew personally, telling the young bride how kind, considerate and friendly they were. She punctuated her statements with little anecdotes and humorous stories and soon the other girl was telling her in detail how she had met, fallen in love and married Big Alec. A few days later, in a much better humor, she accompanied the Indians to the reservation.

Six months afterwards she returned to the hotel and assured Mary and Julia that she was very happy. Big Alec had built a house to her exact specifications. He had furnished it with beautiful things brought in from Louisville. As the wife of the chieftain's son she was not allowed to do any of the work around the house, and the other squaws cooked for her and took care of the chores.

Billy of course knew nothing of this. As extra hand and cavayard rider in Simpson's outfit, he was learning something new every day. Although his own duties were clearly defined, they did not keep him busy full time and he spent many hours learning other jobs. Often he clambered aboard one of the J. Murphy wagons and sat next to the driver. During an easy stretch of the trail he was handed the reins and then he was in his element—Billy Cody, bullwhacker.

When actually driving the team himself, he would be most conscious of the heavy weight of the huge wagon with its load of six or seven thousand pounds of freight. Occasionally he would glance back at the precious merchandise piled to the roof of the wagon box and protected from the weather by two heavy canvas sheets and an overhead covering. This freight space was as big as a large room in the Cody house. When the oxen wearied of pulling the immense burden and slackened their pace, he would crack the bullwhip in the air and holler "wohaw" in the best Western manner.

During the first week or so out he met "Wild Bill" Hickok, the famous scout of the plains—a man who was admired and feared more than any other of the frontiersmen. The first meeting between the young cavayard rider and the noted scout was a dramatic one. Billy was ordered to do some small task by one of the teamsters. The boy was sitting on an ox-yoke at the time, eating his dinner, and did not move fast enough for the surly, overbearing driver. The man cuffed Billy across the back of the head and sent him sprawling to the ground.

Young Cody, incensed by this treatment, sprang to his feet, seized a camp kettle of hot coffee and flung it at the bully. The liquid burned his face and he charged at Billy, filling the air with curses. He trapped the boy against one of the wagons and was just about to grab him when a tall, broad-shouldered man stepped between them. The teamster, who a second before had appeared as ferocious and murderous as a slightly wounded buffalo charging a hunter, halted abruptly in his tracks and became as meek as a lamb.

"You oughta be ashamed of yourself," the newcomer said to the wagoner, "attacking this boy. If you so much as lay a finger on him, I'll kill you."

The bully muttered something about being "sorry" and having "lost my head" and then retreated quickly from the scene. As soon as he had gone, the intruder introduced himself to Billy as Wild Bill Hickok. The boy was thrilled to meet the famous scout and they soon became fast friends.

Wild Bill was an unerring pistol and rifle shot, and he and Billy practiced shooting for hours. Under Hickok's tutelage, Billy soon was a crack shot. But Billy learned something much more important than marksmanship from Wild Bill; in imitating his mentor in every respect he inadvertently became a gentleman. For Wild Bill, though he had killed almost a half dozen men at the time he first met Bill Cody, was a gentle, considerate man. He deplored bravado and bluster in others and was completely devoid of these traits himself. He was soft-spoken and never resorted to vulgarity or blasphemy. He would rather settle a quarrel peacefully than resort to violence. When misunderstandings and disturbances broke out among his comrades, he acted as peacemaker. Though his words were conciliatory and delivered calmly, there was always authority behind them in his powerful well-formed body, and especially in his slender hands that he was always pulling and bending, like the fluttering and thrashing of a bird's wings to keep them supple for gunplay.

A good deal of Wild Bill's gentlemanliness rubbed off on Billy Cody, smoothing the rough edges of his personality, serving as a counter-influence to the rough and ready bullwhackers.

A sudden, unexpected catastrophe struck the Simpson party when it was at a point near the River Platte, about 20 miles from the scene of the Indian attack on McCarthy's outfit. The trail the men were following wound slowly along about two miles from the river. In the intervening space a large herd of about 500 buffaloes grazed in the sun. Without warning a party of Californians galloped out of the west and dashed down upon the herd. The startled buffaloes broke for the trail where the Simpson wagons were moving along. The stampeding animals were upon the bull-train so quickly that the bullwhackers had no time to do anything but hide behind the biggest wagons. Six yoke of Texas steers, pulling the light messwagon behind them, joined the buffaloes. The charging bison would certainly have swept everything out of their way if the main wagons had not been so heavy. The animals did manage to turn some of the prairie schooners completely around, entangling themselves in the reins and gearing.

One huge buffalo bull charged furiously between two yoke of oxen. His horns caught in the heavy wagon chains; with one toss of his massive head he tore the iron links from their sockets; then he raced off into the hills with the yoke chains dangling and jangling in the air, looking like a bloated, misshapen Christmas reindeer on a rampage.

Fortunately no one was seriously injured. The oxen were rounded up, the chuck wagon was recovered with provisions intact and the covered wagons were fixed in record time. The returning gold seekers, who had set off the stampede, were severely chastised and they apologized profusely. Three days later the Simpson train was back on the trail, heading for Utah.

During the week that followed, the bullwhackers discussed buffaloes morning, noon and night. This steady conversational diet did not pall on Billy Cody; on the contrary he thrived on it. From the veteran wagoners he garnered enough facts, theories and information about the buffalo to fill a good-sized book. Billy filed everything he heard away in the back of his mind. He did so completely unaware of the fact that someday he was to be completely identified in the public mind with this animal, that in fact he would take its name as part of his own and be known all over the world as Buffalo Bill.

As much as he was able to find out from the conversation of the teamsters, there was more to be learned from what he saw with his own eyes. Wherever the wagon train went, there were buffaloes. The shaggy beasts sometimes covered the grasslands for hundreds of miles, one all-encompassing blanket of flesh from which thousands of short, stubby, black horns protruded. The bodies of these animals were covered with fine wool instead of hair, much longer on the female than the male. From their very large heads, however, cowlicks of thick, long, matted hair fell down between the horns and over their eyes, giving them a frightful appearance. Beneath the heads, short but extremely wide necks led into two broad, powerful shoulders between which were small humps.[9] Billy soon realized that the buffaloes' short, stubby, wool-covered legs were indeed deceptive for they could move very quickly and propel the animals at such great speed that only the swiftest horsemen were able to keep up with them.

It was neither stampeding buffaloes nor hostile Indians that next threatened the Simpson party. Armed white men —dangerous, dedicated, daring white men—were the cause of their new trouble.

The train had reached the Green River, about 115 miles east of Salt Lake City, and most of the outfit had driven the oxen to a creek about a mile and a half from camp. On the way back they noticed a party of twenty mounted men approaching, heavily armed with double-barreled shotguns, rifles and revolvers. The teamsters anticipated no danger. True, they were out of sight of their home base, but the strangers were white men and therefore no threat.

The leader of the strangers rode forward and was met by Lew Simpson. "Throw up your hands, Simpson," he said, "we've got you covered."

Taken completely by surprise Simpson could no nothing but comply. Wild Bill Hickok, Billy Cody and the other members of the wagon crew also raised their hands above their heads.

The wagon-master recognized his adversary as Lott Smith, a man who had signed on as a teamster with the wagon train a few days before, only to disappear shortly afterwards. Smith readily admitted that he had joined the Simpson outfit merely to find out what supplies they were carrying and what their exact route was to be. Actually, he revealed, he was a leader of the Mormon Danites—the rebellious religionists whom General Johnston had been sent to Utah to subdue.

Lott Smith's men were all members of "The Church of Jesus Christ of Latter-day Saints," founded in 1830 in the United States by Joseph Smith. Ostracized by most American communities which could not understand the advocacy of polygamy by this sect and which resented the challenge to their own fundamentalism posed by the crusading Danites, the Mormons had established a colony at Nauvoo, Illinois. Finally driven from this city by the outraged citizens they had found Zion at Salt Lake City.

The succeeding ten years were fruitful ones for the Mormons. Periodically the church fathers sent wagon trains back to the Missouri River where they picked up scores of converts who had come from eastern states, and carried them back across the desert to Utah.

In 1855 calamity struck. The oasis of plenty that the

Latter-day Saints had established in the West became a bitter desert. Crop failure brought starvation and impoverishment to Salt Lake City. A new crowd of disciples waited at the Missouri for the prairie schooners which were to take them to Zion. But the wagons did not come, for the Mormon church had become bankrupt.

The elders of the church issued what the non-Mormon population considered a cruel edict. Let the newcomers come out by foot, they proclaimed.

And come by foot they did in the year 1856 over the long, hard, Indian-infested territory that extended 1,000 miles from the Missouri River to the Great Salt Lake. More than 1,300 men, women and children—many of whom had traveled all the way from Europe to join the Mormons—began this perilous journey. Many fell by the wayside. The trail to Salt Lake City was lined with stragglers—the ill, the lame, the fever-ridden and the indigent. The roadsides served as burial grounds for the dead. Overturned, two-wheeled carts were the improvised headstones used to mark the graves.

In the public mind cruelty and polygamy were shocking enough, but dictatorial tactics and defiance of Federal authorities were completely reprehensible and called for counteraction. The Mormon leader Brigham Young, the majority thought, was running the territory to suit himself instead of in accordance with Federal laws. General Johnston had been ordered to Utah to support the authority of new officials sent from Washington with orders to whip the Mormons into line.[10]

Lott Smith's band of Destroying Angels, as the Mormons liked to call themselves, herded Simpson and his men back to the main wagon camp. There another surprise was in store for the teamsters. Several hundred additional Danites had surrounded the wagons. The remaining bullwhackers were huddled in a tight group, disarmed, while others of the Mormons were searching the wagons.

The black-bearded Smith ordered the teamsters to return on foot to the Missouri River. He gave them enough provisions to last to Fort Bridger and, in response to Simpson's plea, provided them with one wagon and six yoke of oxen to transport their food. At first he refused to allow them to take any guns or ammunition, but once again the wagonmaster convinced him that it would be a murderous act to force them to walk hundreds and hundreds of miles without weapons for protection in case of Indian attack. Smith relented and gave them revolvers, rifles and bullets.

As the dejected company began the long trek to Fort Bridger, the thirty teamsters looked back over their shoulders and saw smoke and fire rising to the sky, which meant that their wagons were going up in flames.

They made steady progress, averaging thirty miles a day, and finally arrived at Fort Bridger. En route they were lucky, running into no unfriendly Indians. Billy Cody wore out three pairs of mocassins on the return journey and his feet became firmly calloused. The wagoners joked about this and assured him that even though he had to walk back from a wagon trip he certainly was no longer "a tenderfoot."

When they finally reached the fort, they were informed that Smith's forces had captured and destroyed wagons from two other trains going to Utah. Alexander Majors summarized this harassing operation by writing:

> A party of Mormons, under the command of Colonel Lott Smith, had been sent out by the Mormon authorities

> in the rear of Johnston's army to cut off his supplies. They captured and burned three of our trains, two on the Sandy, just East of Green River and one on the West bank of Green River. They gave the captain of each train the privilege of taking one of his best wagons and teams and loading it with supplies to return home or back to the starting point. They committed no outrage whatever toward the men and as soon as the captain of each train told them he had all the food necessary to supply him to get back to the starting point, they told him to abandon the train, and they were set on fire and everything burned that was consumable. The cattle were driven off by the Mormons and those that were not used for beef by the hungry men were returned to the company after peace had been made between the Mormons and the Government. This loss put the army upon short rations for that winter and spring until they could be reached with supplies.[11]

In all, seventy-five wagons loaded with supplies for Johnston's army failed to reach the command.

By the time Simpson and his crew reached Fort Bridger, it was late autumn and the entire party was forced to spend the long, tedious winter there because of the severity of the weather. In addition to the troops stationed at the fort, more than 400 employees of Russell, Majors & Waddell—many of whom had also lost their wagons as a result of Mormon raids—lived in tents and cabins as organized militia companies under the command of wagon-masters.

The Danites were entrenched in the vicinity and effectively cut off supplies from the fort. Before the winter was over all the men were put on three-quarter rations; soon this was reduced to one-half; and finally to one-quarter shares. At one point they were so short of food that it was necessary to kill worn-out oxen and mules.

In later years William Fredrick Cody gave a vivid picture of this trying period. The oxen "were actually so poor," he wrote, "that we had to prop them up to shoot them down. At last we fell back on the mules, which were killed and served in good style. Many a poor unsuspecting Government mule passed in his chips that winter in order to keep the soldiers and bullwhackers from starvation. It was really a serious state of affairs."[12]

The temperature often hit the thirty below zero mark and stayed there for days. Teams of troopers and teamsters would scour the surrounding countryside for fuel. At first the sagebrush and wood were carried back to the fort by mules. Then the men ate the mules, and the firewood was hauled to Bridger on hand-drawn sleds. In desperation, when blizzards heaped up mountains of snow and made the paths impassable, the sleds were burned. Finally the snow melted, and the men and boys went forth again, but with the mules eaten and the sleighs burned, they now carried fuel to the fort on their own backs. "Notwithstanding all these hardships, the men seemed to be contented and to enjoy themselves,"[13] Cody said afterwards.

Early in the spring the Government recalled the Johnston expedition, and the entire personnel of the fort, troopers and teamsters alike, started for the Missouri River. On the way a stop was made at Fort Laramie where the 400 returnees had the first square meal they had eaten in months. It was simple fare consisting of hardtack, bacon, beans and coffee, but of which Cody remarked, "I can honestly say I thought it was the best meal I had ever eaten. At least I relished it more than any other, and I think the rest of the party did the same."[14]

CHAPTER 4

Ambushed by Indians

FORT LARAMIE, an old frontier post, was a veritable story book spot come true for Bill Cody. Three or four thousand Indians lived close by the post, and the youngster visited the camps of the Arapaho, Cheyenne, and Sioux. Fascinating as were these legendary warriors, the boy's full hero worship was reserved for the famous Indian fighters and scouts who made the fort their headquarters. Here he saw Kit Carson, Jim Bridger, and many of the other Western frontiersmen whom he had read about, heard about and dreamed about.

All too soon he was on the move again. Lew Simpson was promoted to the position of brigade wagon-master and put in charge of two large trains, with a complement of 400 men, bound for Fort Leavenworth. In order to detour around a sizable group of hostile Sioux and Cheyenne braves known to be lurking in the area, Simpson ordered the wagons to take the trail down the South Platte instead of following the usual route along the North Platte.

Half the journey was covered without incident. The two trains were traveling fifteen miles apart and Simpson, with the rear party, had to gallop the intervening distance to give his orders to the advance contingent. Two companions were chosen to accompany him—the assistant wagonmaster, George Woods, and the youngest member of the crew, Bill Cody.

At eleven o'clock one morning the three had ridden to within seven miles of the forward unit. Suddenly from the hills behind the barren plateau at Cedar Bluffs a band of Sioux bore down upon them. Escape was impossible on their worn-out mules and there was no place in which to take cover. Simpson quickly dismounted, shot the three mules, slit their throats to stop their kicking, and with the help of Woods and Cody dragged their bodies into a triangle. Then the white men crouched behind this barricade.

The redskins charged furiously, shooting arrows as they drew nearer. The defenders held their fire until the warriors were fifty yards away and then let loose a withering volley with their Yagers. This slowed the Indians but did not stop them. Simpson, Cody, and Woods now brought their revolvers into play, and the Sioux pulled up short and then retreated. Three of their comrades lay dead within twenty-five yards of the barricade.

Again the Indians attacked, and again they were warded off, leaving three additional casualties behind them. Woods received a slight wound, while dozens of arrows had just missed their marks and penetrated the mules' bodies instead.

If the Indians had not abandoned their second attack and retreated to hold a council of war, it is doubtful whether the men inside the fortress of flesh could have survived. The respite, however, gave them the opportunity to reload their weapons and prepare for the next assault. Simpson examined Woods' wound and found that it had not been made by a poisoned arrow. He applied a large quid of tobacco to the puncture, and the wounded man was ready for further action.

A third charge was beaten off. The Indians seemed demoralized by the effectiveness of the defenders' rapidly repeating revolvers. This time two more of their number lay dead on the field of battle.

The wagoners were running out of ammunition. In desperation they tried to strengthen their defenses. They dug up the earth inside the fort with their knives and threw it over the dead animals. In this way they fashioned an effective breastwork.

The Indians did not attack again until nightfall and then they varied their strategy. The red men set fire to the prairie in an attempt to burn out the white men. The buffalo grass was too short to sustain a blaze, but the smoke that arose from the grasslands blanketed the braves and forced Simpson and his companions to keep a sharp lookout for sneak attacks.

Through the night each man behind the dead mules took a turn standing guard while the others snatched some sleep. With the rising of the sun the Sioux charged once more. Simpson, Woods, and Cody directed a murderous volley at them and the Indians galloped back out of range. Inside the fortification feelings of relief mingled with desperation. The ammunition was gone. The only weapons that remained were knives and bare hands. The red men's ignorance of this situation—and the fact that the rear wagon train was long overdue—were their only hopes.

The Indians now dismounted and formed a half-mile circle around the breastwork. Obviously the red men had seen the advance wagons passing the day before and were of the belief that the entire train had gone by. Why brave burning bullets, their strategy seemed to say, when starvation and thirst will force our enemy to surrender or die? Each Sioux warrior sat on his haunches, faced the beleaguered men, and waited.

The morning inched on and still no sign of the wagon train. The sun—a bright, glaring disc in the sky—seemed lower than usual, as if it were curious to take a long, close look at the three huddled defenders pressed against their bulwark of mule flesh and dirt.

And occasionally the men gazed back at the sun: Simpson in bewilderment, as he carefully calculated from its position in the heavens how many hours had passed, and wondered whether the rear train itself had been ambushed by the main body of the Sioux; Woods in desperation, for the rays appeared to be long burning fingers intent upon torturing him by irritating the wound in his shoulder, parching his dust-dry throat, sapping the little strength he had left; Cody in confusion (he was a man because he was doing man's work, he had shot and killed Indians and had held his own with grown men in resisting the rigors of Fort Bridger and the dangers of many trails), for he felt tears well up in his eyes ("kid's tears," he labeled them, but they flowed nevertheless) as he thought of Salt Creek Valley, his home, his mother and the rest of the family, and faced the terrible fact that he might never see them again.

All the boy's fears were suddenly reinforced in a horrible way. He looked over at Simpson and saw him methodically sharpening his knife, slowly stropping the long blade on the side of his boot. The wagon-master's attention would shift from the knife to the sun to the knife to the sun, and there were tears in his eyes too. Though not a word was spoken Billy immediately grasped the meaning of this charade. Simpson had put a time limit on the wagon train's arrival. It was inconceivable that if it did not arrive by noon, it would arrive at all. *Midday was literally the deadline!* If help did not come by then, he was determined to kill his companions and himself rather than fall into the hands of the savages.

The sun was almost directly overhead when the stillness of the late morning was broken by a sharp crack, a sound something like a rifle shot, but slightly different, with its own distinctive quality; a familiar sound, a happy sound, a welcome sound—the crackle of the big bullwhip signaling that the bullwhackers had arrived. First the single crack, then a staccato series of snaps as the teamsters urged their oxen forward, and finally the ping and zing of rifle bullets as the wagoners opened fire on the Sioux.

The Indians jumped on their horses and bolted back into the hills.

Food and water and medicine were given to the valiant three. They recounted what had happened and received the congratulations of the entire crew. The teamsters of the rear train explained how they had been delayed: one of the wagons, overloaded and bulging out at the sides like a fat porpoise, had become lodged between two rocks bordering a narrow part of the trail, and it had taken many hours to pry it loose.

The caravan continued on and reached Leavenworth in the middle of July, 1858. Billy hurried to his home and was given a royal welcome by the entire family who had not seen him for over a year. He was saddened, however, to find his mother in poor health.

Wild Bill Hickok accompanied Billy to the Cody farm

and was received with full hospitality. He soon became enamored of Julia Cody, a beautiful young girl with flashing brown eyes and a perfect peaches-and-cream complexion.

She in turn was tremendously impressed by her famous visitor. She had heard the usual exaggerated stories about "Wild Bill, the Killer" and was amazed to find him gentle, soft-spoken, considerate and kind.

Mrs. Cody, Julia, and the other girls agreed among themselves that they had never seen a more handsome man. He stood six-feet-one-inch tall and carried himself as straight as a Sioux arrow. His shoulders and chest were full and strong; his limbs and torso were slender and supple. But it was his face that left a lasting impression on everyone, male and female alike. His eyes were pure blue; his nose, aquiline and finely-shaped; his mouth, firm and straight-lipped though partially concealed by a tawny mustache. His sun-brightened hair was fourteen inches long, light blond, and fell in ringlets over his shoulders. His clothes were flamboyant yet, given his good looks and powerful frame, in excellent taste. Around his waist Wild Bill wore a silver-studded gun belt in whose holsters he carried a pair of specially tooled, ivory-handled revolvers.[1]

The total man—the face, the figure, the clothes, the guns, the manners, the deportment, the authority, the reputation and the personality—was unforgettable.

Wild Bill proposed marriage to Julia. She was extremely fond of him and highly flattered. She consulted her brother and asked his advice. Billy's words were completely candid and showed a wisdom far beyond his years. "Julia," he said, "Wild Bill is my best friend and a man among men. But he loves the plains, he lives for adventure, and even though he'd try with all his might, he could never settle down. Marrying Bill Hickok and trying to housebreak him would be harder than saddling a grizzly bear."

Julia turned Wild Bill down. Yet the famous frontiersman stayed at the Cody farm whenever he was in the vicinity of Leavenworth, and in letters to his own mother and sisters in Illinois always referred to the Salt Creek Valley house as his home.

Billy Cody remained with his family for many months, taking odd jobs in town, helping run the farm, doing chores around the hotel and sandwiching in a little schooling whenever time permitted or inclination moved him. He curbed his spirit of adventure because of his mother's illness.

Some idea of the problems and privations that confronted Mary Cody in the first years following her husband's death can be gained from the contents of a letter she wrote to an old friend, Mrs. Laurel Summers, in the year 1859. The complete letter reads:[2]

Salt Creek
August 26, 1859.

My Dear Friend;

It is a long time since I have wrote to you, when Mr Cody was at your house 4 years this summer he thought you was in a decline, and I was afraid you was no more, and I wrote to Mr Summers. I knew he still lived as I could hear from him politically. When Mr Cody got home I was reduced to a skeleton looking for death. I took a dreadful cold which settled on my lungs, and anxiety of mind owing to the trouble, sometimes almost killed me, but when Mr Cody died it seemed as though I could not die, my helpless family needed me so much and my only consolation was in Religion. I prayed God to save my husband's soul and he died believing in God.

Mr Cody's infidelity gave way when Sammy died, the conversation of that angel child the night before he died made such an impression on him. I loved that boy too much, I made him my idol.

Everything connected with you brings back to memory by gone days spent in Iowa, and of the dear departed friends now gone. How sorry I was to hear of the death of your little boy, although I trust time has healed the wound. To lose those that are near and dear is trying under any circumstance, but it must be a comfort to feel as I have no doubt you do, that as the home circle narrows here it increases in that better world to which we must all go.

If it were not for that hope the loss of friends would be unbearable. Heaven feels very near to me, I have two angel children there and many loved ones besides.

When Mr Cody died we had the quarter section we lived on, some other property at Grasshopper Falls. Mr Cody could not do much on account of the difficulties here. We lost our horses, all our loose property and Mr Cody's death was occasioned by the trouble.

I missed Mr Cody so much and now although more than two years have passed he is fresh in my memory; and poor dear Martha, I loved her so much she improved with every year and few were so good. She joined the Methodist church one year after we came here and died a triumphant death, remembering all her friends and prayed for all to meet her in a better world.

I have been offered $8,000 for this place, before I built the hotel and fences and broke 100 acres of land.

I have had a great deal of trouble, the house cost me more than I expected and I went security for Martha's husband so I got some in debt and it gave me great trouble. I never owed one dollar before and I can not bear to owe.

Do ask Mr Summers if Mr ——, the sheriff when we left, can pay what he had, I must raise $300.00 and if that could be collected it would help. I never have had one dollar or the offer of help from any one.

The world seemed to forget me and I never wrote; and

this year I should have gotten along well but on account of the drought. It had almost brought famine to many in Kansas. Times are very hard, no money can be gotten for anything and interest is so high.

Willie is one of the smartest and best of boys, he has always been a great comfort to me, and hope he is to be distinguished yet. He is decidedly the brightest of the family.

Julia is good, sometimes I think she could do no better. My children are my jewels and do not laugh at my partiality, I have no one else to love and I am father, mother all in one.

Now do write. I hope you are rich and happy, do let me know. You and Summers were the first I loved in Iowa and I used to think you liked me but sometimes I think no one thinks of me.

Tell Helen to write to Julia.

Your friend
MARY B. CODY.

Toward the end of the summer Mrs. Cody's health was greatly improved and Billy made another trip with a wagon train to Fort Laramie, then on to a new post, Fort Walback, at Cheyenne Pass, and then back to Laramie, all without incident. Billy then threw in his lot with a party of trappers, seeking beaver, otter, wolves and other animals in the vicinity of the fort. Results were poor and in December Mr. Ward, the post trader who had sponsored the expedition, called off the entire project.

Billy Cody wanted to return to Salt Creek Valley in time to spend New Year's with his family. Two of the unsuccessful trappers, Scott and Charley, also were heading for the Missouri River, so the three joined forces. With their three ponies and one pack mule, they made steady progress until a band of Indians hunting on the opposite side of the Little Blue River sighted them one afternoon. The redskins galloped along on one side of the river and the trappers rode along parallel to them on the other. The Indian ponies were fresher and could certainly have caught up to the tired mounts of Billy and his friends, if they had been able to find a suitable place to ford the river. But the water was too deep and the banks too steep. Night came and provided a protective blanket of darkness for the white men.

Yet the entire area was overrun with red men, and Billy and his companions searched for a hideout where they might spend the night. Finally they stumbled upon a low ravine in which there was a cavelike hollow. They climbed into this cavern, spread their bedding in the darkness, and prepared to get some much needed rest. Charley struck a match for a last minute smoke before turning in. The subterranean cave was illuminated for a moment and the three trappers screamed in terror. In William Cody's own words: "We were in the exact center of the most gruesome collection of human skulls and bones I have ever seen. Bones were strewn on the floor of the cave like driftwood. We had stumbled into a big grave where some of the Indians had hidden their dead away from the wolves after a battle."[3]

The men did not tarry to investigate further but saddled their ponies and pushed on through the night and well into the next day. Towards midday, with a heavy snow falling, they reached Oak Grove Ranch where they obtained lodging, good food and drink. The harrowing experience of the evening before, added to the fact that the snow bid fair to turn into a blizzard, encouraged Scott and Charley to go on a drinking binge. For days on end they consumed gargantuan quantities of a potent frontier brew, "tanglefoot," and every night, gloriously drunk, they played cards with the ranchers. Their money flowed into the pockets of the hosts as fast as the gallons of firewater flowed into their own stomachs. Billy wanted to press on to Leavenworth but dared not face the threat of the Indians and the fury of the snowstorm, alone.

At last the blizzard abated, the ranchers refused to accept any more I.O.U.'s from Scott and Charley, and the trio—weeks behind schedule—journeyed on and arrived at their destination early in February.

For another brief period Billy Cody went to school and helped his mother in the work around the farm and hotel, but in the spring a new form of excitement, the Pike's Peak gold rush, lured him away from home and soon he was on the trail again with a party of Leavenworth and Salt Creek Valley boys, seeking fame and fortune in Auraria, Colorado (later called Denver). Using this mushroom town of shacks, tents, Indian lodges, dance palaces and saloons for their base, the youngsters spent two weeks panning in the streams and prospecting in the hills. None of them knew anything about mining and it was no wonder that they abandoned the entire enterprise after two months of failure. Billy Cody somehow maintained his good humor; with a paintbrush he *XXXXX*ed out the words "Pike's Peak Or Bust" which the boys had initially lettered on the side of their prairie schooner and scrawled a revised slogan on the soiled canvas, "Busted, By Gosh!"

The youngsters pulled up stakes and headed for home. When they reached the Platte River they abandoned their wagon for a much more romantic means of transportation. They constructed a raft with which to float down the Platte to the Missouri River and then down the Missouri to Leavenworth. For five days they had smooth sailing;

on the sixth their raft struck a submerged rock and fell to pieces in the middle of the river. With it sank their belongings, but the entire crew swam to shore safely and walked the few miles to Julesburg, a famous ranch.

For Billy Cody the catastrophe proved to be a blessing in disguise. Julesburg had been designated as a way station for the newly organized pony express line. George Christman, one of the leading wagon-masters of Russell, Majors & Waddell, was the Julesburg agent for the line; and the company, Billy Cody's old employer, had originated the entire pony express system.[4] The youngster applied to Christman for a job as rider and was hired immediately.

The Julesburg agent was amused to hear of Billy's experiences in Colorado and pointed out to the boy that ironically enough it was the gold rush which had been directly responsible for the founding of the pony express. The telegraph and the railroad were slowly spreading westward but there was still a need for dependable, swift mail service from the Missouri River to the Pacific. By accomplishing miracles of horsemanship the riders for the new messenger system were able to span the 2,000 miles between St. Joseph, Missouri, and Sacramento, California—across endless plains, a dreary expanse of sagebrush and desert, and two lofty mountain ranges—in only nine days and nights. To maintain this suicidal schedule the company depended "on horse flesh and human nerves"[5]—the steady courage, skill in the saddle, and reliability of eighty daredevil riders. Of these Billy Cody, fourteen-years-old at the time, was by far the youngest.

In his autobiography William F. Cody described the pony express system as being "a relay race against time. Stations were built at intervals averaging fifteen miles apart. A rider's route covered three stations, with an exchange of horses at each, so that he was expected at the beginning to cover close to forty-five miles—a good ride when one must average fifteen miles an hour."[6] Billy was light in weight, he wore the minimum of clothing, he knew how to get the most out of his ponies and he easily met the pace that was set for him. Russell, Majors & Waddell had bought up the best horses for this service, insisted that messages to be delivered by the pony express be written on the thinnest possible paper, and supplied an individual waterproof pouch in which each letter was sealed. This combination of employee skill and company planning brought amazing results.

Billy wrote to his mother and told her how much he liked the exciting life of a pony express rider. She replied immediately and begged him to give up his strenuous, killing job. A postscript to this letter, written by Julia, stated that Mary Cody was seriously ill once again. This decided the boy. He quit the company after two months of service and returned to Salt Creek Valley.

The presence of her son was the best medicine in the world for Mrs. Cody. Her recovery was rapid and complete. When a friend of Billy's, Dave Harrington, invited him to go on a trapping trip in the country around Prairie Dog Creek, Mrs. Cody gave the two teen-agers her blessings and sent them on their way.

They built a cozy dugout for themselves out of poles and sod, constructed a fireplace in the wall, which served as oven and furnace, and made a corral outside for the oxen. Day after day the traps were filled. Dave and Billy spent their time baiting the traps, making rounds and killing their catch, skinning off the pelts, salting the hides and storing away the bounty.

Their first casualty occurred when one of the oxen fell

on the ice, broke his hip and had to be shot. That night, just as they were dozing off, they heard a loud commotion in the corral. Dave rushed out and found a bear killing the remaining ox. He raised his gun, fired, and wounded the animal slightly. The enraged bear left the ox and charged at Harrington.

At this moment Billy rounded the corner of the shack. He snapped his gun to his shoulder and shot. The bear fell dead at Dave's feet. Then the two of them walked over to the mangled ox and put him out of his misery.

Now they had plenty of ox meat in addition to other provisions, but they were stranded 200 miles from home with a dugout filled to overflowing with more than 300 valuable pelts and no way to transport them home. They agreed that one of them would head for the nearest settlement and secure a brace of oxen with which to haul their prizes to a trading post.

Shortly after they made this decision they spied a fine herd of elk. Neither could resist the opportunity to bag at least one of these magnificent animals. They slowly stalked the herd along a creek, and just as they were rounding a bend which would bring them within gun range, Billy slipped on the frozen ground and broke his leg just above the ankle. Writhing in pain on the creek bed, Billy nevertheless managed to force a smile as he requested his partner to shoot him and relieve his suffering, as they had previously done for the oxen.

Harrington carried Billy back to camp and set the fracture with a splint which he made from a wagon bow. He made his patient as comfortable as possible under the circumstances. Then the two of them discussed their next move.

It was decided that Dave was to start for the nearest settlement, 125 miles away, immediately and buy another yoke of oxen with which to haul out the patient and the pelts. Before leaving he placed Billy in the bunk, covered him with blankets, piled all the provisions within reach, and rigged up a sapling-string-cup system by which the boy could get snow through a hole in the lean-to and thus have water. Harrington's last act was to heap up the firewood by Billy's bed.

No sooner had Dave gone than Billy cut a notch in a stick he had at hand. This was to be his makeshift calendar on which he could mark off the days until Dave returned. They had figured that the round trip should take twenty days at the most.

Long day followed long day and Billy had nothing to do but to prepare the few simple meals he needed, read and re-read the Bible his mother had given him, and dream of rescue and home.

Just twelve notches had been cut in the stick when Billy was awakened one morning by a firm touch on his shoulder. Coming out of a deep sleep his first thought was of Harrington, but on completely opening his eyes he looked up into the hideous, red-painted face of a Sioux warrior in full war-bonnet.

The Indian asked the youngster in the Sioux tongue what he was doing there and how many more were in his party. Gradually the dugout filled with other braves while Billy could hear the voices of many more on the outside. The helpless boy thought his time was up.

The Indians suddenly moved apart, and through this aisle Chief Rain-in-the-Face, the old leader of the Sioux, advanced. The redskin recognized Billy immediately as the boy who used to visit his lodge at Fort Laramie, and the youngster reminded the chief that he had often played with his children among the wagon-beds, where they had taught him the Sioux language.

Billy also managed to explain his own predicament to the red man and told him that Harrington was bringing help.

Rain-in-the-Face told him that his warriors were on the warpath and that they planned to kill him. He said further, however, that he would intercede with his braves in Billy's behalf.

A brief conclave followed in which the boy's life hung in the balance. Then the old chief turned to Billy and informed him that they had decided to spare him but that they would take his gun, pistol, provisions and ammunition. The boy asserted that this was another form of taking his life, for without food he could not survive, and without weapons he might not be able to hold off the wolves.

The Indian leader said that this was the best bargain he could make. As for food, he pointed to the carcass of the ox which was hanging on the wall. Then the Sioux braves gathered a great deal of the provisions together and cooked a sumptuous feast. Gorged by this magnificent meal some of the braves curled up on the floor and remained until morning.

On departing the Sioux took all of the sugar, coffee, meat (excluding the ox), flour and cooking utensils. But nevertheless Billy heaved a sigh of relief. The long arm of coincidence, in the person of the old chief, had kept his scalp firmly on his head.

Left without matches he could not sleep for long but had to wake up constantly to feed the fire. On the second day after the Indians had left, a savage snowstorm fell, covering the entire lean-to, swirling under the door, seeping through the water hole, and drifting in between the cracks—making it very difficult to keep the wood supply dry. Desperately Billy did everything in his power to keep the flame going, for in the face of the bitter cold of the blizzard he depended on the fire for life itself.

Each morning he cut another notch on his calendar stick. The twentieth day came, the time when Harrington was due to return. Billy knew well that the heavy snows must have delayed his partner, but he hoped against hope that by some miracle Dave might get through on schedule. Night fell and Harrington did not arrive. Billy checked his food supply and was shocked to find that the ox carcass was almost picked clean. As he threw another log on the fire he saw that there was very little wood remaining.

During the long night Billy was unable to sleep. Wolves howled outside the dugout. Smelling the ox meat inside they ran over the roof, pawing and scratching, trying to get in. Within, Billy felt like the piece of cheese with which a mousetrap is baited.

On the twenty-seventh day his food gave out. On the twenty-eighth the firewood was no more. When he had put the last log in the oven, Billy lay back on his bunk and gazed at the ceiling. He was going to die. Dave had surely been caught in the storm and buried in the snow. All was lost. No food, no firewood, and the wolves waiting . . . waiting.

Somehow Billy mustered his last ounce of courage, rose from his bed and hobbled over to the one piece of furniture in the room, a crude table. He broke it into pieces and shoved some of the wood into the furnace. Fitfully he dozed most of the day. At nightfall he put the last two table legs on the fire. In the flickering light he read a few pages of his Bible. Then he said a prayer for his family and closed his eyes, convinced that he would never open them again.

His sleep was shattered by the most welcome noise he had ever heard, the cheerful sound of Dave's voice as he came slowly up the creek, yelling "Whoa! Haw!" to his cattle. Billy's joy was overwhelming. In his own words: "A criminal on the scaffold, with the noose around his neck, the trap about to be sprung, and receiving a pardon just at the last moment, thus giving him a new lease on life, could not have been more grateful than I was at the time."[7]

Dave called out Billy's name and Billy answered weakly. Harrington soon cleared a passageway through the snow, opened the door and stood before the boy. They hugged each other and for a moment neither was able to say a word.

Finally Billy broke the silence and with a quivering voice told of everything that had transpired since Harrington had left. As soon as the story was finished, Dave went outside, broke up a barrel and started the fire once again. Then he carried in some of the food he had fetched from the settlement and cooked a meal for Billy. While the boy was eating, Harrington recounted his own adventures. His trip had been a terrible one. The blizzard had caused him to lose his way and he had been forced to hole up for three days. Then his cattle strayed and he spent two days trailing them through the blinding snowdrifts. After catching them progress was still painfully slow in the face of the fury of the storm, and the mountains of snow.

A few days later Billy and Dave started for home. The

pelts—300 beavers and 100 otters—were loaded on the wagon. A hammock was rigged up for Billy. And the traps and gear were stowed away.

The journey home was made in good time. On the way they stopped at the settlement where Harrington had obtained the yoke of oxen, and gave the owner twenty-five beaver skins as a rental fee for the animals, a sum then equivalent to $60. The owner's son continued with them to Junction City where he reclaimed the oxen. It was at this place that the partners sold their wagon, furs and gear. They then proceeded by Government mule train to Leavenworth.

Dave accompanied Billy home. Mrs. Cody had feared that her son was dead and was ecstatic to see him and deeply grateful to his rescuer. She insisted that Dave stay with the Cody family and asked him to take charge of the farm. To this he agreed. A few months later, while planting some trees, he caught cold in a drizzling rain, contracted pneumonia and died. The Cody family was stunned at his death: Here was a young man who had made a most perilous journey through ice and snow in the middle of winter to save the life of a friend, only to be struck down by a mild spring rain. His loss was mourned as if he were a son or brother and his body was buried next to Isaac Cody's at Pilot Knob.

CHAPTER 5

Union Scout

THE NATIONAL political cauldron was boiling over in the summer of 1860. The slavery issue threatened to split the country down the middle. Speakers representing both points of view stumped the states and territories, seeking adherents. One of the most noted of these political leaders, Abraham Lincoln, who had been nominated for the presidency at the Republican Convention at Chicago in May, stopped off at Leavenworth to make a speech. He stayed overnight at the house of Mark Delehay, the abolitionist editor, who previously had befriended Isaac Cody and helped him when he was in trouble.

Busy with affairs at the farm and hotel, Julia Cody did not know of the presence of this famous man in Leavenworth. By chance she rode into town that very day and stopped at the Delehay home to chat with her friend Molly. Mrs. Delehay and her daughter ran down the walk in great excitement to greet her. The fabulous Abe Lincoln is inside, they told her, come in and meet him.

Julia had heard her mother say that Mr. Lincoln was certain to be the next president. At the thought of seeing him in person she suddenly lost her composure and became giggly and fluttery. She insisted upon changing from her riding habit. A neighboring girl, Mariah Norton, came to the rescue by lending her a pretty white dress.

Julia was then taken into the house and introduced to Abraham Lincoln. He was most charming and told Molly and Julia that he'd much rather chat with pretty girls than discuss politics. At one point he happened to look out of the window and saw Julia's horse grazing in the yard. He complimented the girl on the beauty of the animal and the magnificence of it strappings. She told him that the ornate saddle and bridle had been a gift from her father, Isaac Cody.

At the mention of Mr. Cody's full name Mr. Lincoln declared that he remembered him well. In an amazing feat of memory he repeated almost word for word the contents of the letter of introduction which Mr. Delehay had written to him for Isaac.

When the Delehay family, their friends and their honored guest went in to dinner, Mr. Lincoln insisted upon escorting Julia and Molly to the table and arranged for them to sit on either side of him during the meal. When the discussion finally turned in earnest to politics, he stated that in his opinion, and in the opinion of the Illinois delegation, Isaac Cody had been the best speaker at the Republican Convention of 1856. Mr. Cody had advanced the position at that time that the Negroes should be freed and allowed to colonize in the South. Mr. Lincoln had been so impressed by the cogency of Cody's presentation that he had adopted this line of argument for himself, and had advocated this policy ever since.

When it was time to go to the hall where he was to

make his official speech, Mr. Lincoln rose from his seat, stooped over and kissed both girls on the forehead.

Julia told her mother and Billy all about her wonderful visit with Abraham Lincoln. Mother and son were both proud that the presidential candidate had spoken so highly about Isaac Cody. Billy announced that he was "for" Abe Lincoln, not as might be expected because of the candidate's principles or record, but because the boy had heard that the lawyer from Illinois was one of the best wrestlers in the country.

The summer heat was unbearable and Billy Cody longed to return to the plains and the mountains. He hired a man to look after the farm, then went to Leavenworth and signed on with Lew Simpson who was leading a wagon train to Atchison. The wagon-master asked Billy to stay on permanently as his assistant but the youngster refused, saying he would leave the caravan at Atchison and attempt to sign on again as a pony express rider.

When they reached their destination, Billy asked Mr. Russell, of Russell, Majors & Waddell, for employment. He was given a letter to Alf Slade, one of the genuine killers of his day and a deadly shot drunk or sober, who was stage agent at Horseshoe Station, thirty-six miles west of Fort Laramie, for the pony express division extending from Julesburg to Rocky Ridge.

Slade was reluctant to hire someone so young, but when told that Billy had ridden two months on Bill Trotter's division, he admitted to having heard of the "youngest rider on the plains" and agreed to give him a trial.

Billy Cody was assigned to a route from Red Butte, on the North Platte River, to Three Crossings, on the Sweetwater, a distance of seventy-six miles.

One day he galloped into Three Crossings, his home station, wet and weary, eager for a good meal and some rest. He learned that the rider who was to cover the next stretch had been killed the night before in a drunken row and that there was no one available to make the trip.

Without hesitation, Billy mounted another horse—the schedule only allowed two minutes for transferring the mochila to a fresh mount—and rode on to Rocky Ridge, eighty-five miles farther on, arriving exactly on time. There he met the rider coming in from the west, took the mochila with the eastbound mail, and rode all the way back to Red Butte, his starting point. During the last twenty miles of his journey the mochila felt as heavy as a sack of rocks. He knew that the letters inside were written on the thinnest tissues and enveloped in oilskins, but for a while he fancied they were inscribed on slate and covered with cast iron. Finally he reached his home base, slumped from the saddle and barely dragged himself to the bunkhouse.

With this one ride Billy Cody became a legend among express riders. He had ridden 322 miles without a formal stop for rest, had averaged fifteen miles an hour, had exhausted twenty different horses on route and had safely delivered the mail. Far and wide this performance was heralded as record-breaking. In the entire history of the pony express it remained as one of the longest, if not the longest, continuous ride ever made by a circuit rider.

To the Indians the pony express symbolized even further incursions of their territory by the whites. The lone riders were the portents of things to come: full wagon trains, the railroad, small settlements, big towns and large cities—less land, less game, less space for the red men. So the warriors lay in ambush for the circuit riders and attacked the express stations in a desperate attempt to halt the advance of their implacable enemy.

Billy had his share of troubles with the Indians. One day as he was leaving Horse Creek, fifteen braves attacked him in a sand ravine eight miles west of the station. Fortunately he saw them coming and dug his spurs into his roan racer, the fastest pony in the stable, and galloped on towards Sweetwater Bridge, eleven miles away. Bullets flew thick and fast around his head at first, but he plastered himself flat along his pony's back and soon had outdistanced his pursuers.

Another surprise was in store for him at Sweetwater Bridge. The stocktender had been killed by Indians during the night. All the mounts had been driven off. Unable to change ponies Billy rode to Ploutz's Station, twelve miles farther on. He had covered twenty-four miles at top speed on one mount, with red men hot on his heels most of the way.

The pace of the Indian attacks against the pony express was accelerated. A stage was robbed and two passengers murdered. Lem Flowers, the assistant division agent, was severely wounded. All along the route from Split Rock to Three Crossings the red marauders harassed the express riders and drove off the stock from the way stations. The company ordered a six-week layoff in which time the operation would be reorganized and the stock replenished.

A party of forty men whose livelihood depended upon the continuance of the express service—stage drivers, pony riders, stock tenders and ranchmen, under the leadership of Wild Bill Hickok who had recently signed on as stage driver for Russell, Majors & Waddell—banded together as an unofficial posse to search for stolen stock and to throw a scare into the Indians. Billy Cody was happy to be in the company of his old friend and mentor and rode with him at the head of the company as it proceeded to the head of Horse Creek, twenty miles from Sweetwater Bridge.

There the party found a fresh trail running north to Powder River, and from examination of the hoofprints definitely ascertained that it had been made by horses which had been stolen from the express line. They followed these tracks for hours until they reached Crazy Woman's Fork, a tributary of the Powder. Here evidence was found that additional Indians had joined the band they were following and that the united party constituted a sizeable number of braves. At most, the combined redskin group could not be more than twenty-four hours in advance of their pursuers.

At Clear Creek the white men saw horses grazing on the opposite bank of the stream. This was in the heart of the Indian country where no whites ever dared to venture, so the Indians had not put out scouts.

Wild Bill's men held a council of war. Their leader explained the strategy: they would wait until nightfall, creep up as close to the camp as possible, gallop through it firing as they rode, and stampede the horses. This course of action was absolutely necessary as they were outnumbered by the red men three-to-one.

The plan was carried out successfully. The warriors thought that the white men had dropped down from the skies, and scattered in every direction as the posse raced through the camp. More than 100 ponies belonging to the pony express were recaptured and a number of Indian horses swelled this amount. Wild Bill and his men returned safely to Sweetwater Bridge with this booty without having suffered a single casualty.

The recovery of the stolen stock was celebrated in typical frontier fashion. For three full days the men were gloriously drunk. The entire party guzzled liquor and gambled, without sleeping at all. The Indian ponies changed hands with every deal of the cards.

On the night of the third day Alf Slade rode in to join the festivities. One of the stage-drivers tried to pull an ace out of his sleeve during a poker game and was shot dead by Slade. The men sobered up immediately. They carried their companion's body out into the field and Alf himself said a few words over the dead man. Then they all piled into the bunkhouse and slept around the clock.

The express service was resumed with the reclaimed ponies. Slade promoted Billy to the position of special or supernumerary rider. In this capacity he was a troubleshooter working out of Slade's headquarters. Whenever a rider was ill, or incapacitated or killed—and whenever Indians threatened one section of the line—Billy Cody would make a special run.

The new job was extremely dangerous but it also gave young Cody many extra hours of free time, which he spent in hunting. One day he headed into the foothills of Laramie Peak looking for bear. As night approached, Billy decided to make camp. He had seen many bear tracks, and had bagged two sage hens which he planned to broil for dinner. At a little mountain stream he found an open place where he built a fire.

Suddenly he heard a horse whinny further up the stream. His own mount was tethered nearby so he hurried over and covered its muzzle to keep it from answering the other steed. Then Billy made his way upstream to discover who his neighbor might be. On rounding a bend of the creek he discovered not one but fifteen horses grazing.

On the opposite side of the rivulet a light shone from the window of a large dugout. Billy Cody crept slowly forward until he was close to the shack. From within came the sound of voices speaking English, which meant that the occupants were white men, probably trappers.

The youngster walked to the door and knocked. Silence. Then one voice asking, "Who's there?"

"A friend," Billy said. "No danger, I'm a white man."

The door opened and a huge, ugly fellow said, "Come in."

The boy stepped fearfully across the threshold, and to quote his own words: "I saw that it was too late to back out, and that it would never do to weaken at that point, whether they were friends or foes. Upon entering the dugout my eyes fell upon eight as rough and villainous-looking men as I ever saw in my life. Two of them I instantly recognized as teamsters who had been driving in Lew Simpson's train, a few months before, and had been discharged.

"They were charged with the murdering and robbing of a ranchman; and having stolen his horses it was supposed that they had left the country. I gave them no signs of recognition however, deeming it advisable to let them remain in ignorance as to who I was.

" 'Where are you going, young man; and who's with you?' asked one of the men who appeared to be the leader of the gang.

" 'I am entirely alone. I left Horseshoe station this morning for a bear-hunt, and not finding any bears, I had determined to camp out for the night and wait till morning,' said I; 'and just as I was going into camp, a few hundred yards down the creek, I heard one of your horses whinnying, and then I came to your camp.'

" 'Where's your horse?' demanded the boss thief.

" 'I left him down the creek,' I answered.

"They proposed going after the horse, but I thought that that would never do, as it would leave me without any means of escape, and I accordingly said, in hopes to throw them off the track, 'Captain, I'll leave my gun here and go down and get my horse, and come back and stay all night.'

"If they have the gun, thought I, they would surely believe that I intend to come back. But this little game did not work at all, as one of the desperadoes spoke up and said: 'Jim and I will go down with you after your horse, and you can leave your gun here all the same, as you'll not need it.'

" 'All right,' I replied, for I could certainly have said nothing else. It became evident to me that it would be better to trust myself with two men than with the whole party.

" 'Come along,' said one of them, and together we went down the creek, and soon came to the spot where my horse was tied. One of the men unhitched the animal and said: 'I'll lead the horse.'

" 'Very well,' said I, 'I've got a couple of sage-hens here. Lead on.'

"I picked up the sage-hens, and followed the man who was leading the horse, while his companion brought up the rear. The nearer we approached the dug-out the more I dreaded the idea of going back among the villainous cut-throats.

"I had both of my revolvers with me, the thieves not having thought it necessary to search me. It was now quite dark, and I purposely dropped one of the sage-hens, and asked the man behind me to pick it up. While he was hunting for it on the ground, I quickly pulled out one of my revolvers and struck him a tremendous blow on the back of his head, knocking him senseless to the ground. I then instantly wheeled around, and saw that the man ahead who was only a few feet distant, had heard the blow and had turned to see what was the matter, his hand upon his revolver. We faced each other at about the same instant, but before he could fire, as he tried to do, I shot him dead in his tracks. Then jumping on my horse, I rode down the creek as fast as possible, through the darkness and over the rough ground and rocks.

"The other outlaws in the dug-out, having heard the shot which I had fired, knew there was trouble, and they all came rushing down the creek. I suppose, by the time they reached the man whom I had knocked down, that he had recovered and hurriedly told them of what had happened. They did not stay with the man whom I had shot, but came on in hot pursuit of me. They were not mounted, and were making better time down the rough *cañon* than I was on horseback.

"At last they had come so near that I saw I must abandon my horse. So I jumped to the ground, and gave him a hard slap with the butt of one of my revolvers, which started him on down the valley, while I scrambled up the mountain side. I had not ascended more than forty feet when I heard my pursuers coming closer and closer; I quickly hid behind a large pine tree, and in a few moments they all rushed by me, being led on by the rattling footsteps of my horse, which they heard ahead of them. Soon I heard them firing at random at the horse, as they no doubt supposed I was still seated on his back. As soon as they had passed me I climbed further up the steep mountain, and knowing that I had given them the slip, and feeling certain that I could keep out of their way, I at once struck out for Horseshoe station, which was twenty-five miles distant. I had hard traveling at first, but upon reaching lower and better ground, I made good headway, walking all night and getting into the station just before daylight,—foot-sore, weary, and generally played out."[1]

Billy immediately woke up everyone at the station and told them what had happened. Slade himself organized a force of twenty men to go after the thieves, and young Cody, tired as he was, went along to lead them to the hide-out. The dugout was deserted and the robbers' trail led off in the direction of Denver. It seemed useless to try to follow the fleeing party and the men returned to Horseshoe Station.

About this time young Cody longed to see his mother and sisters once again. He had been away from home for many months and now decided to go east. In June, 1861 he arrived at Salt Creek Valley and was again very distressed to find his mother in poor health.

The entire Territory was in turmoil. The great human conflagration, later to be known as the Civil War, had broken out that spring. Mark Delehay's old friend, Abe Lincoln, had been elected president, and shortly after his inauguration Fort Sumter had been fired upon and captured by the Confederates. Lincoln had mobilized the regular army and had issued a call for volunteers. All these events had had a profound effect on life in Kansas.

While new, untried recruits—boys who had never known the feel of battle—grappled along the Potomac, the veteran partisans of the free-soil and slavery factions in Kansas and Missouri renewed their own backwoods armed imbroglio. Mary Cody, who had lost her husband in the preliminary skirmishes of this great war, was naturally strongly pro-Union in this conflict. So strong was her faith in the Federal Government that she felt certain the war would be over in a few months.

The town and the fort were important outfitting posts for both the regular army and the volunteers. Billy stood by as his friends, young and old, who also had suffered indignities at the hands of the border ruffians, enlisted in the Union forces. He too was eager to join up but he had made a solemn promise to his invalid mother that he would not become a solider as long as she lived. In exacting this assurance from him she had explained that he was the sole breadwinner in the family. Without his support—and with the farm and hotel doing badly because of the shortage of help and the uncertainties of war—Mrs. Cody and her daughters would be destitute.

Billy had pledged his word that he would not enlist, but nothing had been said, by either mother or son, about the "unofficial" warfare which purely local companies were waging against the Missourians. One of the free-staters at Leavenworth, Chandler by name, organized an expeditionary force for the purpose of invading Missouri and harassing the border raiders. Billy Cody was one of the twenty-five men who joined Chandler in this hazardous undertaking.

Operating under what William F. Cody later admitted to being a mistaken assumption that all Missourians were secessionists because the state was a slave state—an opinion that was wrong because many of the citizens of Missouri did not sympathize with the Southern cause—the punitive party made its initial raid.

The goal of the first foray was to capture all possible horses belonging to Missouri desperadoes. Chandler slipped across the border in disguise a few days in advance of the others. He scouted the countryside and located the farms and stables where the horses were kept. When Billy Cody and his fellow "irregulars" met him on a fixed day, they were given maps indicating where the enemy mounts were to be found, and were told to capture these horses and bring them to a central rendezvous the following night.

The plan worked perfectly. At the agreed hour all twenty-five raiders showed up, each man bringing two or three mounts. They rode quickly to the border and crossed the river into Kansas at an Indian ferry above Wyandotte on the Kansas River.

On subsequent raids the little band repeated this same pattern: always the objective was to round up as many horses as they could safely snare, acting on the theory that the border ruffians would be effectively stalemated if they were forced to operate on foot. Occasionally the Missourians and the free-soilers skirmished but there were no pitched battles.

Some of the Kansans acted against Chandler's orders and extended their operations beyond horse-snatching. They began to burn houses and barns, and instead of taking the captured steeds to company headquarters, kept the mounts for themselves. Federal authorities, who had turned their heads the other way during the period when the invasions of Missouri were exclusively for the purpose of stealing horses from the border ruffians, now sent out Government detectives to investigate. A number of the Chandler group were arrested but Chandler and Cody were completely exonerated.

Mary Cody, when she learned that Billy was engaged in jayhawking, told him it was dirty business (who was to say when justified raids ended and looting and random destruction began?) and made him promise to quit, which he did immediately.

In the meantime Billy's old friend Wild Bill Hickok had single-handedly wiped out the McCanles gang, an outlaw band pretending to be attached to the Confederate army. This courageous exploit made Wild Bill the hero of the hour.

General John C. Fremont appointed Wild Bill brigade wagon-master of several ox trains that the Government had bought from the firm of Jones & Cartwright. Wild Bill chanced to meet Billy Cody in Leavenworth and asked him to join the train as assistant wagon-master. Billy gladly accepted the offer and journeyed with his friend to Rolla, Missouri, where the supply caravan was loaded. They continued to their final destination, Springfield, Missouri, without incident.

On their return to Rolla they heard a great deal about the approaching fall horse races at St. Louis. Wild Bill had brought a fast horse, Old Mountain, along and was determined to match him against the other racers. The two friends pooled their funds and decided to back their steed to the limit. So confident were they in Old Mountain's ability to outfoot all opposition that they not only bet every cent of their money on him but also put up the horse itself as a wager against $250 in cash.

It was decided that Billy, because of his light weight, would be the jockey. During the early part of the race Old Mountain was way out in front but at the midway point he suddenly "quit," and all the other horses in the contest galloped by leaving him far in the lurch. Thus the "country bumpkins" who had tried to take the "city slickers" into camp wound up penniless and horseless in the largest city either of them had ever seen.

Wild Bill immediately went to the St. Louis military headquarters and secured a position as Government scout for which he was given a bonus of $25. He turned this money over to Billy Cody who was too young to be accepted into the scouting service.

The two friends parted, Cody returning to Leavenworth by steamboat, Hickok going to Springfield army headquarters.

Billy arrived at the Cody farm to find his mother in failing health. She was so ill that Julia had taken complete charge of the family and its affairs. Mary, Julia, and Billy held a family conclave, and it was decided that despite his mother's critical condition it would be better for everyone concerned if Billy got another job away from home, where his outstanding talents as horseman and scout commanded a high salary. He left Leavenworth, promising to keep in close touch with the family.

First he was employed to carry military dispatches for the Government, working out of Fort Larned, Kansas. Later he was the assistant to George Long in buying horses for the Union forces. In the spring of 1862 he was hired as guide and scout by Colonel Clark's volunteer regiment, the Ninth Kansas, in its actions against warring Comanche

Plate 1 *Brown Bros.*

Buffalo Bill at 11
—a bullwhacker

Plate 2 *Brown Bros.*

Buffalo Bill at 14
—a Pony Express rider

Brown Bros.

Plate 3

Buffalo Bill
as a young scout

Plate 4 *Brown Bros.*

Kit Carson

Plate 5

Wild Bill Hickok

Plate 6

Chief Rain-in-the-Face

Plate 7 *Brown Bros.*

Buffalo Bill at 23

Plate 8

Ned Buntline (left), Buffalo Bill, and Texas Jack—photographed in the early Sixties

Brown Bros.

Brown Bros.

Plate 9

California Joe, a far western scout, and Buffalo Bill

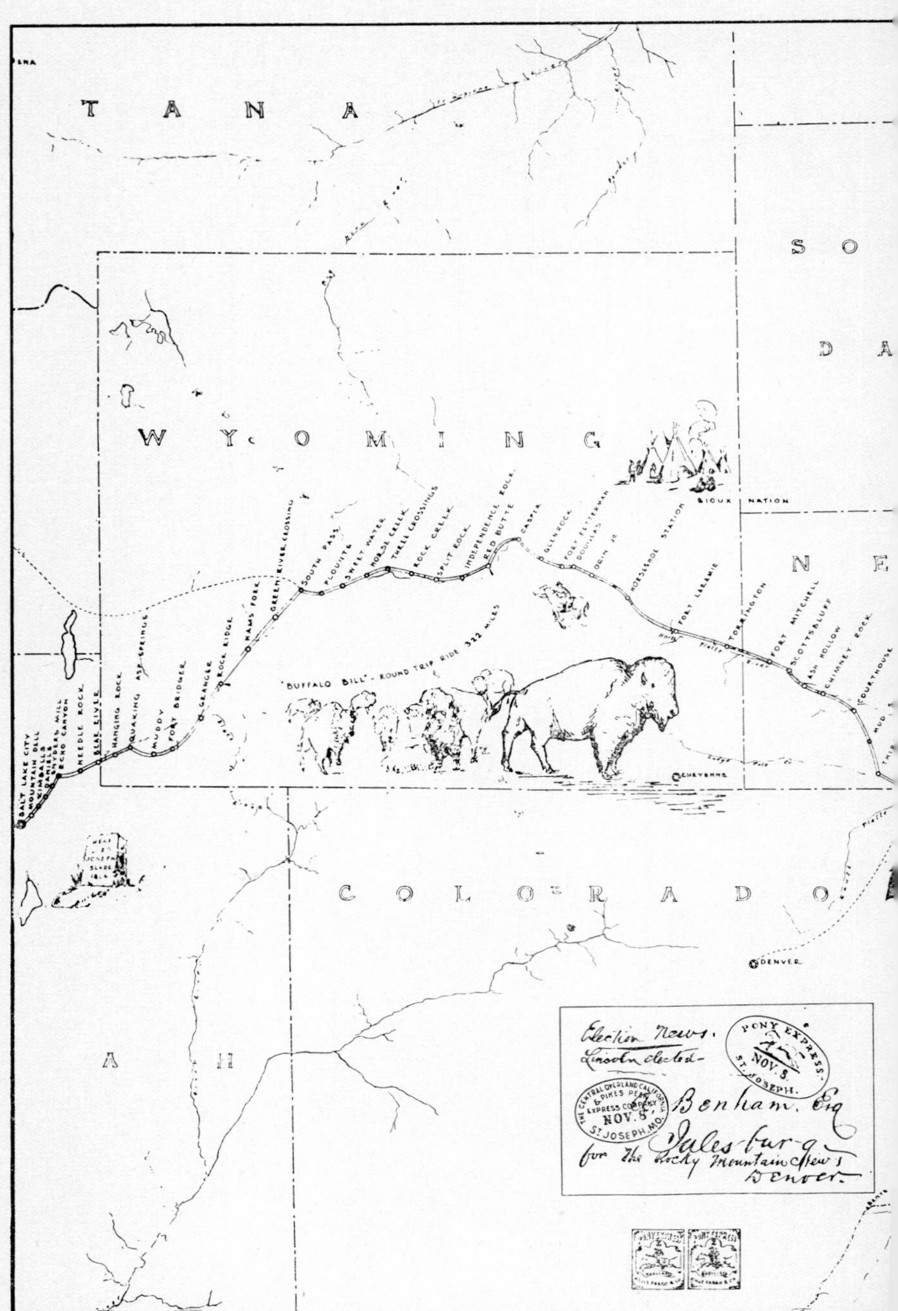
TANA
SO
DA
WYOMING
NE
COLORADO
SIOUX NATION
SALT LAKE CITY
MOUNTAIN DELL
ECHO CANYON
NEEDLE ROCK
BEAR RIVER
HANGING ROCK
QUAKING ASP SPRINGS
MUDDY
FORT BRIDGER
GRANGER
ROCK RIDGE
HAMS FORK
GREEN RIVER CROSSING
SOUTH PASS
SWEET WATER
HORSE CREEK
THREE CROSSINGS
ROCK CREEK
SPLIT ROCK
INDEPENDENCE ROCK
RED BUTTE
CASPER
GLENROCK
FORT FETTERMAN
DOUGLAS
HORSESHOE STATION
FORT LARAMIE
TORRINGTON
FORT MITCHELL
SCOTTSBLUFF
ASH HOLLOW
CHIMNEY ROCK
COURTHOUSE
"BUFFALO BILL" - ROUND TRIP RIDE 322 MILES
CHEYENNE
DENVER
Election News.
Lincoln elected -
PONY EXPRESS
NOV. 8
ST. JOSEPH.
THE CENTRAL OVERLAND CALIFORNIA & PIKES PEAK EXPRESS COMPANY
NOV. 8
ST. JOSEPH, MO.
Benham, Esq
Julesburg
for The Rocky Mountain News
Denver.

Plate 10

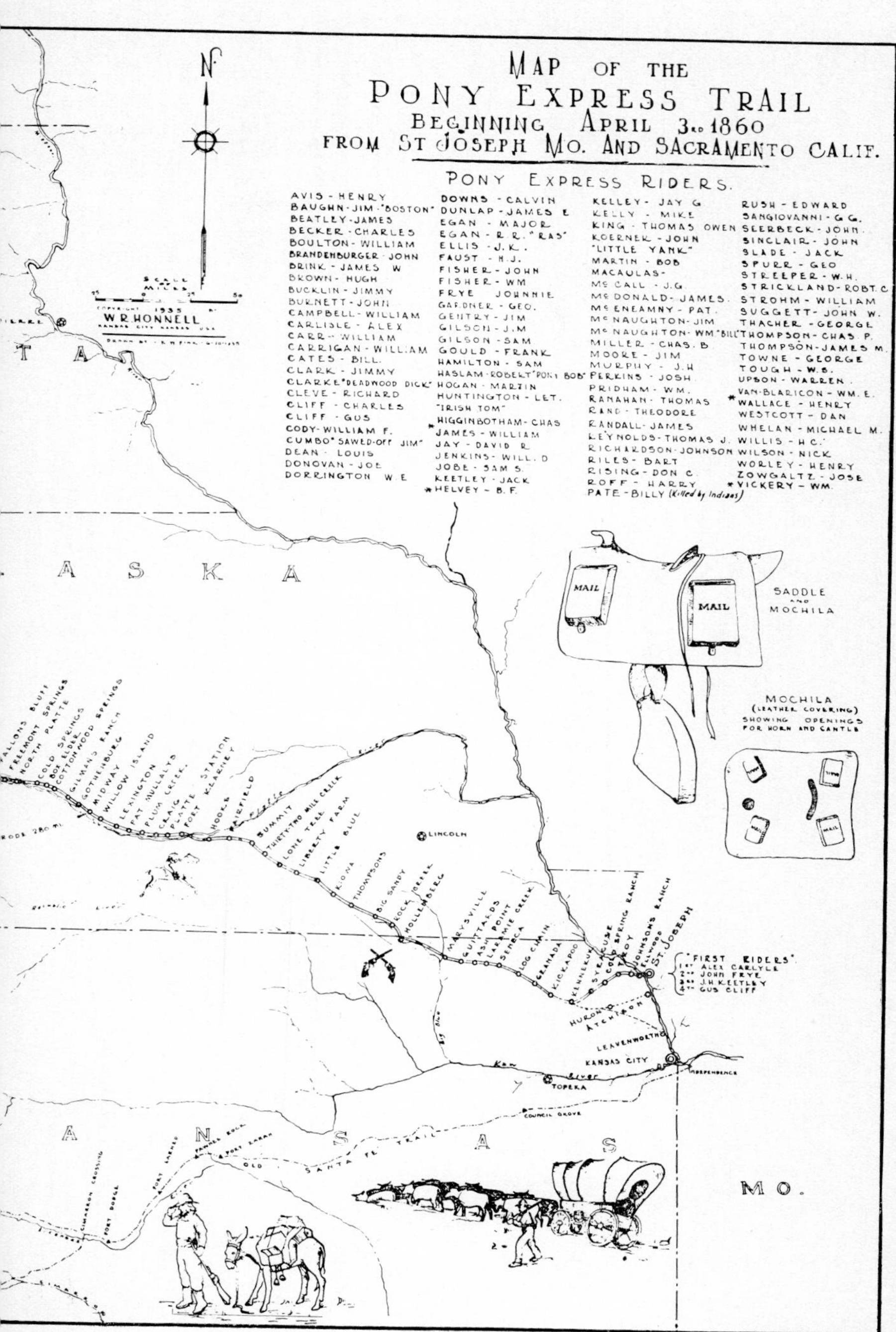

MAP OF THE
PONY EXPRESS TRAIL
BEGINNING APRIL 3RD 1860
FROM ST JOSEPH MO. AND SACRAMENTO CALIF.
N
SCALE MILES
COPYRIGHT 1935 BY
W.R. HONNELL
KANSAS CITY KANSAS USA
PONY EXPRESS RIDERS.
AVIS - HENRY
BAUGHN - JIM "BOSTON"
BEATLEY - JAMES
BECKER - CHARLES
BOULTON - WILLIAM
BRANDENBURGER - JOHN
BRINK - JAMES W
BROWN - HUGH
BUCKLIN - JIMMY
BURNETT - JOHN
CAMPBELL - WILLIAM
CARLISLE - ALEX
CARR - WILLIAM
CARRIGAN - WILLIAM
CATES - BILL.
CLARK - JIMMY
CLARKE "DEADWOOD DICK"
CLEVE - RICHARD
CLIFF - CHARLES
CLIFF - GUS
CODY - WILLIAM F.
CUMBO "SAWED-OFF JIM"
DEAN - LOUIS
DONOVAN - JOE
DORRINGTON W.E
DOWNS - CALVIN
DUNLAP - JAMES E
EGAN - MAJOR
EGAN - R.R. "RAS"
ELLIS - J.K.
FAUST - H.J.
FISHER - JOHN
FISHER - WM
FRYE JOHNNIE
GARDNER - GEO.
GENTRY - JIM
GILSON - J.M
GILSON - SAM
GOULD - FRANK
HAMILTON - SAM
HASLAM - ROBERT "PONY BOB"
HOGAN - MARTIN
HUNTINGTON - LET.
"IRISH TOM"
* HIGGINBOTHAM - CHAS
JAMES - WILLIAM
JAY - DAVID R
JENKINS - WILL. D
JOBE - SAM S.
KEETLEY - JACK
* HELVEY - B.F.
KELLEY - JAY G
KELLY - MIKE
KING - THOMAS OWEN
KOERNER - JOHN
"LITTLE YANK"
MARTIN - BOB
MACAULAS -
McCALL - J.G.
McDONALD - JAMES
McENEAMNY - PAT.
McNAUGHTON - JIM
McNAUGHTON - WM "BILL"
MILLER - CHAS. B.
MOORE - JIM
MURPHY - J.H
PERKINS - JOSH.
PRIDHAM - WM.
RANAHAN - THOMAS
RAND - THEODORE
RANDALL - JAMES
REYNOLDS - THOMAS J.
RICHARDSON - JOHNSON
RILES - BART
RISING - DON C.
ROFF - HARRY
PATE - BILLY (Killed by Indians)
RUSH - EDWARD
SANGIOVANNI - G.G.
SEERBECK - JOHN.
SINCLAIR - JOHN
SLADE - JACK
SPURR - GEO
STREEPER - W.H.
STRICKLAND - ROBT. C
STROHM - WILLIAM
SUGGETT - JOHN W.
THACHER - GEORGE
THOMPSON - CHAS. P.
THOMPSON - JAMES M.
TOWNE - GEORGE
TOUGH - W.S.
UPSON - WARREN.
* VAN-BLARICON - WM. E.
WALLACE - HENRY
WESTCOTT - DAN
WHELAN - MICHAEL M.
WILLIS - H.C.
WILSON - NICK
WORLEY - HENRY
ZOWGALTZ - JOSE
* VICKERY - WM.
MAIL
MAIL
SADDLE AND MOCHILA
MOCHILA
(LEATHER COVERING)
SHOWING OPENINGS
FOR HORN AND CANTLE
A S K A
FREMONT SPRINGS
NORTH PLATTE
COLD SPRINGS
BOX ELDER
COTTONWOOD SPRINGS
GILMAN'S RANCH
GOTHENBURG
MIDWAY
WILLOW ISLAND
LEXINGTON
PAT MULLALYS
PLUM CREEK
CRAIG
PLATTE STATION
FORT KEARNEY
HOOKS
FAIRFIELD
SUMMIT
THIRTY-TWO MILE CREEK
LONE TREE
LIBERTY FARM
LITTLE BLUE
KIOWA
THOMPSONS
BIG SANDY
ROCK CREEK
HOLLENBERG
MARYSVILLE
GUITTARDS
ASH POINT
LARAMIE CREEK
SENECA
LOG CHAIN
GRANADA
KICKAPOO
KENNEKUK
SYRACUSE
COLD SPRING RANCH
TROY
JOHNSON'S RANCH
ELWOOD
ST. JOSEPH
LINCOLN
"FIRST RIDERS"
1ST ALEX CARLYLE
2ND JOHN FRYE
3RD J.H. KEETLEY
4TH GUS CLIFF
HURON
ATCHISON
LEAVENWORTH
KANSAS CITY
INDEPENDENCE
Kaw River
TOPEKA
COUNCIL GROVE
A N S A S
OLD SANTA FE TRAIL
FORT LARNED
FORT ZARAH
CIMARRON CROSSING
FORT DODGE
MO.

H. Zeller

Plate 11 *Brown Bros.*

Chief Yellow Hand

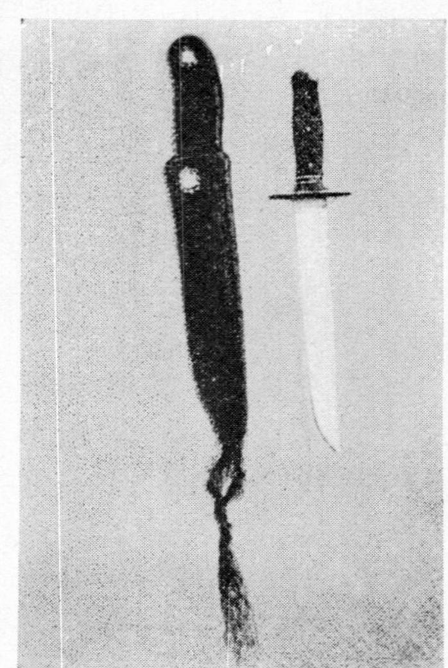

Plate 12 *Brown Bros.*

The knife with which Buffalo Bill killed Chief Yellow Hand

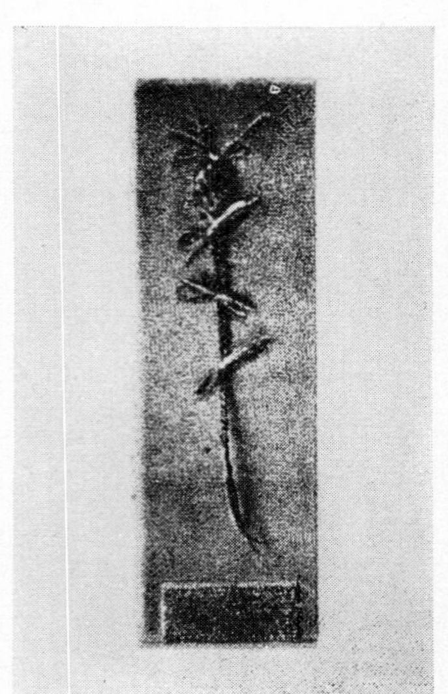

Plate 13 *Brown Bros.*

Chief Yellow Hand's scalp taken by Cody after the Custer Massacre

Plate 14

Gathering and counting buffalo tongues for delivery to the U.S. Army—drawing from "Tenting on the Plains," by E. B. Custer

Plate 15 *Brown Bros.*

Stampede and slaughter of buffaloes on the Kansas Pacific Railroad

and Kiowa tribes along the Santa Fe trail between Fort Lyon and Fort Larned.

In the winter of 1862 he joined a local company, the famous Red-Leg Scouts, commanded by Captain Bill Tuff. This unit cooperated with the regular army along the Kansas borders to protect the Territory from attacks by Quantrell's Missouri freebooters, and by other bushwhackers and guerrilla gangs like the Younger Brothers. Among Billy's comrades-in-arms were such noted Kansas Rangers as Red Clark, the St. Clair brothers, Jack Harvey, and Johnny Frey.

The Red-Leg Scouts were kept very busy. Whenever they found out that the scattered pro-Confederate bands were assembling for a general raid, they would notify the regular troops at Fort Leavenworth or Fort Scott. In addition they countered single actions of the individual bands whenever they could. The guerrillas and bushwhackers robbed banks, attacked villages, burned buildings and bridges, looted and plundered. The Red-Leggers were proud that despite numerous provocations they did not copy the enemy's tactics but restricted themselves to purely defensive fighting.

In December, 1862 Billy was delighted to receive word that his beloved sister Julia had married James (Al) Goodman, a sober, industrious farmer. He sent her his blessings.

In the summer of 1863 Billy Cody quit the Red-Leg Scouts and returned to Leavenworth. Word had reached him that his mother was desperately ill and sinking rapidly. He hastened to the family home where his sister Julia told him that his mother did not have long to live.

Shortly before the end Mary Cody summoned the family attorney, Mr. Douglass, and with all her children gathered around, settled her financial affairs. Julia's husband was appointed guardian over the children and administrator of the estate. Turning to her eldest daughter, she said, "Julia, I want you to be as you have always been, a faithful helper and a mother to the children." Then she spoke to Billy, who was holding her hand, and told him to take special care of his seven-year-old brother Charley. Finally she addressed a few words to the younger children, bidding them to respect the advice and guidance of Julia and Billy, and to show obedience to Mr. Goodman.

With all matters arranged Mrs. Cody said calmly, "I think I have done all that I can do, and will now wait for the Lord's call."

On November 22, 1863 Mary Cody, surrounded by her loved ones, died. She was buried at the side of her husband Isaac, and of Billy's friend Dave Harrington, at Pilot Knob.

His mother's death released Bill Cody from the pledge he had made not to enlist in the regular army while she was alive. That winter the Seventh Kansas regiment, known as "Jennison's Jayhawkers," returned from the war, reorganized and re-enlisted as veterans. Among these soldiers were many of Bill's old friends and neighbors.

On February 19, 1864 William F. Cody, with the consent of his guardian James Goodman, enlisted in the Seventh Kansas Cavalry shortly before his eighteenth birthday.[2]

In the spring of 1864 the regiment was ordered to Tennessee and reached Memphis just after the Union General Sturgis had been badly defeated by the Confederate General Forrest. In May, 1864 General Grant issued a general order to his troops, ordering them to hold fast against the Southern offensive and requesting them to "fight it out on the line if it takes all summer." General A. J. Smith was sent into the field to reorganize Sturgis' army. The revitalized command made a forced march to Tupelo, Mississippi, where General Forrest's troops were defeated in a return engagement.

Bill Cody's frontier training now stood him in good stead. He was put on detached service as a scout and sent out ahead of the regiment when it was ordered to Cape Girardeau, Missouri, to intercept a Confederate force under General Price. For nearly six weeks the two armies skirmished daily.

General Smith sent Bill Cody out to gather information concerning Price's movements, disguised as a Missouri farm boy with a dray horse as his mount. On the second morning Bill spotted a large plantation and decided to ask for a meal. He was readily admitted to the kitchen and was greatly surprised to see a Confederate officer sitting at the table eating bread and drinking milk.

The officer looked up at Bill and said, "You little rascal, what are you doing in those 'secesh' clothes?"

The blue-jeaned boy gasped in amazement for he now recognized the man by his voice, where initially he had been fooled by his perfect disguise. The Confederate officer was his old friend and partner, Wild Bill Hickok. Further words between the two were not possible, for the lady of the house entered the kitchen at that moment. Soon the Tennessee lad and the Southern general were partaking of bread and milk together.

Wild Bill paid the woman for their snack and the pair walked to the gate. "Billy, my boy," said Hickok, as they stood where Cody's horse was tied, "I am mighty glad to see you. I haven't seen or heard of you since we got busted on that St. Louis horse race. I am a scout under General

McNeil. For the last few days I have been with General Marmaduke's division of Price's army, in disguise, as a Confederate officer from Texas."

"That's exactly the kind of business that I am out on today," said Cody. "I want to get some information concerning Price's movements."

"I'll give you all that I have."

Hickok then went on and told Bill all that he knew regarding Price's intentions, and the number and condition of his men, and said, "Here are some letters which I want you to give to General McNeil."

The two soon shook hands and parted, Wild Bill having informed young Cody that he intended to remain a few days longer in this disguise, as he was getting some valuable information.

Bill Cody returned to the Union army and gave his own report and Wild Bill's letters to the commanding general. Then he doffed his blue-jeans and donned his regular uniform, resuming his duties as scout and guide.

A few days later, while riding with the advance guard ahead of the troops, he stopped at a large farmhouse for a drink of water. On the porch was a beautiful lady and her two attractive daughters. There were no men about the place and the women were frightened by the sudden appearance of a Yank on their property. He assured them that he meant no harm and only wanted to quench his thirst.

As he was lifting the dipper to his lips, General Smith and his staff officers came by, closely followed by the main body of the troops. Men began leaving their companies and rushing toward the house. The women huddled in the living room in fright.

Bill walked out into the yard and faced the onrushing men. "Halt!" he hollered, "I order you off this property in the name of the commanding officer, General Smith." The soldiers, recognizing their general's favorite scout, stopped in their tracks and beat a hasty retreat to the road.

The mother and her daughters thanked him profusely and insisted that he stay and eat dinner with them. The prospect of good fried chicken instead of army short rations was an irresistible temptation, and he joined them at the table. Just as he was being served a second helping there was a muffled movement behind him and he turned in his chair to face three double-barreled shotguns leveled at his head.

Before he could utter a word, the women sprang between him and the men with the guns, shouting, "Father! Boys! Lower your guns. Don't shoot him. He saved our house and maybe our lives."

The father and his sons put their weapons aside and sat down at the table. The women told them how he had protected their house from pillage at considerable risk to himself. The old man shook Bill's hand, thanked him for what he had done, and sat and chatted as the boy finished his meal.

When the youngster left the house, the entire family presented him with a bottle of peach brandy as a personal gift to General Smith.

For a time Smith's forces had Price's troops hemmed in near Kansas City but the wily Southerners broke out of the trap and the scene of battle shifted to the vicinity of Fort Scott, Kansas. While the rival armies were skirmishing here one day, Bill Cody was amazed to see two Confederate officers on horseback suddenly bolt from the rebel ranks and dash straight toward the Union line. Both sides fired at the two men, one of them fell dead from his horse, but the other kept coming.

"Hold your fire!" Bill shouted to his comrades. "He's one of our men. It's Wild Bill Hickock."

Wild Bill it was, resplendent in the dress uniform of a Confederate general. He was taken to the tent of General McNeil and General Pleasanton. He reported to them that General Price was putting up a bold front but that his command was actually weak and demoralized. The generals immediately ordered a full-scale attack. For two hours the Union soldiers drove the enemy before them—until nightfall gave the opposition time to re-form its ranks.

Bill Cody and Wild Bill had a bang-up reunion. Wild Bill told his friend that he had left the Confederate ranks just in time, for the secessionist soldiers had begun to suspect he was a Union spy and had been watching him very closely. His one regret—outside of the fact that the other scout who had fled with him had been killed—was that he had been unable to escape earlier in the day when his intelligence about the weakness of Price's army would have enabled the Union troops to crush the enemy in one sustained blow.

In later years William F. Cody wrote, "From this time on, Wild Bill and myself continued to scout together until Price's army was driven south of the Arkansas River and the pursuit abandoned."[3]

During the time Bill was scouting with the Union forces, there was no lack of excitement for the rest of the Cody family at the Salt Creek Valley farm. Goodman had divided feelings: he wanted to enlist in the army yet he was reluctant to leave the homestead and the hotel without a man-in-charge.

Julia decided the issue. "Now Al," she said, "never mind about me. I will look after things here . . . and if I had been a man I would have gone to war long before this."

Captain Will Howe, a family friend of the Cody's, backed Julia up. "Come on, Goodman," he said, "and don't worry. Julia can manage this end of the line as well as you can."

With these assurances Goodman marched off to war and joined in the fighting against Price. But as he left he wondered: Will the big span of mules be stolen without able-bodied men around? What will become of the pen full of fattening hogs when the corn supply runs out? How can Julia take care of the hotel with so many other duties to occupy her?

He need not have worried. Julia met every emergency with good sense and effectiveness. Her first act was to quarter the mules in an out-of-the-way farm building where no one would ever think of looking for them. She kept only her own riding pony close to the main house.

Shortly after her husband's departure Julia saw a party of Union soldiers ride into her yard. One of them started for the corral, intent upon requisitioning her pony for army service, but Julia intercepted him. She explained that this was the only horse she had.

The trooper ignored her and began to put a bridle on the pony. Julia drew a revolver from her belt and pointed it at his head. The soldier dropped the reins but refused to leave the corral. Julia turned to an officer standing nearby and said, "Captain, if your man takes my horse, there'll be a small war right here." Then pointing to a jaded mule that someone had left in the corral, she added, "He can take that old plug."

"Well, John," said the Captain, "you'd better take the

mule and be done with it." The soldier, with an embarrassed grin on his face, pulled the run-down animal from the corral and the men rode off.

Julia invited two women neighbors and an elderly couple who were afraid to remain in their own homes alone to live with her during the emergency period. The price of good meat had skyrocketed to thirty cents a pound which Julia could not afford to pay with so many extra mouths to feed, so she hired a young boy to help her slaughter and dress the hogs, one by one, as they were needed for food.

With her sisters Eliza and Helen, whom she had maintained at school in Leavenworth until the war forced it to shut down, she husked an entire field of corn in fast time. Thus there was fodder for the hogs and food for the table.

Everything went smoothly until one evening when two drunken men rode up to the house and declared that they had been sent to notify the noncombatants that Price had hacked his way through the Kansas militia and was on his way to Leavenworth to sack the city and burn the fort. One of the women became hysterical and screamed, "We're lost! We're lost!"

Despite her own fears that the report was true Julia quieted the woman. Then she seized a pistol from the mantle and ordered the men to scat. The intruders didn't wait for a second warning but reeled drunkenly out into the night.

No one in the Cody household slept a wink that night. In the morning Julia rode to the fort and was informed that just the opposite of what she had been told was true. The Seventh and Ninth Kansas regiments had defeated

Price's force in a pitched battle. So thorough had been the rout that the militia was returning home.

After October, 1864 Bill Cody saw no more active fighting with the Union forces. He was ordered to St. Louis where he was put on detached service at military headquarters. In the late spring he was assigned to assist with the work of the Freedmen's Relief Society, an organization established in March, 1865 by the War Department to supervise and manage all abandoned land and to take care of all matters pertaining to refugees and freed-men.

It was the special job of Bill Cody and his side-kick Wild Bill to find homes for the war refugees as soon as they arrived by riverboat in St. Louis.

It was during this period that Bill Cody, now nineteen-years-old, met and fell in love with a beautiful young lady, twenty-two-year-old Louisa Frederici. The young soldier had many hours of free time at his disposal and spent every possible minute with Miss Frederici.

At the close of the Civil War in 1865 Bill was discharged from the army and returned to Leavenworth. Al Goodman had also been mustered out of service, safe and sound, and was back running the farm and managing the hotel. Little Charles Whitney Cody, the youngest member of the family, who Bill had assured his mother he would personally protect, had succumbed to typhoid fever when that disease ravaged the nation at the height of the war period. Bill paid a visit to the child's grave and placed a wreath on the headstone.

Young Cody did not remain at home for long. His thoughts and his dreams were always in St. Louis with Louisa Frederici. He told Julia about this woman he loved. His sister bade Bill go to St. Louis right away and join

Louisa. He traveled to Missouri by stagecoach and hurried to Miss Frederici's home.

The youth of action, who nevertheless had talked old Chief Rain-in-the-Face into saving his life and who seldom was at a loss for words, was tongue-tied as he attempted to convey his feelings to Louisa. He stuttered and stumbled, and then stopped trying altogether, standing abjectly in front of her in complete silence.

At this moment the girl smiled at him and the warmth of her expression melted the icy obstruction that seemed to block his throat. "Louisa," he blurted out, "I love you . . . I love you very much . . . and I want you to be my wife." Then she was in his arms and her lips met his.

Finally he gave her a chance to speak. "Billy," she said, "Billy Cody, I've been waiting to hear these very words since the first minute I met you. I love you, and I'll marry you whenever you want me to." The young man did not wait to hear another word but sealed her lips once again with a kiss.

CHAPTER 6

Buffalo Bill...Shoots to Kill

THE YOUNG LOVERS sent a letter to Julia, telling her of their engagement. They received a return message from her, wishing them the best of luck and the maximum happiness. In a postscript she wrote that the one thing that marred her own gladness on the receipt of the news was the fact that Mary Cody was not alive to rejoice with her.

Now that he was about to accept the responsibilities of marriage Bill decided to accumulate a nest egg. He looked up his old friend Bill Trotter and hired on with him as a stage driver on the route from Kearney to Plum Creek, a road which ran past the very place where he had killed his first Indian. Both passengers and mail were carried in the Concord coach, drawn by four fine grays, that Bill drove.

A friend of Bill Cody's once said: "He is the only man I ever saw who can sit on a coach box and hit all four of his horses with one motion. No trout fisher ever cast a fly as gracefully as Colonel Cody can toss the beeswax into a refractory off-leader."[1]

Bill drove the stage over this route until February,

1866,[2] but while bounding over the dreary route day after day his thoughts turned continually toward his promised bride. One day on pulling into Kearney he was informed there was a letter waiting for him. The message was from lonely Louisa in St. Louis, urging him to give up the hard life of stage driver and return to the East where he could follow another calling.

Bill resigned at once, went straight to Missouri, and spent a week at his fiancée's home. Then on March 6, 1866, at eleven o'clock in the morning, they were married. Louisa Frederici was a most beautiful bride. Bill Cody, twenty-years-old a few days before the wedding, was a handsome bridegroom. Straight and slim (almost six-feet tall), with fair complexion and brown eyes, he wore his brown hair down to his shoulders. In keeping with his imminent entrance into adulthood and marriage, he had started a mustache and goatee, while driving stage for Trotter, and the fuzz on his upper lip and the fringe under his chin were his pride and joy. He was wearing Western clothes. Though spotlessly clean and well-pressed for the occasion, they contrasted sharply with Louisa's traditional white wedding dress.

An hour after the ceremony the ecstatic couple boarded the steamer *Morning Star* for their honeymoon journey to Leavenworth. On board, things did not go well. The members of an excursion party from Lexington, Missouri went out of their way to snub Mr. and Mrs. Cody. After dinner, when Bill led Louisa proudly out to the dance floor, most of the other passengers immediately walked to the sidelines. Louisa burst into tears, while her husband was completely confused.

In the morning some light was thrown on the mystery. A gentleman from Indiana struck up a conversation with

Bill Cody and informed him that the Missourians had told all the people aboard that he had been a Kansas jayhawker, and that as one of Jennison's house-burners he was a notorious outlaw, bandit and looter.

Bill was powerless to counter this base canard. He did have the satisfaction however, of telling his informant that he had been a soldier and scout in the Union army, that he had participated as an "irregular" in defensive actions against the border ruffians, and that his family, especially his father, had been the victims of the very type of outrages at the hands of lawless men, which the people of the excursion party had lyingly ascribed to him.

The man from Indiana told Bill's story to his fellow passengers. Some of them came up to the Codys and shook their hands, apologized for the rudeness of the others, and wished the honeymooners well.

At one point along the way the steamer stopped at a wild-looking landing to take on wood for the boiler. A group of twenty horsemen galloped through the timber, shooting at the crew members—freed Negroes who were gathering the wood. The deck hands quickly jumped onto the boat, and the captain hastily backed the steamer out into the river.

The riders lined the bank and their leader shouted, "Where is that black abolition jayhawker?" No answer came from the steamboat which was now on its way again at full power.

Later Cody learned that some of the Missouri excursionists aboard ship were bushwhackers. Afraid to attack him themselves, they had wired ahead to twenty of their friends, also bushwhackers, to meet the boat at the landing and kill Cody.

Louisa was most discouraged by the new turn of events

and began to wonder if her husband might really be a hoodlum and outlaw. Bill tried to put her mind at rest, and in desperation wired ahead to his own friends at Leavenworth to arrange a "genteel reception" for his bride.

His friends and family turned out in force. More than sixty people welcomed them when they disembarked at Leavenworth. A brass band thumped out "Here Comes The Bride" in good old-fashioned style. Years later William F. Cody recalled the happy ending of their hectic honeymoon, when he wrote: "That night we were given a big banquet to which my soldier chums and their wives were invited. My wife had a glorious time. After it was all over, she put her arms around my neck and cried: 'Willy, I don't believe you are an outlaw at all.' "[3]

Julia Goodman put the official stamp of approval on the new member of the Cody family when she said to Bill, "We all love sister Lou."

Bill made a valiant attempt to settle down and run a steady enterprise. He rented "Valley Grove House," the hotel his mother had originally built, changed its name to "The Golden Rule House," and took up the profession of innkeeping.

But the lure of the plains was too strong. In September he sold his interest in the hotel, left his wife and his sister Nellie in a comfortable house in Leavenworth, and started for Saline, Kansas, then the western terminus of the Kansas Pacific Railroad being built across the prairie.

On the way he stopped off at Junction City where he met his old friend, Wild Bill Hickok, who was scouting for the Government in the region around Fort Ellsworth (afterwards renamed Fort Harker). Cody accompanied

Wild Bill to the fort, where he too secured employment as a scout.

During the winter of 1866 Cody scouted in the territory around Fort Ellsworth and Fort Fletcher. In the spring of 1867 he was transferred to Fort Hays.

On one occasion General George A. Custer, who had come west to accompany General Hancock on an expedition against the Indians, stopped off at Fort Hays and requested the commanding officer to provide him with a scout to guide him to Fort Larned, sixty-five miles away.

Bill Cody was selected for the job and reported to General Custer the following morning, mounted on a big mouse-colored mule. Custer was in a hurry and made some disparaging remarks about his scout's mount, but Bill assured him that the animal could hold its own against the army horses. Despite the general's skepticism, the journey began.

For the first fifteen miles Cody had difficulty keeping out ahead of the well-mounted company. General Custer was riding a thoroughbred Kentucky stallion which kept right at the mule's heels. When the Smoky Hill River had been forded, however, the situation changed. There among the sand dunes Bill urged his mule forward and when the party arrived at the halfway mark, Custer's entire command was strung out behind the scout. Several times Bill had to wait for the others to catch up.

At the end of the trip Custer congratulated Cody on his "magnificent mount" and vowed never to say an uncomplimentary word about any mule again.

On Bill Cody's return to Fort Hays he was immediately sent back into the field. Indians had raided the Kansas Pacific railroad, killing six men and running off 100 horses and mules. Major Arms and the Tenth Cavalry, a Negro regiment, were ordered to pursue the marauders, and Bill Cody went along as guide and scout.

On the second day out they saw a party of Indians a mile away on the opposite bank of the Saline River. The Major placed his one heavy fieldpiece—a mountain howitzer—on a hill, left twenty men to guard it, and led the rest of his command across the river to engage the enemy.

No sooner had Major Arms' main body of troops forded the river than they heard shouting and shooting behind them. Looking back, they saw that their gun-guarding party was being attacked by over 100 redskin warriors.

Major Arms and his men immediately turned back to help their comrades. They drove off the Indians and took up defensive positions on the hill, next to the cannon. The main enemy force had crossed the river and now charged full speed at the men around the howitzer.

A violent battle raged. More and more Indians converged on the hill from all over the surrounding area. In a matter of minutes the soldiers of the Tenth Cavalry were trapped. Many troopers were wounded, including Major Arms; five or six cavalrymen lay dead on the field of battle; and still the enemy kept pouring reinforcements into the conflict.

The major, who had been lying under the cannon since receiving his wound, asked Cody if he thought there was a chance to break through the circle of red men. Bill replied that there was a possibility, and the retreat was ordered.

The troopers mounted their horses. Led by Bill Cody, they galloped headlong against the thinnest arc of the Indian circle. The redskins wavered and broke, and the men of the Tenth crashed out of the trap. The Indians

pursued them, shooting down additional soldiers. Finally darkness came and a soundly beaten body of men staggered back to the fort.

The time had come for Bill to make another attempt at establishing his own business. A daughter Arta had been born to the Codys on December 16, 1866, and the proud father was determined to give up the life of a plainsman and settle down.

Opportunity knocked in the person of William Rose, a contractor for the Kansas Pacific railroad. Rose was enthusiastic about the notion of laying out a town site one mile from Fort Hays, on the west side of the Big Creek, adjacent to where a railroad crossing was to be constructed. He told Bill Cody all about his plan and offered him a partnership; the scout liked the proposition and the real estate firm of Rose and Cody was established.

Not only were the partners going to sell choice corner lots at $50 apiece (giving the other acreage without charge to anyone who would build and reside thereon), but they also planned to establish a general store, which they would own and run.

An engineer surveyed the land and staked out the plots. The entrepreneurs christened the town Rome. Settlers poured in. In two months the town had boomed to 200 dwellings, three or four stores (in addition to the highly successful Rose-Cody emporium), and a good hotel. Louisa and little Arta came to live with Bill and were temporarily quartered in the back of the store until the magnificent house which he was building would be finished. Rose and Cody were convinced that they were on the way to becoming millionaires.

Instead of achieving wealth, they went broke. The bust,

when it came, was even more spectacular than the boom. A well-dressed gentleman stopped at their store one day, introduced himself merely as Dr. Webb, and congratulated them on the success of their flourishing little town. He then asked if they would consider taking in a third partner. The town founders turned him down flatly. Webb then informed them that he was an agent for the Kansas Pacific railroad and that it was his job to find suitable town sites along the line. He warned that if they refused to share the proceeds from sales of land and lots with the company, he would be forced to establish a rival town nearby.

The partners were adamant in their refusal and Dr. Webb went on his way.

Three days later the golden bubble burst. The entire town of Rome—frame buildings, stores, lumber, furniture—was carted eastward to the new railway division town of Hays City. Only the Rose-Cody general store remained, but there were no customers. All the citizens of Rome had stampeded to the new community.

Cody and Rose were "reduced to the ragged edge of poverty."[4] Dr. Webb had done the trick. He had invited the citizens of Rome to visit the location where a new community, Hays City, was to be built and sent wagons to fetch them. At the town site he made a speech, telling the people that the railroad would construct roundhouses and machine shops at Hays City, providing permanent employment for many men. He boasted that in a short time the town would be one of the most important business and commercial centers on the plains. The Romans came, saw, heard—and remained in Hays City. It was Cody and Rose who were conquered.

A discouraged Louisa packed up her belongings and returned to Leavenworth with Arta. A chastened Bill Cody hitched his fleet horse Brigham to a scraper, and with his ex-partner Rose, graded five miles of roadbed for the railroad. As the recent realtors and merchants pushed wheelbarrows in the broiling summer sun, blisters appeared on their hands. A fine state of affairs, indeed, they thought: from Rome to ruin; from race horse to work animal; from merchant princes and founding fathers to ordinary laborers.

Dr. Webb visited Cody and Rose, became fast friends of both, and eventually presented each of them with two first-class lots in Hays City. The good doctor had never killed a buffalo and begged Bill to take him on a hunt. Cody was only too happy to comply; chasing buffaloes was a welcome change for him from the rigors of railroad grading; Brigham too felt much more at home on the plains.

Bill explained to Webb that in a sense it was even more degrading for Brigham to serve as a Percheron than it was for Cody himself to do menial, manual work. He told how he had bought the horse from a Ute Indian, and had named him after the Utah Mormon leader, Brigham Young. "The best horse I ever saw for buffalo chasing," said Cody. "It is a fact, that Brigham would stop if a buffalo did not fall at the first fire, so as to give me a second chance, but if I did not kill the buffalo then, he would go on as if to say 'You are no good, and I will not fool away my time by giving you more than two shots.' "[5]

Under Bill Cody's expert tutelage Dr. Webb soon became an accomplished buffalo hunter. The two men participated in many exciting chases after bison. Occasionally, when the hunters encountered roving, hostile bands of Indians, roles were reversed and they became the hunted. But the swiftness of their mounts and the skill of Bill Cody as hunter and scout carried them safely through every scrape.

Webb was tremendously impressed by Bill Cody and Brigham. He told everyone he knew that the combination of the sure-shot Cody and the splendid steed Brigham made an unbeatable buffalo hunting team.

One day one of the railroaders spied a herd of buffaloes, and informed Bill Cody of this fact. There was a shortage of meat for the railroad workers at the time, and the scout resolved to bring back some fresh buffalo steak. Brigham was standing by without bridle or saddle, but Cody mounted him nevertheless and rode toward the herd, armed with a new weapon, a late-model, improved, breech-loading needle-gun, which he called "Lucretia Borgia." One of the track-layers followed him with a wagon to fetch the meat.

As he rode toward the herd, he met five officers, recent transferees to the fort, who were also after the same animals. They asked sarcastically if he were out after buffaloes. When he answered "Yes," they poked fun at Brigham (who in fact was an unprepossessing mount, looking more like a workhorse than a racer), saying that he'd never catch anything on such a plug. Charitably, they said that inasmuch as they were after game just for the sport, they would be happy to turn the buffalo carcasses over to him, after they had taken the tongues and tenderloins for themselves.

The officers dashed toward the herd which was a mile away. Cody saw that the animals were heading for a creek, and started for the water to intercept them. When the eleven animals arrived at the watering place, Bill was waiting. Hundreds of yards away the cocksure soldiers were still galloping after the elusive bison.

The scout urged Brigham forward and in a few seconds rider and horse were alongside the rear buffalo. He raised Lucretia Borgia and downed his target at the first shot. Brigham knew exactly what to do next. He bounded to the side of each buffalo in turn and soon the entire herd was downed, eleven animals killed in twelve shots.

Cody's triumph was sweet indeed. Writing about it years later he asserted, "As the last one dropped my horse stopped. I jumped to the ground. Turning around to the astonished officers, who had by this time caught up, I said: 'Now, gentlemen, allow me to present you with all the tongues and tenderloins from these animals that you want.' "[6]

The members of the military party were loud in their praise of Cody's skill. Captain Graham, the senior officer of the group, said that he would be stationed at Fort Hays for a long time and told Bill that he would like him to serve as guide and scout for all of his expeditions.

The opportunity to accompany Graham into the field came much sooner than either expected. That very evening the Indians raided the camp of Cody and Rose, and made off with six of their best horses. The following morning Bill rode to Fort Hays to seek assistance in recapturing the animals. Captain Graham and a company of 100 Negro troopers from the Tenth Cavalry were ordered to track down the redskins.

At first the hoofprints of the Indian mounts and the tracks of the stolen horses were difficult to follow. But toward evening, when the red men obviously believed they were safe from pursuit, the marks became much clearer and Cody had no trouble discerning the trail. By sunset Bill had pushed far out in advance of the cavalrymen. He rode down a little ravine toward the Solomon River, where he believed the red men would be camping for the night.

After dismounting, he crept silently down to the water and spied a herd of horses, the stolen ones too, grazing about a mile away. He returned to the main company and informed Captain Graham of his findings. The officer ordered his men to move stealthily forward through the woods and then to rush upon the Indian camp, as soon as they reached open ground.

The soldiers were just about to start their charge when one of them became so excited at the prospect of real action that he shot off his gun accidentally The noise of the rifle, and the crackling of the underbrush that followed, gave the Indians ample warning. They leaped to their horses and escaped in the darkness.

The troopers pitched their tents for the night. In the morning they desultorily followed the red men's trail for a while. But the chase was futile: the braves had made a forced march through the night while the cavalrymen slept, and were too far ahead for Captain Graham's men to catch them.

The bugler blew retreat and the soldiers rode wearily back to Fort Hays. The impetuous trooper whose premature shot had given the alarm to the Indians paid the penalty for his carelessness by being forced to make the long journey to the post on foot.

Hays City now replaced Saline as the Western headquarters of the Kansas Pacific railroad. Daily an army of laborers of more than 1,200 men climbed aboard a string of flatcars and clattered to the end of the track that had been laid the previous day. With them, they took all the necessary raw materials for a town: canvas, board, store-fronts, hammers, saws, nails, ropes, housewalls, bedding, barrels, bricks, bottles and Bibles. While the majority of the men set down ties and rails all day, a special building crew remained behind to erect a special makeshift town. At sunset the railroad men returned to the newly-constructed community and ate, drank, danced, gambled, fought and slept there. On the following morning the building crew would become wreckers, pulling down the jerrybuilt structures, packing the prefabricated equipment and tools on the flatcars, and transporting everything to the point where the road men had put down the last tie the afternoon before. There and then the entire operation was repeated.[7]

Providing food for this hungry army was a major problem. The railroaders didn't particularly like vegetables and "fancy victuals." Meat was what they wanted and meat was what the Goddard Brothers, who had contracted to feed the men, aimed to give them.

The buffalo was a convenient, walking meat market. Not only were his tenderloins and hump steaks succulent and tender, but also the softer parts and internal organs—the kidneys, testicles, tripe and tongue—were delicacies, and according to the tracklayers, delicious. In the sixties the plains were black with 15,000,000 buffaloes. Especially were they plentiful in the spring when the animals, as part of their annual migration, ranged northward across western Kansas, devouring all the available grass and stamping out wide, dirt roads as they wandered.

The Goddards were seeking an experienced and dependable buffalo hunter. From soldiers at the fort like Captain

Graham, from civilians like Dr. Webb, and from their own trackhands they learned of Bill Cody's prowess. They arranged an appointment with him at Hays City, told him they needed an average of twelve buffaloes a day, and offered him the job. It was dangerous work. Buffaloes stampeded easily; a wounded bull on the loose was as dangerous as a runaway locomotive; the Indians, to whom the bison represented not only a meat market but also an entire department store—bedding, clothing, shelter, horse equipment—made the buffalo hunter their chief target, knowing well that the eradication of these animals by the white men would in effect mark their own death.[8] In the light of these dangers, and on the basis of his own proved skill as hunter and scout, Cody demanded a top salary of $500 a month, to which the firm agreed.

From the day that Cody accepted the position he was a marked man: the recipient of praise and adulation from the railroad workers, who saw in him the incarnation of security and heroism; the target of the hostility and venom of the Indians, who hated the hunter as a harbinger of doom, for he provided food for the construction gangs that were putting down the tracks over which the iron horse would come—the iron horse which threatened to crush all Indians before it.

His popularity with the workmen was demonstrated by a quatrain which was sung and chanted whenever he passed:

> Buffalo Bill, Buffalo Bill
> Never missed and never will.
> Always aims and shoots to kill
> And the company pays his buffalo bill.[9]

The name stuck. First the railroaders, then the soldiers, and finally his civilian friends started calling him Buffalo Bill.

The Indians showed their feelings toward him in actions, not words. A band of thirty braves jumped him one morning at Smoky Hill River, twenty miles from the fort, where he was scouting the movements of a huge herd of buffaloes. In the nick of time the hunter wheeled his horse about and lit out for Fort Hays. Brigham, though he had already covered over twenty miles that day, seemed to know that the situation called for extraordinary speed. He literally flew over the plains. But the Indians were well-mounted on fresh horses, and one of their number, a brave astride a spotted pony, gained steadily on Cody.

This lead warrior had a rifle and sent bullets whizzing past Bill's head, much too close for comfort. The other pursuers strung out behind their leader, and posed no threat. But the spotted pony had closed the gap rapidly and was less than 100 yards behind. Suddenly Buffalo Bill pulled Brigham up short, turned in the saddle, and raised Lucretia Borgia to his shoulder. At the crack of the rifle, down went the spotted steed.

Seven of the other Indians had cut down drastically the distance between Cody and themselves in the time it took for the hunter to drop their leader, and they now spattered the air around him with a fusilade of bullets. Miraculously, neither he nor Brigham was hit. On sped the hunter and his horse until they came within three miles of the railroad track, where a company of soldiers was protecting the working crew.

The cavalrymen leaped to the saddle and rode to the rescue. Buffalo Bill left his horse with the workmen, climbed on a fresh mount and joined the troopers in pursuit of the Indians. Now the situation was reversed: the white men had the fresh horses while the warriors' steeds were exhausted from their wild gallop across the prairie. Captain Nolan and his soldiers of the Tenth Cavalry quickly gained on their foes. Before the red men had fled five miles the cavalrymen caught and killed eight of them. The rest escaped into the hills.

When the Tenth reached the spot where Buffalo Bill had shot the spotted pony, it was discovered that his bullet had cleaved the animal's forehead dead center. "He was a noble animal," Cody said, "and ought to have been engaged in a better business."[10]

In the meantime the section crew had given Brigham a careful rubdown, had walked him back and forth as if he were a derby winner, and had made him an extra special supper. When Cody returned, he walked over to where the horse was tethered and fed him some extra lumps of sugar and an apple, for once again the horse had saved his life.

On most of his hunts Buffalo Bill was accompanied by Scotty, his skinner-butcher, who followed him at some distance in a light wagon drawn by a pair of mules. When Cody made his kill, he signaled to Scotty who would come rattling up to do the dirty, bloody work of skinning and butchering the buffaloes.

Scotty approached the nearest animal with his ripping knife in hand. Then he prepared to "undress" the bison. This meant slitting the skin from tail to neck along the belly, and then cutting down along the inside of each leg. Next a slit was made all around the neck. The cut along the belly was widened until a channel four-inches-wide ran from neck slit to tail.

Now the actual undressing occurred. Scotty placed a lasso over the animal's head, pulling it taut just below the ears so that the noose fitted into the slit around the neck. The rope was tied to a horse which faced the buffalo's tail. Scotty smacked the steed across the buttocks, the horse bolted towards the rear of the bison and in one quick pull yanked the hide completely off.[11]

Once the buffalo had been skinned, Scotty butchered it and then placed both meat and hide in the wagon. The work was hard, the skins and steaks were heavy, but Scotty did his job quickly and well and was a most valuable partner for Bill Cody.

One day the hunter and his assistant had made a very successful kill in the vicinity of the Saline River. Cody had downed fifteen bison and he signaled to Scotty who then rattled up in the wagon to do the butchering. As the skinner drew near the dead animals, a party of thirty Indians galloped toward the two men from the head of a nearby ravine. Immediately, Buffalo Bill and Scotty put into effect a plan of action they had previously worked out for just such an emergency. The hunter's horse and the butcher's mules were unhitched and tied to the wagon. The buffalo carcasses were piled around the wheels to form a protective wall. Then the white men scurried under the wagon.

When the red men were 100 yards away, Bill and Scotty directed a raking fire at them. The Indians pulled their ponies up short, and then slowly circled the wagon, firing as they rode. The mules and the horse were killed almost instantly.

For their part, the ambushed men downed three red warriors. The main body of the Indians retreated to plan the next move.

As soon as the attackers were out of range, Buffalo Bill crawled from under the wagon and set fire to the prairie on the windward side. This constituted Part Two of the defense plan. Smoke rising from the plains was the prearranged signal to the soldiers guarding the railroad, indicating that Buffalo Bill was in danger.

The red men did not realize that this smoke signal was a call for help. They continued shooting at the cooped up defenders. An hour passed. Suddenly, a cavalry company galloped into view. The Indians saw the reinforcements, hastily mounted their own ponies and sped off down the canyon of the creek. The soldiers did not give chase but instead escorted Buffalo Bill and Scotty back to camp.

The next antagonist to challenge Buffalo Bill was a friendly enemy, Billy Comstock, chief of scouts at Fort Wallace, Kansas, who was General Custer's favorite guide. The officers at Wallace were convinced that Comstock was more worthy of bearing the name "Buffalo Bill"—they claimed he had no equal as a buffalo hunter—and in behalf of their champion challenged Bill Cody to a shooting match. Unofficially, the title, "Buffalo Bill," was at stake; officially, a purse of $500 would go to the winner.

Cody readily agreed to the contest.

The two men were to hunt for eight hours, beginning early in the morning. A referee was to follow each contestant on horseback to keep count of the number of animals killed. The hunter who was able to down the greater number of buffaloes during the allotted time period would be declared the victor.

Posters announcing the match were nailed up all along the route of the railroad. News of the forthcoming contest spread as far as the Mississippi. On the appointed day crowds of people descended upon the hunting ground, twenty miles east of Fort Sheridan, where the plains were level and the buffaloes abundant. A special train arrived from St. Louis, bringing over 100 spectators. Among these were Mrs. Cody and Arta. From the fort, the entire throng journeyed to the field of battle in wagons and on horses. Once there, they were requested to watch the proceedings from a grove of trees, from which they might easily see what was going on without the buffaloes in turn seeing them.

Bill Cody was extremely confident. He knew that old Brigham was the best horse in the West for buffalo hunting. He rated Lucretia Borgia far superior to any other rifle for killing bison from horseback. Comstock, Cody knew, owned a Henry rifle with which he could fire more rapidly than was possible with Lucretia Borgia. This advantage was more than offset, he thought, by the fact that his own Springfield could hold 70 grains of powder and 470 grains of lead, giving it much greater fire power. The Indians, fearing the strength of the 48-caliber Springfield, had dubbed it, "Shoot today—kill tomorrow."

The referees spotted a huge herd of buffaloes. The contestants hastily agreed that they would both go into this herd at the same time. And the hunt was on.

As soon as Cody and Comstock approached the massed animals, the bison separated. Comstock went after the bunch to the right, Cody the one to the left. The difference in shooting styles between the two men immediately became apparent. The Fort Wallace chief of scouts employed the usual method for killing game: he shot at the rear buffalo, and then the next, and the next, as they bounded along in a straight line. The Union Pacific hunter, for his part, galloped to the front of the herd on the right-hand side of the animals and shot to the left-hand, the natural direction for a mounted rifleman. On this occasion of the "first run" of the contest, as he had on so many previous occasions, Cody unerringly picked out the leader of the herd. The other animals always followed this leader, grazed near him and depended upon him. The ability to always single out the lead buffalo was a rare quality in a hunter indeed, one that was purely instinctive. The rifleman, who somehow magically was able to select the leader, could never explain or teach this skill to someone else. Cody picked out and downed the leader with one sure shot.

With the leader dead and the hunter crowding in from the left, the herd milled around in a circle. Round and round the brutes ran, shaggy spokes on an ever turning wheel, the dead leader at the hub. As they circled, Cody picked them off one by one, concentrating on those which tried to break away from the ring, and soon thirty-eight buffaloes lay dead in a comparatively small circle. As William F. Cody himself said, "I had 'nursed' my buffaloes, as a billiard-player does the balls when he makes a big run."[12]

Comstock, in the meantime, using his straightaway, shoot-the-rear-animals-first system, had killed twenty-three bison. These buffaloes were strung out on the ground over a nine-mile trail.

With the score of the initial run thirty-eight to twenty-three in Cody's favor, the hunters took time out and joined the visitors from St. Louis in drinking champagne.

Refreshments over, Cody and Comstock returned to the hunting ground. This time they spied a smaller herd, made up of cows and calves, quicker in their movements than the bulls. Cody killed eighteen of these animals while

Comstock dropped fourteen. Thus the total stood at fifty-six for the former and thirty-seven for the latter, when a respite was taken for lunch and more champagne.

The contest resumed in the afternoon. Cody was so far in the lead that he permitted himself the luxury of giving the spectators an exhibition of trick riding. A gasp went up from the onlookers when they saw the hunter put his saddle and bridle in a wagon and then mount Brigham, guiding the horse only by the sound of his voice and the touch of his hand. One pretty young lady tried to dissuade him from hunting a new herd in this manner, but Cody told her, "That's nothing. Old Brigham knows as well as I what I am doing and sometimes a great deal better." Then he dashed toward the buffaloes three miles away.

Shooting from the windward, he downed twelve of the brutes. For the final kill he drove a buffalo in the direction of the watchers. Screams of fright rose from the men and women as the great beast bounded at them. The buffalo was thundering along at express-train speed, head lowered, small eyes gleaming from beneath matted hair. At what seemed the very last second, Cody galloped up to its head and shot it right through the eye.

The bison stopped in its tracks, threw up its head, lurched backwards a step or two and then keeled over dead. Later, Cody explained to the admiring guests that if he had aimed for the heart instead of the eye, the buffalo might have been able to charge on for hundreds of yards, which meant that it could have attacked the crowd.

Comstock's total during the same run had been nine buffaloes. This brought the official tally to sixty-nine for Cody and forty-six for his rival. At this point Comstock's backers gave up the ghost. The referee proclaimed William F. Cody the champion buffalo hunter of the prairies.

On his return to the railroad headquarters, Buffalo Bill presented the company officials with the best heads from the big hunt. This was always his custom, for the railroad executives had the heads mounted and placed in stations and hotels all along the line as an advertisement for the road.

In May, 1868, the Kansas Pacific had been pushed as far as Sheridan, Kansas. Construction was abandoned for a while and Buffalo Bill's services were no longer needed. In one year alone he had killed 4,280 buffaloes for the company; in the entire eighteen-month-period that he supplied the track men with fresh meat he had shot 4,862 bison, as well as many deer and antelope. It was an enviable record, one of which Cody was justly proud. Almost 5,000 buffaloes killed, not in wanton destruction, not for fun or sport, but only so that the track crews building the great Kansas Pacific railroad might have food.

CHAPTER 7

Mission of Mercy

FORT LARNED, Kansas had become one of the principal outposts from which United States soldiers maintained the peace and security of the frontier. Dick Curtis, an old-time scout and friend of Bill Cody, was chief of scouts at the fort and in charge of guiding the small complement of men constituting the permanent personnel—two companies of infantry and one troop of cavalry—keeping order on the plains. Buffalo Bill signed on as scout and guide at this post.

Before he went to Larned, Cody settled some personal affairs. He took his family to Leavenworth, where he provided his wife and daughter with a comfortable home. Then he arranged for the disposition of old Brigham. He was reluctant to expose his favorite mount to the strenuous grind of scouting. Instead, he raffled Brigham off. The winner, Ike Bonham, took the horse to Wyandotte, Kansas and entered him in a four-mile-race against five thoroughbreds. As had happened many times to Brigham in the past, the other riders called him a "poky plug"; and as had occurred so often previously, Brigham swept past the other steeds and easily won the race, gaining a purse of $250 for his proud new owner.

Buffalo Bill soon realized that the troops stationed at Fort Larned were sitting on a powder keg. Several hundred lodges of Kiowas and Comanches were located within shouting distance of the fort. The braves were restless. Their chiefs, Santanta, Lone Wolf, Kicking Bird, and others, treated General Hazen, the commandant, in an insulting and sullen manner. An explosion was imminent; one word by any of the chieftains might set off the fuse.

As General Hazen's special scout, Buffalo Bill accompanied him on a tour of inspection of neighboring Government outposts. When the party reached Fort Zarrah, thirty miles from home base, Hazen requested his soldiers, twenty infantrymen and Cody, to remain at that point. He had decided to push on to his next stop, Fort Harker, without escort.

The scout received permission to return to Larned alone. Riding a mule, he proceeded without incident to a halfway point, Pawnee Rock, when a group of well-mounted Indians in full war paint approached him. Despite their bellicose appearance, the forty warriors all raised their hands in the air and shouted, "How? How?"

Bill recognized them as Indians he had seen at Larned that very morning and held out his hand to their leader. His handshake was accepted; the fingers of the red man tightened suddenly on his and he was jerked violently forward in the saddle. Another Indian grabbed his mule by the bridle. With a wild yell the rest of the redskins pressed in upon him. One yanked Bill's revolvers from their holsters; a second snatched his rifle; another hit him over the head with the blunt end of a tomahawk, knocking him senseless.

Some time later he woke up to find himself tied to the mule. One Indian was pulling the animal along while another was lashing it from behind. Directly ahead was a river. On the further side, moving toward them, was a horde of mounted warriors in battle regalia.

The band that had captured Cody forded the river and converged with the main body of warriors. Whooping and hollering with delight they dragged Cody up to the chiefs and principal warriors. Buffalo Bill immediately recognized one of these men, the cruel, ruthless, wily old chief, Santanta.

Santanta was the spokesman for the red men. He asked Cody where he had been and what he was up to.

Buffalo Bill answered that he had been out after a herd of "wohaws," knowing that the Indians had been without meat for several weeks and were eagerly awaiting a herd of Government cattle that had been promised them.

Santanta's curiosity and interest were aroused. He asked where the cattle were, and Buffalo Bill said "a few miles back." The chief's paint-covered face broke into a broad grin when Cody told him that he was General Hazen's personal envoy, sent ahead to inform the chief that the herd was on its way and that it was intended for his people. The chief's smile disappeared as swiftly as it had come, however, when Cody warned him that the great white chief would be very angry when he learned how rudely his personal representative had been treated.

Now it was Santanta's turn to lie. He maintained that the entire incident had been a joke, an attempt on the part of the younger warriors to test the white man's courage.

The Indian then asked Buffalo Bill to ride out to meet the cattle—to which Cody readily acquiesced, informing

Santanta that these were General Hazen's exact orders. With his firearms restored, and after having firmly refused the chief's offer to provide him with an escort of young braves, Bill crossed the river, knowing that this would give him a good three-quarter-mile start on the Indians if they decided to follow him.

In fording the water he rode the mule at a leisurely pace so as not to arouse suspicion. On reaching the further bank he looked back over his shoulder and saw a band of fifteen Indians about to enter the river on the other side. Nevertheless, Cody acted as if nothing were amiss and urged his mount into a gentle lope toward the place where he had claimed the cattle were.

Once he had crossed the ridge and was no longer in view of his pursuers, he wheeled his mule in the direction of Fort Larned and set out at top speed. Soon he reached a high point in the trail and gazed backwards. The Indians, after a few minutes of confused searching, realized in which direction he was running and now were in hot pursuit.

Mile after mile the chase went on. The warriors were gaining. When Bill arrived at Ash Creek, six miles from the fort, his lead had been cut to half a mile. At the four-mile point the fort came into view and Cody heard the boom of the evening gun. The mule was tiring. At Pawnee Fork, two miles from the post, the scout saw that the red men had shaved one quarter of a mile off the distance between them. After crossing the stream and lighting out for home, he rode right into the arms of some soldiers in a Government wagon. Quickly, he told them what was happening.

Denver Jim, a scout who was with the soldiers, shouted, "Drive the wagon into the trees and we'll wait for 'em."

This was done. Bill Cody also hid by the side of the road. Soon the red men came dashing up, their horses white with lather. The soldiers waited until a few Indians had ridden by and then opened fire on the others. Two of the braves were dropped by this first volley. The rest of the Indians scattered in all directions. Buffalo Bill and the wagon load of soldiers returned safely to the fort.

Bill Cody gave the officers at Larned a complete account of what had transpired with Santanta. They in turn informed him of what he already suspected: the Kiowas and Comanches had joined forces and were on the warpath, and old Santanta was their leader.

Dispatches telling of the critical situation confronting the small garrison at Larned had to be taken through the Indian-infested country and delivered to General Sheridan at Fort Hays. None of the scouts was willing to brave the darkness of the night, the approaching storm and the danger of marauding red men in unfamiliar territory. Finally, although he was exhausted from his encounter with Santanta and his men, Buffalo Bill allowed himself to be drafted for the job, insisting only that he be furnished with a good horse because he was "tired of dodging Indians on a Government mule."[1]

The best horse in the fort was given to Cody, he strapped the dispatch bag over his shoulder, and at ten o'clock in the evening he began his journey. He would be forced to stick to the path that led directly to Fort Hays, for the terrain on both sides of the road was hilly and treacherous. Yet—and Bill knew that this was the great hazard in taking the straight route—somewhere on the road ahead, probably in the vicinity of Walnut Creek, a large party of red men were encamped.

Writing of this trip years later, William F. Cody said: "My greatest danger was that my horse might run into a hole and fall, and in this way get away from me. To avoid any such accident I tied one end of my rawhide lariat to my belt and the other to my bridle. I did not propose to be left alone, on foot, on that prairie."[2]

A wise precaution indeed, for suddenly the horse stepped into a prairie dog's hole and fell, throwing Cody over his head. The animal scrambled to its feet and started to gallop away. But not far—suddenly it came to the end of its rope and Buffalo Bill was firmly anchored at the end of the lariat. The scout climbed back on, and was on his way again.

Cody kept to the path and traveled at a steady pace until he neared a ravine leading into Walnut Creek. He detoured off the road to by-pass the Indian camp. One minute he was picking his way carefully through some trees; the next second he was right in the center of the red men's ponies. They whinnied, snorted, pawed the earth and then crashed off in every direction into the trees and bushes. A dog barked loudly and nipped at the heels of the horse Cody was riding.

The woods were suddenly alive with Indians, all running toward the spot where the horses were tethered. A few of them caught some of the ponies, mounted them and set out after Buffalo Bill. The scout hadn't stopped for an instant. Having blundered into the enemy he now attempted to speed his way out of the trap, despite uneven ground and snapping branches.

The darkness which had blinded him into stumbling upon the Indians now camouflaged his flight. Soon the red men were swallowed up in the inky darkness; Buffalo Bill cut back to the main road, the old Santa Fe trail. At daybreak he was ten miles from Fort Hays. Shortly after reveille he rode into the post.

Cody handed the dispatches to General Sheridan personally and was invited to stay for breakfast. Bill begged off and rode into Hays City instead, where he visited friends, napped for an hour and had refreshments. Then he returned to Fort Hays.

At the fort he joined a group of scouts who were talking together. General Sheridan, they said, wanted an important message taken to Fort Dodge, ninety-five miles away. A bonus of several hundred dollars had been offered to the scout who would volunteer to make the trip. No one was willing to go, for the Indians had murdered the last three men attempting to carry dispatches over this route.

Cody went immediately to the general's headquarters and said to Sheridan, " 'General, if no one is ready to voluteer, I'll carry your dispatches myself.'

" 'I had not thought of asking you to do this, Cody,' said the general. 'You are already pretty hard-worked. But it is really important that these dispatches should go through.'

" 'If you don't get a courier before four this afternoon, I'll be ready for business,' I told him. 'All I want is a fresh horse. Meanwhile I'll get a little rest.' "[3]

But he didn't get rest. He ran into some of his cronies at Hays City and spent the time with them instead.

During his absence from the fort, no volunteer had come forth. So Bill Cody hit the trail again, heading for Dodge. The scout rode all night without meeting any Indians. At daylight he approached Saw Log River, having covered seventy-five miles of his journey.

A company of Negro cavalry, under the command of

Major Cox, was stationed on the river bank. Cody made his identity known to the sentry and was taken to the major's tent. After an hour's sleep and a meal, he mounted a fresh horse. He rode on to Fort Dodge, twenty miles away, and arrived there at ten in the morning without having seen a single Indian.

After handing over his dispatches, he had a reunion with Johnny Austin, chief of scouts at the post, who informed him that red men were on the warpath throughout the area and were especially numerous along the Arkansas River between Fort Dodge and Fort Larned. He considered it a miracle that Cody had not been ambushed.

In the face of the Indian uprisings it was essential that communications be constantly maintained between the various frontier outposts. In this instance, reports had to be sent from Dodge to Fort Larned. Once again scouts were reluctant to hazard the dangerous ride. Buffalo Bill, anxious to return to his home base, sent word to the commanding officer through Austin that he would take the dispatches to Larned. No fresh horses were available so Bill mounted a Government mule and as darkness came on started for home.

At Coon Creek, thirty miles out of Dodge, he left the main wagon road and traveled parallel to it, knowing that Indians might be lying in wait for dispatch bearers on the main thoroughfare. At one point he stopped for water. As he bent down to the stream to drink, the mule jerked away and headed back to the main road toward Fort Larned.

Buffalo Bill hurried after him. But the mule, cantankerous, ornery and very tricky, jogged along just fast enough to keep in front of his recent rider and just slow enough to tease Cody in trying to catch him. Mile after mile, the mule and the man moved along. Bill cursed himself for having neglected to tie one end of his lariat to the animal's bit. He cursed the mule for refusing to stop and be caught. He cursed his own rotten luck that was forcing him to try to cover the distance between Coon Creek and Fort Larned, thirty-five miles, on foot. Again and again as he felt anger rise in his chest, Cody thought of shooting the mule. But always discretion got the better of anger. The sound of the shots would certainly bring a horde of red men down upon him. And besides, the mule was serving as a convenient freight animal for the heavy saddle.

More than anything else Buffalo Bill did not want to be caught on the road when morning came. So he walked fast and the mule trotted along a few feet ahead of him. As the sun's first rays appeared in the east, Bill reached the top of a hill overlooking the valley of Pawnee Fork where Fort Larned was located. When the morning cannon roared, the mule and his pursuer were within half a mile of their goal. Close enough, Bill thought, close enough. He raised his rifle and fired at the mule. Again and again he shot until the animal was dead. Then carrying the saddle into the fort, he delivered the messages.

After hours and hours of sound sleep, he was awakened by Dick Curtis. The chief of scouts told him that General Hazen had returned and was eager to have dispatches taken to General Sheridan at Fort Hays. Buffalo Bill said he was more than willing to do the job. For he realized that his dispatch-carrying activities were approaching a scouting record. General Hazen said that he didn't think it was necessary for Bill Cody to kill himself with trail weariness, when there were so many legitimate dangers—Indians, bad trails and horrible weather—that might cause his death. Nevertheless, he consented to let him go.

At nightfall Buffalo Bill left Larned for Hays. This proved to be the easiest journey of all. The next morning he rode into Sheridan's post and delivered the official letters.

The news of Cody's record breaking, marathon scouting adventures spread rapidly. The story of the mileage covered, the riding speed, the multiplicity of trips telescoped into a few days, and the impossible conditions under which he had traveled, became a frontier legend. At the drop of a drink his fellow scouts, the old pros, would summarize what had happened: Buffalo Bill had pushed from Larned to Zarrah and back, sixty-five miles, in twelve hours (they added ten miles to account for the distance covered when the Indians had dragged him across the Arkansas River); in the next twenty-four hours he had ridden from Larned to Hays, sixty-five miles, in eight hours; during the succeeding twenty-four hours he had traveled from Hays to Dodge, ninety-five miles; the following night he had gone from Dodge to Larned, thirty miles on mule and thirty-five miles on foot, in twelve hours; and on the last night he had journeyed sixty-five miles from Larned to Hays. All in all, the scouts pointed out, he had ridden and walked 365 miles in fifty-eight hours, averaging six miles an hour.

Most impressed by this amazing performance was General Sheridan himself. He appointed William F. Cody head guide and chief of scouts for a Fifth Cavalry expedition against the Dog Soldier Indians, a band of Cheyennes who were looting and murdering in the Republican River region. The commander of the expeditionary force was Colonel William Royal.

On the fifth of October, Colonel Royal's troops left Fort Hays and began their march to the Beaver Creek country. "It was a beautiful command," declared Buffalo Bill, "and when strung out on the prairie with a train of seventy-five six-mule wagons, ambulances and pack mules, I felt very proud of my position as guide and chief of scouts of such a warlike expedition."[4]

Late in the afternoon of the second day, when they had made camp on the south fork of the Solomon River, the colonel asked Cody to kill some buffalo. Bill agreed and asked for a wagon to go along with him to carry back the meat. Royal countered, "Kill your animals and then I'll send the wagon."

Cody went out, shot many buffaloes and on his return told the colonel to send out not one but many wagons to pick up the meat.

The following afternoon Buffalo Bill was sent out to kill more bison. This time he did not ask for wagons. He rode out some distance from camp and came upon a small herd of buffaloes. He cut seven out of the herd and headed them straight for Colonel Royal's tent. The colonel heard the thundering hoofs and ran out to see what was happening. Cody drove the animals to within fifty feet of the officer and then shot them down in rapid succession.

Royal was very angry and demanded an explanation.

"I didn't care about asking for wagons this time, Colonel. I thought I would make the buffaloes furnish their own transportation," Buffalo Bill replied.

The colonel smiled wryly but made no further comment.

One day fused into another. Bill Cody was kept busy hunting and scouting. A new commanding officer, Brevet Major General E. A. Carr, senior major of the regiment, arrived to replace Colonel Royal. With him came the celebrated Forsythe Scouts, led by Lieutenant Pepoon, a regular-army officer. This change of leadership in no way altered the basic plan of the expedition—to track down and pacify all marauding Indians in the Republican River area.

When the troops reached the south fork of the Beaver, they discovered a fresh Indian trail. They followed it for eight miles until they came to a bluff on which was ensconced a large number of red men. General Carr immediately ordered Company M, under the command of Lieutenant Schinosky, a reckless Frenchman, to join with Pepoon's scouts in attacking the enemy.

In his eagerness to engage the redskins, Schinosky led his men more than a mile in advance of the main force. There Pepoon and Schinosky were set upon by a charging contingent of over 400 Indians. The white men were getting the worse of the battle when Carr and the rest of the soldiers dashed up to join the fray.

The red men also poured reinforcements into the battle and it was soon apparent to Buffalo Bill that almost a thousand braves were in the engagement. General Carr was amazed to see that the Indians were willing to risk everything in one full-scale onslaught. Usually the red men preferred to employ hit and run tactics.

Bill Cody had the answer. The Indians, he maintained, had been completely surprised by the presence of a large force of soldiers in the territory. Their willingness to lock horns with the soldiers was in reality a kind of delaying action; they were trying to gain time so that their families and villages could escape into the hills.

All day the conflict raged, and far into the night. When

morning came, the soldiers set out in pursuit of the fleeing enemy. They soon came upon the remnants of the Indian village, and Buffalo Bill's theory was substantiated. All evidence pointed to the fact that the redskin settlement had been made up of over 500 lodges.

During the next two days the soldiers occasionally caught up with the rear guard of the fleeing red men and sporadic fighting took place. But the retreating tribe was traveling at top speed and the white men never overtook the main force. The trail was cluttered with camp kettles, furs, robes, tepee poles and other heavy articles which the Indians had cast aside in their haste to escape. The red warriors not only fled during the day but also began to make forced marches by night. Finally, after Carr and his soldiers had reached the Republican River and then made a cut-off northward towards the Platte, the general realized that the Indians had divided up into many small parties, all rushing headlong out of the area. The chase was abandoned.

Orders were given for the command to return to Fort Wallace. One stretch of the trip was twenty-five miles in length, from the Republican River to the headwaters of the Beaver, a day's journey. Bill Cody, as guide, was with the advance guard. At about two o'clock in the afternoon General Carr overtook his chief scout and asked how far it was to their destination. Buffalo Bill estimated the distance at about eight miles.

The general then informed him that Pepoon's scouts were maintaining he was leading the command in the wrong direction, that the Beaver was at least fifteen miles away and that if they kept to Cody's course, they would hit the Beaver, but at a place where it was completely dry.

Buffalo Bill insisted the others were wrong and promised

that he would lead them directly to a beaver dam, big enough and strong enough for the entire command to cross. There would be plenty of water on both sides of this dam, he promised, to allow all the soldiers and their animals to bathe and drink to their hearts' content.

Bill was right. They hit the water-filled Beaver exactly eight miles further on. That night camp was made at a little creek, a tributary of the Beaver. Not finding it marked on his military map, General Carr officially named it Cody Creek. Pepoon's scouts drank to Buffalo Bill's health and told him they were very glad that they had followed his directions instead of their own.

On the following day Cody was ambushed by a party of Indians as he rode out in front of the soldiers. He crouched behind his dead horse and picked off two of the red men as they tried to come in for the kill. In the nick of time Pepoon's scouts charged down upon the red men who whirled and galloped away. That evening Buffalo Bill drank to the health of the Forsythe Scouts.

On their return to Fort Wallace, the soldiers had little to do but wait for orders. Buffalo Bill spent his time hunting for buffaloes.

In a few days dispatches arrived at the fort from General Sheridan ordering Carr's troops to Fort Lyon on the Arkansas River, where they were to be outfitted for a winter campaign in the Canadian River country. The command left Wallace early in November, 1868 and arrived at Lyon late in the month.

Carr's men were immediately ordered to go on a mission of mercy.

Three weeks before Carr's command arrived at the new post, General Penrose and a force of 300 men had left

Lyon to survey Indian strength in the area. He had taken no wagons with him; all his supplies were on pack mules. In the days that had passed since he had gone into the field, no word had been received from him. Carr was told to find him as quickly as possible, for it was certain his meager supplies were running out. Buffalo Bill was especially concerned in reaching Penrose in time, for his old pal Wild Bill was one of the scouts on the survey expedition.

For three days Carr's command followed the missing soldiers' trail without difficulty. On the fourth day the troopers were caught in a blinding blizzard at a place called Freeze-Out Canyon and were forced to hole up for twenty-four hours.

When the storm stopped, all traces of Penrose's march had been obliterated. Carr ordered Cody to take four men and try to find some sign that would indicate the direction in which Penrose had gone. Shortly after Buffalo Bill and his comrades started their scout, it began to snow again. Despite the awful weather they found one of Penrose's old camps on the Cimarron River, about twenty-five miles away from Freeze-Out Canyon. Though it was late and the snow was coming down heavily, Cody decided to head back right away to inform Carr of his discovery. If he were able to bring the news before nightfall, the rescue party could get an early start in the morning. Leaving the other scouts at Penrose's old camp to enjoy some venison they had shot during the day, he battled through the snowdrifts and reached camp at eleven o'clock that night.

A light was still burning in General Carr's tent and Cody reported to him that signs of Penrose had been found. The general was overjoyed at the news; he bade his orderly prepare a hot supper for the scout and then arranged for Bill to spend the night in his quarters.

In the morning the entire command struck out for the Cimarron River, where Buffalo Bill's fellow scouts were waiting. On route the drifts were so deep that often the soldiers were forced to dig their way through. At sundown they sighted the Cimarron and soon found the scouts' camp, where a roaring fire was burning as a welcome for them.

On the following day they picked up faint traces of Penrose's trail. And on the day after this they found out that the missing general and his 300 men could not be far away. For Buffalo Bill, riding out in front of Carr's men, suddenly heard someone calling his name. It turned out to be one of the soldiers of the Tenth Cavalry. A moment later two other soldiers of Penrose's command crawled out of the bushes. These cavalrymen were deserters who had left their outfit in the lurch sixteen days before, when there were no more rations, and were making their way towards Fort Lyon. The deserters were starved and lost; they had no idea of Penrose's whereabouts. But their plight—and report on the sickness and starvation which had blighted Penrose's soldiers—spurred the rescue mission on to superhuman efforts.

Major Brown, with two companies of cavalry and fifty pack mules, hurried forth the following morning to bring provisions to the lost troops. Buffalo Bill, in questioning the deserters, had gleaned one thing from their garbled tale: Penrose might be in the vicinity of Polladora Creek. Cody went along as guide, and on the third day out found Penrose's famished soldiers encamped on the Polladora. Many of the men had raging fevers. More than 200 mules had died. The lost troopers, in desperation, had eaten the dead animals.

The reunion of the two forces was a very happy one. Wild Bill and Buffalo Bill sat around the campfire well into the night—even after the others had turned in after gorging themselves with a sumptuous feast—bringing each other up-to-date on adventures and activities since last they met.

Soon General Carr's soldiers came up in force and the general took command of the combined troops. He arranged for even more wagons to bring additional supplies from Fort Lyon and to transport Penrose's exhausted troops to their permanent headquarters.[5] Then he selected 500 of his own best men and horses and headed south to the Canadian River. Buffalo Bill accompanied them as guide.

For several days Carr and his men scouted along the Canadian but found no Indians. Then slowly, because the horses were tired and run-down, they started back to Fort Lyon, stopping at various other posts along the way. Finally, Wild Bill and his scouts brought fresh animals to Carr's command. Fort Lyon was reached in March, 1869. Buffalo Bill rested with the rest of the men for thirty days, a respite that General Carr said they all richly deserved.

Bill Cody was eager to see his wife and child, and requested a leave of absence. He was given a month's leave to visit his family in St. Louis. Carr instructed the quartermaster, Captain Hays, to allow Cody to take his horse and mule to Sheridan, 140 miles away. At Sheridan, it was understood that Bill would go on by train to his final destination.

Instead of putting the animals in the Government corral at Fort Wallace, as per orders, Buffalo Bill found it more convenient to leave them with an old friend Perry, a hotel keeper at Sheridan.

Mrs. Cody and her daughter were overjoyed to see Bill, even though Louisa was shocked by her husband's appearance.[6] His long mustache and tiny goatee were striking but not shock provoking. It was the length of his hair that upset her; it was matted like an unruly lion's mane and hung straggly and thick down over his shoulders. When she questioned him, he answered that this was the fashion on the plains, that one couldn't claim to be a scout if one's hair wasn't shoulder length.

Louisa doubted her husband's statement, but strangely enough he was speaking the exact truth. It had become a point of honor among Indian fighters to let their hair grow long so as to really give the red men something to scalp, if they were captured. Short hair was the sign of a coward. Long hair meant that its wearer was willing to give the redskins an even break. All this was part of the scouts' own ironic code: Find them and fight them, but never cheat an Indian!

In deference to his wife, Bill Cody spruced up a bit and bought himself some new "store clothes." Louisa's good cooking soon put "flesh on his bones." Fattened up, rested, and very happy, Buffalo Bill bade farewell to his family and headed back to Sheridan to get his horse.

His happiness changed to confusion and then to anger when he learned that his horse and mule had been seized by the army officials, that he had been accused of selling Government property to a civilian, and that his friend Perry faced arrest for being a receiver of stolen goods. The quartermaster's agent, who had instigated this entire action, had also told General Bankhead, commander at Fort

Wallace, and Captain Laufer, the quartermaster there, that Cody had fled the territory with the money he had gained from the illegal transaction.

Buffalo Bill gave the quartermaster's agent a good thrashing. The informant then ran to the fort and reported this incident to the general.

Bill rode to Wallace and demanded his animals. General Bankhead ordered him off the post A bitter quarrel ensued and Cody finally left. That night, while the scout was sleeping in the Parker House nearby, he was awakened by a squad of armed soldiers, forced to dress immediately, and shepherded to the fort, where he was thrust into the guardhouse at two o'clock in the morning.

The next day he demanded to see General Bankhead, under whose order he had been incarcerated. This request was refused. Bill decided to go over the general's head and composed a long telegram to General Sheridan, explaining his predicament. Instead of sending it, the telegraph operator took the message to Bankhead who tore it into tiny pieces.

Cody then went to the telegraph office with a guard and insisted the wire be sent. The entire matter was turned over to the commandant again, who summoned Bill to his quarters. The general realized he had no right to deny the scout permission to communicate with General Sheridan, but he did not want to have the message delivered, for its contents were highly critical of him.

First, he offered to allow Buffalo Bill to leave Wallace, providing he not get in touch with Sheridan. Cody said No. Next, Bankhead asked if he would proceed to Fort Lyon right away in case his horse and mule were returned. Again Cody refused, explaining that he had affairs to settle at a nearby town. Finally, the general received Cody's promise that the quartermaster's agent would not be bothered again. This was the only condition Bill was willing to meet in return for his release. With this moral victory, Bill reclaimed his animals, settled his business, and then rode to Fort Lyon, arriving there two days later.

General Carr was very glad to see his favorite scout, had in effect been waiting for him two weeks to carry out a special assignment. Thieves had stolen from the fort four mules and eight horses, among them Carr's favorite charger and Lieutenant Forbush's black racing mule. At a point some distance from the post the tracks of the stolen animals had suddenly disappeared. Nevertheless, Carr was certain that Cody could pick up the trail.

The following morning Buffalo Bill rode with Bill Green, Jack Farley, Long Doc, and three other scouts to the place where the hoofprints stopped. Cody then directed his party to ride around in ever-widening concentric circles. This the scouts did and the trail was found.

It was soon apparent that the horse thieves, whether Indians or whites, were experienced frontiersmen. Occasionally, to confuse possible pursuers, the fugitives had led the stolen horses, one by one, in different directions through the woods, only to effect a rendezvous later on at an agreed upon place. This caused the scouts to follow many blind trails and slowed their progress considerably.

Finally, the robbers abandoned these tactics, obviously feeling that they had covered their traces completely. It was now a simple matter for Buffalo Bill and his helpers to keep on their tracks, which led to the Arkansas River, down it to Sand Creek, and across that stream in the direction of Denver.

Four miles from Denver the scouts lost the trail. But now it didn't matter, for they were informed that mules and horses answering the description of the stolen animals had passed by just two days before. Besides, Buffalo Bill was aware that a large horse auction was held at Denver every Saturday and he was certain that the thieves would try to unload their booty there.

For two days Cody and the other scouts camped outside of the city, not wanting to arouse suspicion. Early Saturday morning, before anyone was in the streets, they slipped into the city and registered at Ed Chase's hotel, securing a room that overlooked the auction corral. From the window Buffalo Bill saw one of the old packers from the post, Williams by name, ride into the ring on Forbush's mule. He was leading another animal, a horse newly branded with the initials "D.B.," under which the letters "U.S." could faintly be seen.

The auction began. When Forbush's mule was put on the block, Bill walked through the crowd of bidders and took Williams into custody. The other scouts showed the auctioneer their credentials and confiscated the Government mule and horse.

The question remained: Where was the rest of the stolen stock and did Williams have an accomplice? The prisoner refused to talk so the scouts took him to a wooded area three miles from the city, flung a lasso over a tree limb, and threatened to hang him if he didn't tell where his partner and the remainder of the stock were hidden. For four of the five minutes of the time allotted to him the man was silent; then with one minute to go he poured out the information: his partner was hiding out in a house three miles from Denver, on the banks of the Platte.

The whole party rode to this house and surrounded it. Buffalo Bill pushed open the front door and walked inside. He caught the other criminal, Bill Bevins—who also had been a packer at the fort—and relieved him of his rifle. In the yard in back, the scouts found the rest of the mules and horses.

The two crooks were taken back to Denver where they were locked up for the night. On the following day each was tied to a mule and the return journey began.

That evening, camp was made at Cherry Creek, seventeen miles out of Denver. The scouts and the prisoners slept in a row, feet to the fire. The captured men had been docile and there seemed no necessity to chain them, especially since the scouts took turns guarding them all through the night.

At three o'clock in the morning there was a terrible commotion. The scouts awoke to find Farley, the man on watch, sprawled in the fire. Williams had kicked him into the flames while Bevins had jumped up, leaped over the fire, and was running away into the darkness.

Buffalo Bill knocked Williams down with the butt of his revolver. Green started after Bevins, firing as he ran. Bevins escaped into the brush but in the process dropped one of his shoes. Nevertheless, it was impossible to follow him by night. The brush was too thick and the woods too dark.

At the first sign of daylight Cody and Green saddled the two fastest horses, and leaving Williams with the others, followed Bevins' trail, plainly visible in the snow. The scouts knew that he couldn't travel very fast with one bare foot, especially because the woods were dotted with prickly pears which sent their sharp needles above the snow.

The trail was soon spotted with blood, where the pear points had pierced the fugitive's foot. Despite this severe handicap, the length of his strides, as clearly defined by the prints on the snow, showed that he was making good time.

After following these tracks for twelve miles, the scouts saw Bevins crossing a ridge about two miles ahead. When Buffalo Bill and his fellow scout reached the same ridge, Bevins was sliding on loose rock down a divide that led to the South Platte. The river at this point was deep and swift, and Buffalo Bill knew that if Bevins once reached the water, chances of catching him were slim. He spurred his horse forward, came within shooting distance, and ordered the fugitive to halt or be shot. Bevins calmly sat down on a rock and waited for the two scouts to approach.

When Cody confronted the criminal, the scout readily admitted that if Bevins had had fifteen minutes more head start, he never would have been caught.

Recalling this chase in one of his autobiographies years later, William F. Cody wrote: "Bevins' run was the most remarkable feat of the kind ever known, either of a white man or an Indian. A man who could run bare-footed in the snow through a prickly pear patch, was certainly a 'tough one'; and that's the kind of person Bill Bevins was. Upon looking at his bleeding foot I really felt sorry for him. He asked me for my knife, and I gave him my sharp-pointed bowie, with which he dug the prickly briars out of his foot. I considered him as 'game' a man as I had ever met."[7]

Buffalo Bill loaned his own horse to Bevins, while he

took turns with Green in riding the other. Back at camp, they breakfasted and then the entire party resumed the journey.

That night they stopped at an abandoned cabin near the Arkansas River. There was no reason to keep close watch on Bevins; his foot was swollen to a great size. As for Williams, it did not seem possible that he would be able to get away from the cabin, with a guard always on duty, so they did not bind him to his bunk.

All of the scouts turned in, except Long Doc who sat up, revolver in hand. At about one o'clock Williams asked Doc if he might step to the door for a moment. Doc assented, holding his revolver on the prisoner all the while. In a flash Williams leaped out into the darkness and disappeared. Doc fired after him but missed.

The other scouts woke up just in time to see Doc coming back into the cabin, cursing a blue streak. Williams had gotten clean away and there was nothing that could be done about it.

On their return to Fort Lyon, General Carr congratulated them on the success of their mission, even though Williams had escaped. Bevins was taken to Bogg's Ranch, on Picket Wire Creek, to await trial. But before he was brought to court, he too escaped.

CHAPTER 8

The Killing of Tall Bull

THE FIFTH CAVALRY, under the command of General Carr, was transferred from Fort Lyon to the Department of the Platte. New headquarters for the outfit was to be Fort McPherson, Nebraska, from which point the Fifth was expected to carry on large-scale operations against the Indians. On the march from Lyon to McPherson, Buffalo Bill rode well ahead of the soldiers, guiding them through the dangerous territory.

At the north fork of the Beaver, Cody discovered tracks scattered all over the valley on both sides of the creek and estimated that an entire village of Indians, at least 3,000 men, women and children, had recently passed that way.

When Carr heard his chief of scouts' report, he ordered his entire force to make camp in a low ravine so that the red men might not catch sight of them. Lieutenant Ward, twelve soldiers and Buffalo Bill were sent forward to ascertain how fast the warriors and their families were moving.

The scouting party soon found out that the red men were proceeding slowly, hunting as they went along. Cody galloped back to General Carr and told him to attack immediately before the redskins could take alarm and flee. "Boots and Saddles" was sounded and all the troops, except two companies which were left to guard the supplies, rode swiftly ahead.

After a five-mile gallop, the Fifth Cavalry sighted hundreds of Indians advancing up the creek to do battle. The red men were deployed in a thin line on both sides of the stream, a line that stretched as far as the eyes could see. Carr immediately ordered his men to concentrate their attack against the thinnest segment of this line, thereby driving a phalanx of horses and troopers right past the defenders to the ultimate objective, the Indian village itself.

This movement would have been successfully executed if it had not been for the daredeviltry of Lieutenant Schinosky, in command of Company B. Instead of obeying the order, he charged upon the red men on the left flank, engaging them in hand-to-hand fighting, while the rest of the troopers catapulted through the weakest spot and charged down on the village.

Soon General Carr realized that Schinosky and his company were surrounded by 500 warriors. A halt was called to the main advance; the entire Fifth Cavalry wheeled around and went to the rescue of the entrapped company.

Valuable time was consumed by this relief action. The Indians had reformed their lines, in depth, and fought a stubborn delaying action to give their squaws and children the opportunity to escape. At nine o'clock in the evening General Carr called it a day and set up camp for the night.

In the morning not an Indian was in sight. All along the creek, as the Fifth pressed northeast towards the Republican River, were signs of the red men's hasty flight. All day the troopers kept on the trail of the escapees; toward evening fleeing Indians could be seen in the distance.

Just before noon the Fifth caught up with 300 braves. The battle started in a narrow ravine, where the outnumbered red men had an advantage, but soon spilled out over the broad prairie. Here the white men were able to bring their superior numbers into play and in a short time the enemy was being driven into the hills. The redskins scattered in all directions, leaving behind their exhausted ponies.

General Carr later described in his own words what occurred next:

> Reaching the scene we could see the Indians in retreat. A figure with apparently a red cap rose slowly up the hill. For an instant it puzzled me, but on seeing the horse I recognized it as Cody's Powder Face, and saw that it was Buffalo Bill without his broad-brimmed sombrero.
>
> Upon closer inspection I saw that his head was swathed in a bloody handkerchief, which served as a bandage as well as a chapeau, his hat having been shot off, the bullet plowing his scalp badly for about five inches. He was bleeding profusely—a very close call, but a lucky one. The advance guard had been relieved, the Indians severely punished, with a loss on our side of only three killed.
>
> Our greatest need was supplies, which the hot trail had sidetracked. As the country was infested with Indians, and it was fifty miles to the nearest supply point, Fort Kearney, on consultation with Cody he decided it would be best to undertake the job himself, a point characteristic of him, as he never shirked duty or faltered in emergencies.
>
> I gave him the best horse in the outfit, and when twilight arrived he, after patching up his head a little, was off to bring relief and meet us at a point Northwest about a day's march.
>
> These were about the most definite directions any scout

got in the trackless wastes of those days, and it showed the peculiar sixth sense or acumen, possessed by experienced army officers and scouts, like Cody, and why, in the wide terrestrial seas of the great plains, they rarely ever missed connections. Cody made a ride of fifty miles during the night, arriving at Fort Kearney at daylight.

He had chased and fought Indians all day, been wounded, and when through his rare frontier instinct, he reached us he had been almost constantly in the saddle and without sleep for forty hours. Pretty strenuous work.[1]

After returning to Fort McPherson, the Fifth Cavalry remained there for ten days, resting and preparing for a new action against the Indians. Years later, Brigadier General E. M. Hays recalled the scope and intent of the campaign when he wrote:

> Early in May 1869, the Republican River Expedition, under Brevet-Major General E. A. Carr, consisting of seven troops of the 5th Cavalry and a battalion of friendly Pawnee Indians—the latter under Major Frank North, an experienced Indian fighter, left Fort McPherson, Nebraska to operate against the renegade Sioux, Cheyenne and Arapahoe Indians, known as "Dog Soldiers," and led by the fierce and savage chief, Tall Bull, who had been creating terror and dismay amongst the settlers living in the exposed frontier countries of Kansas, Nebraska and Colorado, and was the scourge of that whole territory, capturing and killing women and children, and in many instances torturing them in the most fiendish manner.
>
> General Carr, who was selected to follow and chastise these Indians, was a noted Indian fighter, with a thorough knowledge of Indian character and methods.[2]

Buffalo Bill was fascinated by the Pawnee scouts. He respected their soldierly skill, their trailsmanship and the alertness and alacrity with which they responded to each of Major North's commands, delivered to them in their own tongue. He was amazed at the variations they had effected in the basic, regular cavalry uniform: some of them wore heavy overcoats; others sported black opera hats with fancy brass accoutrements attached; some had on only regulation pantaloons with nothing above the waist; others didn't even bother with pants but were covered merely by breechclouts; some had ripped the cloth legs out of the pantaloons, leaving just leggings exposed; and others eschewed moccasins and boots, wearing big brass spurs on their heels as a kind of ankle jewelry.

And it was not very long before Bill Cody saw the effectiveness of the Pawnee scouts in an actual fight. When the command was encamped on the Republican River near the mouth of the Beaver, a party of fifty Sioux warriors attacked the mule herd, which had been taken down to get water, in an attempt to stampede it. Buffalo Bill jumped on his horse, certain that he would be the first on the scene. But he was mistaken. The Pawnee soldiers, not waiting for formal orders from the officers, had already counterattacked and were routing the astonished Sioux.

The Pawnees chased the enemy braves for fifteen or twenty miles, killing several warriors. At first Cody's excellent mount was some distance in front of the Pawnees. Suddenly one pursuing warrior sped by Bill, mounted on a big, yellow buckskin pony. When they had returned in triumph to the camp, Cody sought out the Indian who owned the swift horse and traded with him for the buckskin. Buffalo Bill named the mount Buckskin Joe, and Brigham had a worthy successor.

For his part, Buffalo Bill soon gained the respect and esteem of all the Pawnees. He accompanied a number of the Indian scouts on a buffalo hunt. He stood by and watched twenty of them surround a herd, dash in among the animals, and kill thirty-two bison. Another herd appeared. At Cody's request, Major North kept the Pawnees back while he galloped to the head of the herd. Using his famous force-them-to-circle method, he dropped thirty-six buffaloes, killing one brute with nearly every shot. The bodies of the dead bulls lay close together in a small circumscribed area. The Indians were most pleased at this demonstration and from that moment on called him the Big Chief.

The Fifth Cavalry and the Pawnee scouts took a westward course up the Republican. Two companies of Pawnees, under Major North, and three companies of cavalry, under Colonel Royal, made a scout north of the river. The main body of troops waited their return at Blacktail Deer Fork.

The Pawnees came galloping back into camp—followed by the regular cavalrymen—singing, yelling and waving their lances. They had come upon the rear guard of what appeared to be a large party of warring Sioux. The Pawnees, though outmanned, had jumped the Sioux and had killed four of them.

Next day the trail of the Sioux was picked up again. For several days the Fifth Cavalry kept close on the tracks, and from the amount of prints and the number of campfires passed, it became obvious that this was the largest force of Indians the soldiers of General Carr had ever followed. And wherever the Indians had camped the mark of a woman's shoe was found, proving that the Sioux had a white woman as their captive.

As the Fifth pressed closer to its prey, Buffalo Bill and

six Pawnee scouts proceeded ten miles out in front of the main command to locate the Indian camp, so as to be able to give the troops the necessary information with which to launch an effective attack. At last Cody and his squad peered carefully over the top of a large hill and saw the Indian village down below in the sandhills south of the South Platte River, at a place called Summit Springs.

The news that the enemy had been found was then delivered to General Carr. In the general's own words:

> On Sunday, August 11th, 1869, I was thinking of going to the river to water my horses when Buffalo Bill came back and said: "I have seen the village, it is over a ridge away from the river valley." We had not seen the trail for some time.
>
> They had followed an old custom of turning along the ridge where we had dismounted to cross it, and going over high ground so that any one approaching on it would be visible from camp.
>
> Cody's idea was to get around beyond, and between them and the river. He changed horses quickly and went on, and I took the gallop for several miles through the deep sand and got on top of a sandhill. Some Pawnees away off on the left on the bluff beckoned me and I went. The Pawnees pointed over the ridge and said: "Hoss! Hoss!" I saw what looked like a band of ponies but said: "No, Buffalo Bill." They said: "No, no, hoss, hoss." They took my glass and looked, "Yes, hoss." I looked and sure enough there were ponies grazing, and the camp was no doubt below.[3]

General Carr returned to his troops and ordered them to "Tighten saddles and prepare for action." Then following his chief of scouts' suggestion, he led his men to the north, bypassing the Sioux village. When the soldiers were between the Indians and the river, they doubled back and pushed to within a mile of their objective without being sighted. The cavalrymen drew up in battle formation on a high hill overlooking the camp.

"Sound the charge!" the general told the bugler.

Silence.

Again the order, but in the excitement the bugler had forgotten the notes of the call.

Quartermaster Hays jumped into the breach, snatched the bugle from the dazed soldier's hand, and blew the call for charge.

The Indians were just preparing to move camp when the hordes of soldiers swooped down from the hill. The braves were completely surprised and offered only token resistance. As the Pawnees, stripped naked and riding bareback for the occasion, and the cavalrymen, spic and span in their best blue uniforms, galloped through the village, shooting at everything they saw, the Sioux—men, women and children—scattered in every direction, panic-stricken. In a short time the village was completely in the hands of the Fifth Cavalry.

General Carr ordered an inventory taken of the spoils of war. A quick count indicated that 140 braves had been killed, 120 squaws and papooses had been taken prisoners, 200 lodges, replete with a large quantity of robes, equipage, provisions and buffalo meat, had been captured, and 800 of the Sioux's horses and mules had been rounded up.

Meanwhile, the Sioux warriors had rallied in the hills and now they returned to do battle. One Indian, a chief on a large bay horse, seemed to be spearheading the Sioux attack. Buffalo Bill resolved to kill the red man, knowing that the death of this firebrand would break the back of the redskin counterattack.

Plate 16 *Culver Service*

Buffalo Bill on Charlie, his favorite horse
from the painting by William De La M. Cary

Plate 17 *Brown Bros.*

Louisa Frederici Cody
Wife of Buffalo Bill

Plate 18 *Brown Bros.*

Sisters of Buffalo Bill
Seated: Lidia and Julia Cody
Standing: May and Helen (Nellie) Cody

Plate 19

Kit Carson Cody
Son of Buffalo Bill

Plate 21

Irma Cody
Daughter of Buffalo Bill

Plate 20

Arta Cody
Daughter of Buffalo Bill

Plate 22

Orra Cody
Daughter of Buffalo Bill

Plate 23 *Brown Bros.*

Outfit worn by Buffalo Bill, and his famous "Lucretia Borgia" gun, at the time of the great hunt arranged for the Grand Duke Alexis of Russia

The swift action that followed is graphically described by General Carr:

> Buffalo Bill had got pretty well around the village when he went in on Captain Price's right. He had with him two soldiers and a Pawnee. He saw the women and children hiding in ravines and sand washes. As he advanced he saw a chief charging about and haranguing his men, and as he came near, Buffalo Bill shot him off his horse and got the horse. This was the celebrated race horse "Tall Bull" which he, Cody rode for a long time, and won many exciting races. When he came into camp, Mrs. Tall Bull said that was her husband's horse. On this occasion the Indians had two white captives, Mrs. Alderdice of Missouri, whom they killed during the fight and Mrs. Weigel of Kansas (whose husband was killed at the time of her capture) who had been shot in the back with a pistol bullet, which broke a rib, was deflected and passed around and lodged below her left breast. Fifteen hundred dollars in gold, silver and green backs, which was gathered in the camps, was given her and she went back, remarried and "proved" up on her claim.
>
> Next morning we dug a grave and buried Mrs. Alderdice, the surgeon reading the service. After the fight I entertained the chief's wife and family at tea and learned that the chief was named Tonka Haska, Tall Bull; he had three wives but only one was with him, a fine looking squaw, the daughter of a chief, and her little girl of eight years. When they were surprised, he tried to get away with them, but she said he looked back and saw the destruction of his band, which was his pride and said: "My heart is bad, I cannot endure this. I will turn back and get killed. You escape and treat the white woman well and when peace comes she will intercede for you." He turned back, firing as he charged and by Cody's unerring rifle he fell.[4]

In addition to receiving the swift horse Tall Bull as his reward for shooting the Sioux chief, Cody was also given

—when the captured horses and mules were distributed among the officers and men—a fast pony called Powder Face. Another honor—not a material one but cherished by Buffalo Bill just the same—was presented to him by the enemy itself. From that day forward, all the northern Indians bestowed upon William F. Cody the *nom de guerre,* Prairie Chief.

But the battle of Summit Springs did much more than bring renown and reward to the slayer of Tall Bull; it brought fame and praise to General Carr's entire command. News of the battle had been telegraphed to the entire nation. When the troops arrived at Fort Sedgwick, high army officers were waiting to extend their personal compliments and official commendation to the Fifth Cavalry. All agreed that it had been a most significant victory: Tall Bull and the Sioux had long terrorized settlers and travelers in the Kansas-Colorado-Nebraska area. "This campaign and engagement resulted in ridding the frontier borders of these states from hostile Indians, and bringing peace to the distracted settlers."[5]

In the days—and even the years—that followed the battle of Summit Springs, additional tributes to Cody's strategy in outflanking the Sioux and bravery in killing Tall Bull were forthcoming from participants in the fight and principals in the army.[6] By word of mouth, by official memoranda, by personal letters and by casual reports the exploits of Buffalo Bill were made known to people in the East.

The extension of the railroad and the efficiency of the telegraph were bringing the thrill of the frontier to Boston, New York, Philadelphia and Washington. Newspapers reported the campaigns against the Indians in vivid detail.

To the soldiers of the Fifth Cavalry, the fighting at Summit Springs had been bloody, grueling work. To the great American public, safe and secure far from the perilous plains, the defeat of Tall Bull and the Sioux had been a great spectacle; Carr was the man of the hour and Cody was soon to become a national hero.

Brigadier General E. M. Hays heralded Cody's guidance and daring at Summit Springs as "the greatest of the many great achievements of this wonderful scout."[7] General Carr's feelings about his chief of scouts, finally written down in a letter in 1883, were crystallized by Cody's actions at Summit Springs:

> From Cody's services with my command, steadily in the field, I am qualified to bear testimony as to his qualities and character. He was very modest and unassuming. He is a natural gentlemen in his manners, as well as in character, and has none of the roughness of the typical frontiersman. He can take his own part when required but I never heard of his using a knife or pistol, or engaging in a quarrel when it could be avoided.
>
> His personal strength and activity are very great, and his temper and disposition are so good that no one has reason to quarrel with him.
>
> His eyesight is better than a good field-glass; he is the best trailer I ever heard of, and also the best judge of the lay of the country—that is, he is able to tell what kind of country is ahead, so as to know how to act.
>
> He is a perfect judge of distance, and always ready to tell how many miles it is to water, or to any place, or how many miles have been marched.
>
> Mr. Cody seemed never to tire and was always ready to go, in the darkest night, or the worst weather, and usually volunteered, knowing what the emergency required. His trailing, when following Indians, or looking for stray ani-

> mals, or for game, is simply wonderful. He is a most extraordinary hunter.
>
> In a fight Mr. Cody is never noisy, obstreperous, or excited. In fact I never hardly noticed him in a fight. When I happened to want him, or he had something to report, he was always in the right place, and his information was always valuable and reliable.
>
> During the winter of 1866, we encountered hardships and exposure in terrific snowstorms, and sleet. On one occasion that winter, Mr. Cody showed his quality by quietly offering to go with some dispatches for General Sheridan, across a dangerous region where another principal scout was reluctant to risk himself.
>
> Mr. Cody has since served with me as post guide and scout at Fort McPherson, where he frequently distinguished himself.
>
> I consider that his services to the country and to the army, by trailing, finding and fighting Indians, thus protecting the frontier settlers, and by guiding commands over the best and most practicable routes, have been valuable.[8]

Although the battle of Summit Springs was a crushing defeat for the red men, it by no means put an end to Indian outrage and atrocity. A band of braves raided O'Fallon's Station on the Union Pacific, killing several section hands and running off some stock. Two companies, under Major Brown, were ordered into the field by General Carr, and Buffalo Bill was assigned to accompany them.

On the day previous to the start of the pursuit of the raiders, the famous dime-novelist and writer, Edward Zane Carroll Judson, better known by his pseudonym, Ned Buntline, came to Fort McPherson to interview Major Frank North, leader of the Pawnee scouts. Buntline was seeking background material for one of his new novels or magazine serials. He had read in the papers about the battle of Summit Springs and was particularly impressed by the unorthodox activities of the Pawnees.

Major North had little respect for writers and referred him to Bill Cody instead. The scouts were taking their midday siesta. Buntline crossed the parade ground, poked beneath one of the wagons, and roused Bill out of a sound sleep. A twenty-three-year-old giant, tall and handsome with long hair falling below his shoulders, crawled out from under the wagon, rubbed the sleep out of his eyes, and shook hands with the man who was to be his "discoverer." In this most pedestrian way, Buntline, the writer, met Cody, the plainsman, and thus began an association which was to have far-reaching consequences for both.

Buffalo Bill invited Colonel Judson to go along on the chase after the redskins. Cody loaned the author his own mount, Powder Face. The scout was surprised at the novelist's riding skill, shooting ability and courage during the scouting trip. The tracks of the fleeing raiders led to the North Platte, tracks that Colonel Judson easily followed. And when they reached the river itself, the troopers were forced to swim their horses across the swollen waters. Buntline, on Powder Face, was the first man over.

The scouting expedition itself was a failure; the Indians had had too great a headstart. During the few days they were out on the prairie, however, and on the return journey to the Fifth Cavalry's new home base, Fort Sedgwick, the two men became fast friends. Buntline was a good talker; he spent hours telling the young scout of his own Civil War adventures, his experiences at sea, and his activities during the Seminole War. He was also a good listener; he plied Bill Cody with hundreds of questions and the younger man found himself pouring out the entire story of his life.

Once back at the fort, Buntline was caught up in the excitement of Buffalo Bill's horse racing activities. One of the officers at the post, Lieutenant Mason, owned a racer which he thought was faster than Tall Bull. He challenged Cody to a race, a half-mile dash, proposing a side bet of $500. Bill accepted. Other officers and civilians wanted to bet against Cody, and he covered all wagers until he didn't have a cent left.

Then in quick order Bill matched Tall Bull against the fastest steed of the Pawnee scouts, and Powder Face against a fast pony belonging to Major Lute North, winning both contests and picking up sizeable purses and many side bets each time.

After Buntline returned to the East, promising to write to Buffalo Bill and receiving the same promise from the scout, Cody found it more difficult to drum up competition. So he evolved a handicap for himself; in each race he would ride Tall Bull bareback. And during the ride, while galloping at top speed, Cody would swing to the ground and then back on to the horse, eight times in a row in rapid succession. This made his task more difficult and more spectacular, yet he continued to win and soon the Pawnee scouts and the regular officers would not bet against him under any circumstances.

Indications were that the entire command, which had again been transferred to Fort McPherson, would remain at that post for an indefinite length of time. Therefore, Buffalo Bill sent for his wife and daughter to join him, and built a small cabin for them outside the stockade.

W. H. McDonald, later a prominent banker at North

Platte, Nebraska, in a recent interview clearly recalled the Cody family reunion:

> In 1869, Col. W. F. Cody, "Buffalo Bill" came to fort (Fort McPherson) as chief of the Scouts for the Fifth United States Cavalry. Mr. Cody brought his wife and 3-year old daughter, Arta with him. I delighted in carrying the little Cody girl in my arms, as if she were my sister.[9]

In the winter, Bill Cody was shown an advertisement in the *New York Weekly* announcing a forthcoming serial by Ned Buntline, to be called "Buffalo Bill: The King of Border Men—the Wildest and Truest Story I Ever Wrote."[10] In a short time the scout was reading each successive episode of his own life story with avidity and amazement. "Wild" the installments certainly were; Buntline had allowed his fertile imagination to create a superman in frontier clothes. "True" the episodes were, only in snatches and patches; whenever Cody would discover the skeleton of himself under the rash of purple prose that Buntline had written, he would immediately lose himself again in the torrent of outlandish adventures and superhuman feats of derring-do that the novelist claimed "Buffalo Bill" had accomplished.

True or false, hyperbole or understatement—it made no difference to the American reading public. For readers throughout the land, the fictional character fused with the actual man, and Buffalo Bill became a hero everywhere.

With plenty of time on his hands, Cody spent days on end hunting deer, antelope, elk and buffalo. A party of Englishmen, most prominent of which was Boyd Houghton, well-known caricaturist from London, spent some time shooting big game in the vicinity of Fort McPherson.

Buffalo Bill was the guide for these visitors, and they returned to England with thrilling memories of their hunts with the great scout.

Indian trouble broke out again. General Duncan was put in charge of a pacifying expedition, and Buffalo Bill went along as scout. Cody's old comrades-in-arms, the Pawnee Scouts, under their leader Major Frank North, were part of this command. The only other white scout on the expedition was John Y. Nelson, whose Indian name was *Sha-Cha-Cha-Opoyeo,* in English, "Red-Willow-Fill-The-Pipe." Nelson and Cody were pals, and worked well together as a team.

One day Major Frank North and Buffalo Bill rode out in front of the command to find a suitable camping place for the soldiers. A good site was found near Prairie Dog Creek, not far from the location of the dugout where Cody had been injured with a broken leg many years before while on a camping trip with Dave Harrington. Bill rode to the top of the hill, where the troops would be sure to see him when they came up, and stretched out on the ground to rest.

A series of shots brought him to his feet. Major North came galloping into view, followed by more than fifty Indians. Bill mounted his horse, fired a shot or two over his shoulder, and then joined North in fleeing from the red men. The Indian bullets came awfully close: one clipped Cody's whip right out of his hand; another pierced his hat, parting his hair as it passed.

The Indians, on fresher horses than those of the white men, were on their heels when a company of soldiers, under the command of Lieutenant Valkmar, came dashing up. The red men pulled up their ponies and fled.

Major North kept riding towards the main command until he reached a point where he knew he could be seen by the Pawnee scouts. Then he rode around in a circle. This was a sign to his men that hostile redskins were near.

Now the entire command—Pawnee scouts, regular army, Valkmar's company, Buffalo Bill and John Y. Nelson—lit out after the Indians. Three stragglers were caught and killed.

The chase continued the following day. The troopers caught up with an old squaw whom the tribe had left on the prairie to die. Nelson recognized the old woman as a relative of his wife. From her, they learned that the escaping red men were known as Pawnee Killer's band and that they had recently massacred a surveying party of eight white men.

The soldiers drove Pawnee Killer's braves across the Platte River. Then they returned to the fort, bringing the abandoned squaw with them. Later she was sent to spend her remaining days at Spotted Tail Agency.

During Cody's absence, his wife had given birth to a son. Although the boy was born on November 26, 1870, he was still unnamed when Buffalo Bill returned to the post a few weeks later. The proud father had been in constant correspondence with Ned Buntline and wanted to call the child Elmo Judson, after his friend. But the officers at the fort outvoted him and christened the boy Kit Carson Cody.

About this time petty offenses were being committed in the vicinity of the post by civilians over whom General Emory, commandant at the stockade, had no jurisdiction. At the general's request, Buffalo Bill accepted the position of justice of the peace.

Cody knew nothing about law but he possessed a highly developed sense of justice and fair play. And more important, perhaps, on the frontier, he had the strength, the reputation and the name to make his decisions stick. On one occasion, a poor immigrant came to Cody and asked him to recover his one and only horse, which had been driven off the night before when a large herd of horses had passed his camp. The herd boss had refused to return the horse, claiming it was one of his own stock.

Buffalo Bill picked up Lucretia Borgia, saddled Buckskin Joe, and with the immigrant started after the herd boss. They soon caught up to him.

The herd boss demanded that Cody serve him with a writ of replevin, and then he would return the animal. Bill answered that his gun was his writ.

One of the herders took the boss aside and whispered in his ear that the constable was Buffalo Bill. Immediately, the thief handed over not only the immigrant's horse but some money as well to cover "court costs."

Shortly after this, Cody was called upon to perform a marriage ceremony. One of the sergeants at the fort was getting married and he considered it only fitting and proper that his old side-kick Buffalo Bill do the honors.

Bill put on his best clothes. Then he went to the house where the service was to be held, armed with the Statutes of Nebraska. Many of the officers from the post were in attendance. They drank to the health of each other, to the happiness of the prospective bride and groom, to the glory of the army, to the victory at Summit Springs, to the prosperity of everyone's sisters, cousins and aunts, and to the success of Bill Cody as justice of the peace.

When the time came for the ceremony itself, it was

little wonder that Buffalo Bill was in such a haze that he was unable to find the marriage law anywhere in the statute book. Drawing in a big gulp of air, he turned to the bridegroom and asked, "Do you take this woman to be your lawful wedded wife, to support and love her through life?"

"I do," was the reply.

Addressing the bride he said, "Do you take this man to be your lawful wedded husband through life, to love, honor and obey him?"

"I do," was her response.

He then told them to join hands.

Cody took another deep breath of air and then said, "I now pronounce you man and wife, and whomsoever God and Buffalo Bill have joined together, let no man put asunder. May you live long and prosper. Amen."

Among the first to press forward to congratulate him on this inspired improvisation were his sisters Helen and May Cody who had come to McPherson for an extended visit with their brother and his wife. The unusual marriage ceremony they witnessed was a portent of things to come, for they too were to meet their future husbands while at the post.

CHAPTER 9

On Stage, Mr. Cody

BUFFALO BILL and the other professional buffalo hunters were often disgusted and enraged, during the years 1873 and 1874, as they saw their noble profession being desecrated by rank amateurs, by sadists masquerading under the name "sportsmen," and by week-end shooters. As late as 1871 the plains had been covered with a veritable blanket of moving bison. Two years afterward the prairies were clogged with the putrefying carcasses of these animals, wantonly destroyed by the slaughterers-come-lately.

The professional hunters killed the buffaloes to gain meat or hides. Rigorously they maintained a clear-cut code of conduct: the number of bison shot during any one period must not exceed what was required to fulfill the basic needs of the community; no animal should be left lying on the hunting ground, but must be transported back to camp or town; and above all, there must be no hunting just for hunting's sake.

The amateurs had no such strictures. Their one desire was to kill as many bison as possible. When nightfall came, the "sportsmen" did not go home. Instead, they set fires by water holes and waited for the buffaloes to come and drink. All through the night, the massacre of the animals would continue. Not only men participated in this "sport," but also women and children. As one old hunter put it, "Seems to me there's more people out shootin' than there are buffaloes to shoot at. Soon there'll be no animals left and they'll just have to shoot each other."

The cruelest part of this entire business was the shooting of buffaloes from railroad cars.[1] For a hundred-mile stretch along the Kansas Pacific the trains chugged slowly over the prairies, parallel to thousands of buffaloes. Especially was this true during the spring and fall when huge herds made the railroad route their stamping grounds. The trigger-happy travelers would shoot at the animals through the open car windows. With every weapon imaginable—breech-loaders, carbines, muskets, pistols, revolvers, squirrel rifles, and shotguns—the passengers fired at the lumbering beasts. Hitting bison was child's play; it was almost impossible to miss. Killing them was another matter; for every brute that fell dead right away there were at least twenty others which stumbled away into the ravines and valleys to die. From the plains and the gulleys arose the all-encompassing, all-pervasive stench of decaying flesh, the stink of the dead and the dying.

Buffalo Bill and the other legitimate hunters did everything in their power to curb these excesses. But their warnings and their counteractions went for naught. They could only maintain their own integrity amid the general madness.

Genuine sportsmen would seek out these veteran hunters as guides. These sportsmen wanted the thrill of shooting buffalo from horseback, instead of from the safety of railroad cars or water-hole blinds, and the pleasure of eating bison steaks afterward or knowing that the meat and hides would be turned over to soldiers or needy civilians.

One of these parties, gentlemen hunters from New York, came West in a special train to try its luck at shooting buffaloes. The men were all friends of General Sheridan and included, among others: James Gordon Bennett, of *The New York Herald*; Dr. Asch, of General Sheridan's staff; Colonel J. Schuyler Crosby; General H. E. Davies; Samuel Johnson; Carroll Livingston; Captain M. Edward Rogers; Quartermaster-General Rucker; General Anson Stager, of the Western Union; and Charles Williams, editor of *The Chicago Journal*.

Sheridan had asked Buffalo Bill to act as guide for the hunt. The scout dressed up flamboyantly for the occasion: light buckskin suit, elaborately decorated crimson shirt, and white sombrero. After being introduced to the Easterners, he showed them the elaborate camp outfit that had been prepared for the occasion: sixteen wagons to carry baggage supplies and food (two of these wagons had been earmarked to haul ice for the wine); three or four ambulances, horsedrawn, to transport the guns and to serve as carriages if the hunters tired.

From September 22 to October 2 the Easterners spent their days and nights on the plains. Under Buffalo Bill's expert instruction and guidance, every member of the party killed his share of buffaloes. In the evening the tired tenderfeet gathered around the campfire and feasted on their kill for the day.

A typical menu at one of these gargantuan meals included:[2]

Soup
Buffalo Tail

Fish
Broiled Cisco; Fried Dace

Entrees
Salmi of Prairie Dog; Stewed Rabbit; Filet of Buffalo aux Champignons

Vegetables
Sweet Potatoes, Mashed Potatoes, Green Peas

Dessert
Tapioca Pudding

Wines
Champagne Frappe, Champagne au Naturel, Claret, Whiskey, Brandy, Ale

Coffee

The members of the hunting party were so impressed by the affability and competence of Buffalo Bill that they invited him to New York for a visit. Bennett went one step further; he promised to pay the scout's expenses if he were to come East.

No sooner had the visitors from New York left than Cody was ordered by General Carr to guide three companies of the Fifth Cavalry, one company of Pawnee Scouts, and some friends of General Emory—a Mr. McCarthy from New York and two Englishmen—on a twenty-day scout. The expedition had two objectives: to hunt for fresh game and to find hostile Indians.

Plenty of game was sighted and killed, but no redskins were encountered. McCarthy was disappointed, and kept saying he wanted to "see action." Finally, Buffalo Bill manufactured some action for him; he prevailed upon the

Pawnee scouts to disguise themselves as hostile Indians. When McCarthy saw the "enemy" warriors charging down upon him, he turned tail and galloped towards camp. Even when the joke was disclosed, he still refused to ride out in front with the scouts but insisted on staying close to the main command.

Back in the East, James Gordon Bennett was printing reams of publicity about Buffalo Bill, some true, some imaginary, in his paper, designating Cody as the "beau ideal of the plains."[3] And Ned Buntline was turning out yarn after yarn with Buffalo Bill as the hero.

In January, 1872 newspaper correspondents descended in droves upon Fort McPherson to cover an event in which Buffalo Bill was to play a prominent part. Grand Duke Alexis of Russia was touring America on a good will mission. The nineteen-year-old royal youth announced that he would like to hunt buffaloes on the Western plains, and General Sheridan was selected to see that this wish was granted.

Bill Cody was chosen to serve as guide for the hunt. As part of the preliminary preparations, he journeyed to the lodge of Spotted Tail, famous chief of the Sioux, to prevail upon him to bring his warriors and chiefs to Red Willow Creek, the site selected for the Grand Duke's camp, to welcome "the great chief from across the water."[4] The chief agreed to come.

On the morning of January 12, 1872 the royal train pulled into North Platte, and the Duke and his companions were greeted by officers and soldiers from the fort, with impressive ceremony. General Sheridan introduced the Grand Duke to the man who was going to teach him everything about shooting buffaloes, Buffalo Bill.

Then the entire party rode to Camp Alexis, arriving there late in the afternoon. Spotted Tail, true to his word, was waiting for the noble visitor with a whole band of his chiefs and braves. That evening the red men performed their spectacular war dance in full battle regalia.

Hunting began the next day. Cody loaned Alexis his own favorite horse, Buckskin Joe, for the occasion. A large herd was sighted. Buffalo Bill and the royal party approached the animals stealthily from the windward. Then the scout smacked Buckskin Joe across the rump and hollered to the Duke, "Go get one!" Alexis was overanxious and fired at one of the bison from 100 yards away. He missed.

Buffalo Bill explained that he had not gotten close enough to his quarry. The next time the Duke rode swiftly along with the herd, closed in on a large bull, held his gun almost against the animal's flank, and pulled the trigger. The buffalo fell dead, much to the Duke's delight.

The next day Spotted Tail requested the big chief from across the sea to hunt along with one of his own men, the famous chief, Two Lances. Alexis was astonished, as was the entire party, when Two Lances shot an arrow clear through the body of a large buffalo, and the royal visitor gladly accepted the arrow as a souvenir.

During the days he hunted on the plains, Alexis killed eight buffaloes. He wanted to stay longer but admitted that this was impossible, given his tight touring schedule. On the way back to the railroad station, the Duke rode with General Sheridan in a double-seated open carriage drawn by six frisky cavalry horses. Alexis wondered how a real stage driver would handle the team, so Sheridan asked Cody to take the reins.

Buffalo Bill climbed into the driver's seat, flicked his

whip over the horses' heads, and away they went. As they started down a steep hill, the steeds were going so fast that Cody had all he could do to keep them on the trail. There were no brakes on the carriage; every time the hind wheels hit a rut the vehicle bounced frighteningly a few feet into the air. When they finally reached their destination, after three miles of jounce and bounce, the Duke climbed down gingerly, shook hands with the scout, and wanly thanked him for the ride.

Before he left, the Duke presented Bill Cody with a magnificent coat of fine Russian furs. Subsequently, Alexis telegraphed to his jewelers in New York and had them make and send Buffalo Bill a set of cuff links and a scarf pin studded in diamonds and rubies, each piece in the shape of a buffalo as big as a half dollar.

Bill Cody rode back to Fort McPherson with General Ord. On route the general offered Bill an officer's commission in the regular army, but Cody refused, declaring that he preferred the life of a scout.

Back at the post, General Sheridan urged Cody to accept James Gordon Bennett's invitation to visit New York. Bill secured a thirty-day leave from General Ord, wired Bennett and told him he was coming East. He received $500 from the editor to pay his expenses.

The scout's first stop was Chicago. There Colonel M. V. (Mike) Sheridan, General Philip Sheridan's brother, met him. Reporters swamped the scout and he was kept busy answering questions. Colonel Sheridan finally shooed the newsmen out. Then the colonel informed Bill that there was going to be a ball in his honor that night at the Riverside Hotel, and asked him whether he had a dress suit. When the scout answered No, Sheridan took him to Marshall Field's and assisted him in selecting appropriate evening wear.

Cody thought he should get a haircut but the colonel vetoed this. Sheridan told Bill it would be proper, however, for him to purchase a top hat for the occasion. This time Buffalo Bill refused. A startling compromise was effected: the scout wore white tie and tails, patent leather shoes, and topped the entire getup with his favorite Stetson.

At the ballroom itself the scout was presented to a bevy of beautiful women. Instead of bowing to each of them, as he saw the other men do, he shook hands all around. In truth, he was afraid to bow, thinking he might burst the seams of his shiny, tight evening clothes.

Bill was unfamiliar with the newfangled dance steps, so to make him feel at home an old-fashioned quadrille was added to the program. Stiffly, and with much difficulty, the scout managed to get through this number. Then he slipped into the cloakroom and remained out of sight for the rest of the evening.

On the following morning, when it was time for him to take the train to New York, Cody informed the colonel that he just couldn't make it, that he was returning to the sagebrush. Sheridan listened sympathetically, all the while steering the scout swiftly and firmly toward a Pullman car. Bill was still protesting when the train pulled out of the station; he was on his way to New York.

A few of his hunting companions met him in the Big City and he was escorted to the Union Club. After an informal reception there, Bill and his party, accompanied by a covey of newspapermen who scribbled down the scout's every word, went over to the Brevoort to visit Ned Buntline. The novelist and the plainsman were very happy to see each other again, and the writer insisted that the scout be his guest during his stay in the city.

Buffalo Bill was taken everywhere and shown everything. Wherever he went, he was treated as a celebrity. His modesty and friendliness brought him admiration and respect.

Breakfasts, luncheons and dinners were held in his honor. One night he saw Edwin Booth in a Shakespearean play; the next evening he attended a musical, "The Black Crook," at Niblo's Garden, as the guest of James Gordon Bennett. He was wined and dined by politicians and industrialists, theatre people and society leaders. All the papers reported his every move, especially Bennett's *Herald*.

Cody's greatest triumph came at the Bowery Theatre on February 20, when he attended the opening-night performance of a drama based on his own life, "Buffalo Bill, the King of Bordermen," adapted by Ned Buntline and Fred G. Meader from Buntline's *New York Weekly* serial.

The play itself was a pastiche of every Western cliche and abounded in fights between noble scouts and bloodthirsty red men, and noble scouts and villainous bandits. Obvious, yes; incredible, yes; but the crowd and Buffalo Bill loved it.

Between the acts the audience learned that the real Buffalo Bill was in the theatre, a spotlight was turned on him, and everybody in the house cheered, stamped and hollered. At the end of the show the crowd refused to leave if Cody wouldn't make a speech.

The bashful plainsman was led onto the stage by Mr. Freleigh, the producer. Bill looked at the vast sea of upturned faces. He babbled incoherently—even the orchestra leader didn't understand a word he was saying—but the audience didn't care. That the great hero of Summit Springs was standing before them in the flesh, was sufficient. Wave after wave of applause rolled up to the scout on the stage. Tears filled his eyes and he beat a hasty retreat back to Buntline's box.

Freleigh cornered Cody and offered him a salary of $500 a week to play the part of "Buffalo Bill" himself. Bill, still shaking from his first experience with an audience, refused, saying, "You might as well try to make an actor out of a Government mule."

His sojourn in New York was cut short by a telegram from General Sheridan. Recalcitrant Indians had raided settlements in the vicinity of Fort McPherson, and Cody was needed back at the post to guide the Third Cavalry—which had replaced the Fifth—in punishing the marauders.

Bill bade good-by to his friends and took the train to Chicago. From there he traveled on to McPherson. Immediately he joined the troops in the field under the command of Captain Meinhold and Lieutenant Lawson. Soon, with Texas Jack (T. B. Omohundro), another scout at the post, he was riding out in front of the soldiers, following the trail of the retreating redskins.

On the second day out the tracks appeared fresher and clearer, indicating that the red men were not far away. Captain Meinhold made camp and then ordered Buffalo Bill to choose six men and go in search of the Indians.

Cody and his companions discovered the Indian camp about a mile away and galloped right in among the tepees. Red men ran out of the tents, were fired at by the scout and the soldiers, and shot at the white men in return. Other Indians on the other side of a stream started to the rescue of their friends. Bill urged Buckskin Joe across the creek to meet them, at the same time shouting to one of the soldiers to have the men dismount and follow him into battle.

Before the troopers could reach the creek, two braves on horseback closed in on Buffalo Bill, firing as they approached. Cody shot one down. The other brave wheeled and ran. Bill gave chase, and as he did so he felt blood running down his forehead. He put his hand on top of his head; his scalp had been creased by a bullet. He realized that the Indian he was chasing had caused the wound. Cody dug his spurs into Buckskin Joe, caught up with his assailant, and killed him with one shot through the head.

Meanwhile the dismounted cavalrymen had crossed the stream and had engaged the Indians in hand-to-hand combat. By the time Captain Meinhold arrived with reinforcements, six Indians had been killed by the advance guard. One soldier was dead, and Buffalo Bill slightly wounded. When the main command came close, the red men fled from the scene. Some of Meinhold's men, led by Cody, were sent in pursuit, but to no avail.

Shortly afterward the Third Cavalry returned to Fort McPherson.

For his part in this action against the Indians, William F. Cody received the Congressional Medal of Honor on May 22, 1872. The basis for this recognition of his gallantry in the engagement at Platte River was a report written by Captain Charles Meinhold, Troop B, 3rd U.S. Cavalry, dated Fort McPherson, Nebraska, April 27, 1872.[5]

That section of the report which pertains to Cody's bravery reads:

> Mr. Cody had guided Sergeant Foley's party with such skill that he approached the Indian camp within fifty yards before he was noticed. The Indians fired immediately

> upon Mr. Cody and Sergeant Foley. Mr. Cody killed one Indian, two others ran toward the main command and were killed. While this was going on Mr. Cody discovered a party of six mounted Indians and two lead horses running at full speed at a distance of about two miles down the river. I at once sent Lieutenant Lawson with Mr. Cody and fifteen men in pursuit. He, in the beginning of the chase, gained a little upon them, but after running more than twelve miles at full speed our jaded horses gave out and the Indians made good their escape.
>
> Mr. William Cody's reputation for bravery and skill as a guide is so well established that I need not say anything else but that he acted in his usual manner.

After this exciting episode at Platte River, life at Fort McPherson seemed dull and uneventful. Occasionally a sporadic Indian raid broke the tranquility, and the troopers, with Buffalo Bill as guide, went out to punish the offenders. Periodically parties of hunters from New York, Chicago and Omaha sought out the services of the great scout. But these minor interruptions were mere flecks of incidental foam on a great ocean of routine calm.

In the fall of 1872, while Bill was out in the field on one of these scouts or hunts, his friends, without his knowledge, made him their candidate to represent the twenty-sixth district in the Nebraska legislature. Although he was a Democrat, and the state was largely Republican, it first appeared as though the non-campaigning Bill Cody had won.

Two historians, writing of the election, explain what happened:

> William F. Cody, better known as Buffalo Bill, was the democratic candidate for member of the house from the twenty-sixth district and according to the returns of the board of canvassers of the district he was elected by a major-

ity of forty-four votes. The report of the committee on privileges and elections disclosed that the clerk of Harlan county had neglected to transmit the returns of the election in that county to the canvassers of Lincoln County as he was by law required to do. The committee found that by counting the votes of Harlan County, D. P. Ashburn, Cody's opponent, was elected by a majority of forty-two votes. The house therefore decided to "go behind the returns" of the canvassers and seat Ashburn. Mr. Cody did not appear to claim the seat.[6]

An event of much more importance to Buffalo Bill than this on-again, off-again election was the birth of his third child, a second daughter, Orra. Louisa's parents in St. Louis expressed a wish to see the new member of the Cody family, and Mrs. Cody decided she would pay them a visit. Bill's sisters, Helen and May, had married—the former to A. C. Lester, a cattleman, the latter to Edward Bradford, an engineer. Both women had established homes of their own.

With his wife and children away, with his sisters no longer dependent on him for food and lodging, and with activities on the prairies reduced to a standstill, Buffalo Bill decided to attempt a major experiment. Ned Buntline had been begging him to try his luck as an actor. Just before Louisa left for St. Louis, Cody showed her Ned's last letter. "Mamma," he told his wife, "I know I'd be a fizzle at legislatin'. I don't know just how bad I'd be at actin'. I guess maybe I'd better find out."[7] Buntline had requested Bill to come to Chicago with some genuine Westerners and real Indians, but acting on a spur of the moment decision Cody arrived in the Windy City with only one companion, his old scouting partner, Texas Jack.

The reunion of the plainsman and the writer turned into a comedy of errors. Ned was flabbergasted that Bill didn't have twenty Indians in tow. Cody was amazed that Buntline had overlooked one little matter: he had neglected to write the play in which the scouts were to perform. Nevertheless the two men soon laughed off these "minor shortcomings" and made preparations to present a bold front to the manager of the Chicago amphitheatre, Jim Nixon, at whose establishment the play was to be presented.

Nixon was furious when he was told that there were no Indians and no script. Buntline had promised the manager that he would supply the company, the drama and the billboard art. Nixon had said that he in turn would furnish the theatre, the attendants, the orchestra and local printing. The playwright-producer was to receive sixty percent of the gross, and the amphitheatre owner was to get forty percent. Now, Nixon thundered, the deal was off.

Buntline inquired what the theatre rent was for one week.

"Six hundred dollars," was the answer.

Ned counted out the required amount of greenbacks and tied up the theatre for one week. Then he hurried off to his hotel with Buffalo Bill and Texas Jack, and in four hours' time had written *The Scouts of the Plains,* a rip-roaring melodrama. Hotel clerks were drafted to write out the principal parts for each of the actors. Then Bill and Jack set about the grim business of learning their lines while Ned went out to round up twenty men to play the roles of Indians in the production. Buntline couldn't be too particular about whom he hired; it was already late Thursday afternoon and the drama was scheduled to open the following Monday night.

Late in the evening, after having hired his actors and having signed up Mlle. Morlacchi to appear as Dove Eye, the beautiful Indian girl, Buntline returned to the hotel to drill the scouts in their parts. He found two discouraged plainsmen who were making plans to return to the prairies, convinced that they'd never be able to memorize their words. The writer painted vivid verbal pictures of imminent fame and fortune which would accrue to them, and the scouts agreed to stay.

Rehearsals were impossible affairs. The scouts forgot their lines, stepped on each other's cues, and with the appearance of the "red men" on stage, "attacked" the enemy so realistically that the actors threatened to walk out en masse if the scouts didn't pull their punches.

On opening night, December 16, 1872, all seats were filled and standees pressed against the railings in the rear. When the curtain rose, the "good guys," Buffalo Bill, Texas Jack and Ned Buntline (playing the part of Cale Durg, an old trapper), were spotlighted center stage. Cody had the first speech but he couldn't remember a word.

Buntline came to the rescue. "Where have you been lately, Bill?" he asked.

"I've been out on a buffalo hunt with Milligan," the dazed scout answered. This answer, ad-libbed and not in the script, brought down the house. Milligan was a very popular Chicagoan, who with friends, newsmen and army officers occupied front row seats. He had indeed been on a recent hunt with Cody—all the Chicago papers had covered the event in full. Buffalo Bill had nervously peeped out at the audience before the curtains had parted, and had seen Milligan. Now, unconsciously he responded with the true, real life answer to Buntline's "in character" question, and the audience loved it.

When the applause died down, Ned continued to feed

Buffalo Bill and Texas Jack leading questions. The scouts staggered and stammered but somehow managed to get through the first act. Just before the curtain came down, the feathered, war-painted supers in their cambric pantalets rushed on the stage. "The Indians are attacking!" Bill yelled, and he and Jack fell upon the "red men" with a vengeance and "slaughtered" everyone of them. This action brought the crowd up cheering, and the shy scouts retired to their dressing rooms with the thunder of approval in their ears.

The second act was much like the first. The "dead Indians" were resurrected and in subsequent attacks were killed again in a variety of ways: by pistols, rifles, lassos, bowie knives and bare hands. In the final act Cale Durg was in turn killed by the red men. The death of the trapper was revenged by Buffalo Bill and Texas Jack who decimated the entire company of Indians with their bowie knives. The final curtain brought the blood bath to an end; during the whole performance neither Buffalo Bill nor Texas Jack had once delivered a complete line exactly as it had been written in the original script.

Popularly and financially the show was a huge success. Opening night box office receipts amounted to $2,800, insuring substantial profits. And the audience demanded curtain call after curtain call from the happy actors, and jammed the streets outside the amphitheatre after the show to catch a final glimpse of the heroic scouts and the noble trapper.

Critically the drama was panned. The *Chicago Times* stated that if Buntline had actually spent four hours in writing this play, it would be difficult to ascertain what he had been doing all that time. The *Inter-Ocean* also rapped

Ned as a playwright and as an actor, declaring it was unfortunate that he had been killed off in the second act when he could have been erased in the very first scene.

Theatre owner Nixon induced Buntline to take him on as a partner. At the end of the Chicago run the troupe pulled up stakes and went on to St. Louis where the play opened at the Grand Opera House on Monday, December 23. The theatre was packed to the rafters: society swells and ordinary workingmen mingled in the throng, all present in response to the irresistible lure of the Wild West. Louisa Cody had bought a third row seat without letting her husband know. What happened next can best be reported in her own words:

> I was sitting in the third row and Will saw me. He came forward, leaned over the gas footlights, and waved his arms.
>
> "Oh, Mamma!" he shouted, "I'm a bad actor!" The house roared. Will threw me a kiss. . . .
>
> And after that, when I went to see my husband in his new role as actor, I chose a seat in the farthest and darkest part of the house. But it did little good. For invariably Will would seek me out, and invariably he would call: "Hello, Mamma! Oh, but I'm a bad actor."[8]

Bad actor or not, the crowds loved Buffalo Bill and the St. Louis stay was most successful.

City after city took *The Scouts of the Plains* (retitled at one point *Scouts of the Prairie*) to its heart. In Cincinnati, at Pike's Opera House, thousands attended and hundreds were turned away. In Albany, upstate New Yorkers stormed Cody's hotel lobby and refused to leave until Buffalo Bill said a few words to them. In Boston, 1,400 Yankees turned out to view the Westerners during the one-week run, paying $16,200 for the privilege.

The show moved into New York for the acid test. In addition to the principals the cast now totaled 120 people. To add to the illusion of the authentic West Buntline planned for the scouts to make exits and entrances on horseback. Unfortunately, the physical layout of Niblo's Gardens, where the drama opened on March 31, 1873, precluded the use of live animals, but the play received whopping audience approval just the same.

The *Herald* and the *World* joined in roasting the production, yet both papers had left-handed compliments for Cody.

The *Herald's* critic wrote:

> The Hon. William F. Cody, otherwise "Buffalo Bill," occasionally called by the refined people of eastern cities, "Bison William," is a good-looking fellow, tall and straight as an arrow, but ridiculous as an actor.[9]

The *World's* reviewer blasted the play but had kind words for Bill:

> The Hon. W. F. Cody enters into the spectacle with a curious grace and a certain characteristic charm that pleases the beholders. He is a remarkably handsome fellow on the stage, and the lithe springy step, the round uncultured voice and the utter absence of anything like stage art, won for him the good-will of an audience which was disposed to laugh at all that was intended to be pathetic and serious.[10]

But the plain people of New York City, and many of the fancy ones as well, ignored these critical evaluations. By word of mouth the news went out: the show is a humdinger; the action is fast and furious; Buffalo Bill is great. Night after night the theatre was filled. When the troupers left Broadway for Philadelphia and other points, they did so secure in the knowledge that they had conquered the biggest city of them all.

The tour wound up at Port Jervis, New York, on June 16, 1873. Bill Cody counted the money he had been able to lay aside and discovered that he had saved $6,000.

The applause of the fans, the magic of grease paint and the security of having lots of money to take care of himself and his family lured Buffalo Bill back to the boards for the 1873-1874 season. Cody decided to go it alone without Buntline. He organized his own company and hired Major John M. Burke as his manager. And he talked his old partner, Wild Bill Hickok, into joining the troupe.

Starting their tour in New York, Buffalo Bill, Texas Jack, Wild Bill Hickok and the other actors traveled from town to town, city to city and state to state, bringing their Western extravaganza to the view of thousands. From the beginning, however, Cody had trouble with Wild Bill. There was only one genuine Indian in the cast; the rest of the red men were again unemployed New York actors who were eager enough to get steady work, even when it meant dying three times a night behind the anonymity of layers of war paint. As bad luck would have it, the real redskin was a relative of two Indians, Chief Whistler and the chief's nephew, both of whom Wild Bill had killed near the Republican River two years before.

Trouble broke out. The Indian was slow in "dropping dead" when Hickok shot at him with his pearl-handled revolvers. The make-believe red men followed the lead of the reluctant warrior and also took their time in dying. Occasionally, the real redskin made threatening gestures towards the scout. Finally, Wild Bill took matters into his own hands.

At Rochester, New York he bought some sand-shot cartridges. Instead of loading his guns with blanks, he put the sand-shot in his pistols and went on stage. When the fake Indians and the real red man took their time in biting the dust, Wild Bill peppered their bare legs with the stinging shot. The actors shrieked genuine screams of pain, jumped over the footlights and ran howling through the audience with the scout at their heels. The crowd was thrilled, believing it was all part of the performance, but their enthusiasm changed to anger when they were told by a bewildered Buffalo Bill that the show was over.

Cody caught up with his friend and discussed the whole matter with him. Hickok vowed further revenge against the balky Indian; Cody insisted he forget the feud; Wild Bill quit the show.

Reluctantly, Buffalo Bill bade farewell to his old pal. The supers, suffering from powder burns on their legs, returned to the cast, and the company pushed on to the next city. With less excitement but more *esprit de corps* the troupe finished its tour in Boston on May 13, 1874.

During the summer layoff Bill Cody returned to the plains and signed on as scout for seven companies of cavalry and two companies of infantry under the command of Colonel Anson Mills of the Third U.S. Cavalry. The soldiers scouted in the Powder River and Big Horn territories for a number of weeks. Outside of a few minor skirmishes with the Indians the expedition was uneventful.

Upon its return to headquarters Buffalo Bill left the command and journeyed to New York. There he organized another theatrical company. Texas Jack was not available and Bill was the only star. A new vehicle had been tailored for his talents, *Scouts of the Plains or Red Deviltry As It Is,*

—written by Hiram Robbins—and the new play was received favorably by audiences in all the principal cities of the nation. At the close of the tour Buffalo Bill returned to Rochester, his permanent Eastern place of residence, and spent the summer with his family.

In the autumn of 1875 producer-actor Cody and his touring company hit the road again. Texas Jack had returned to the group and was featured in the production. On April 21, 1876, while playing in Springfield, Massachusetts, Buffalo Bill received a telegram just as he was going on stage. The wire, signed by an old friend of the Cody family, Colonel G. W. Torrence of Rochester, stated that Bill's son, little Kit, was dangerously ill. The curtain remained down while Cody hastily consulted with his manager, Major Burke. Train schedules were checked and it was decided that Bill would take the nine o'clock train that evening for Rochester. In the time-honored tradition of the stage Bill Cody played his role during the first act as if nothing untoward had happened. Then, during the intermission, the scout stepped out of character, explained to the sympathetic audience what had occurred and told the customers that Major Burke would finish the play in his stead. Bill hurried to the train and arrived at Rochester at ten o'clock in the morning and was met at the depot by Moses Kerngood, an old friend, who accompanied him to the Cody home.

Bill was shocked to find his little boy, usually so active and alert, lying unmoving in bed. The child's large dark eyes were glazed. Perspiration had plastered his mass of curly hair close to his head.

All day the scout cradled Kit in his arms. At six o'clock in the evening the boy died.

Plate 24

Sioux Warriors at the Battle of Wounded Knee

Plate 25 *Bettmann Archive*

Buffalo Bill's Wild West and Congress of Rough Riders of the World lithographic poster, 1899

Plate 26 *Bettmann Archive*

Buffalo Bill show poster, 1900

Howard Athenæum Programme

SEASON OF 1881-82.

FRANK WRIGHT .... STAGE MANAGER
B. F. TRYON .... TREASURER
Harry Saxton........................ Leader of Orchestra

Week Commencing MONDAY, APRIL 10th,
MATINEES, WEDNESDAY and SATURDAY

After many campaigns on the frontier, decorated by achievements which have won the highest evidences of distinction from

AMERICAN GENERALS AND FOREIGN PRINCES,

BUFFALO BILL

HON. W. F. CODY,

Will appear in his new and powerful Border Drama, taken from scenes in Buffalo Bill's past life, and written expressly for him by John A. Stevens, author of "Unknown," entitled the

PRAIRIE WAIF

A STORY OF THE FAR WEST.

SCENERY........................BY........................ALBERT C. ROBERTS
MECHANICAL EFFECTS........ " ....E. B. HARRIS
GAS AND CALCIUMS........ " ....GEO. BOWMAN
PROPERTIES........ " ....W. O'BRIEN

BUFFALO BILL, Representing Three Distinct Western Characters........................Hon. W. F. CODY
ONITA........................Miss LYDIA DENIER
SADIE........................Miss NELLIE LINGARD
MARK STANLEY........................Mr. W. J. BALIE
JIM HARDY.... } Danites. { ....Mr. ROBERT NEIL
JACK HARDY.. } Danites. { ....Mr. HARRY MELMER
HANS........................Mr. JULE KEEN
CAPT. RUSSELL........................Mr. J. LEWIS
GEN. BROWN........................Mr. T. J. QUINN
E. OVERTON, a Sutler........................Mr. R. D. DORSEY
LIEUT. SAUNDERS........................Mr. HARRY IRVING
LIEUT. WHITE........................Mr. GEO. HANCOCK
JACK CASS........................JERRY
LONE DEER.... } Winnebago Chiefs, by { ....LONE DEER
YELLOW HAND.. } ....YELLOW HAND
FLYING CLOUD.. } ....FLYING CLOUD
CHIEF BEAR..... } ....CHIEF BEAR
HE-NU-KAW, Indian Maiden, by........................HE-NU-KAW
SPOTTED HORSE, Pawnee Chief, by........................SPOTTED HORSE
BOY CHIEF OF THE PAWNEES........................HARRY B. BURGESS
Soldiers, Danites, Indians, &c.

ACT I. Prairie Waif.
A lapse of one year between 1st and 2d Acts.
ACT II. Home of Buffalo Bill.
An interval of one month between 2d and 3d Acts.
ACT III. The Attack and Defence.
ACT IV. The Rescue.

In Act IV, a Genuine Band of Indian Chiefs will appear in their wild and weird Songs and Dances, as follows:

THE SCALP, SUN, HORSE, SQUAW,

And other Dances, under control of Eddie Burgess, Interpreter and Boy Chief of the Pawnees.

Mr. CODY, Buffalo Bill, will give an exhibition of Fancy Rifle Shooting, in which he is pre-eminent and alone. NOTE. — The audience will please take particular notice of the twenty different positions that Mr. Cody holds his rifle in making his fancy shots.

Plate 27 *New York Public Library*

Show Program, Boston, 1882

Wild West!

BEACON PARK

—FOR A SHORT SEASON—

Commencing, MONDAY, July 2.

PROGRAMME.

CODY AND CARVER - - Proprietors
JOHN M. BURKE........................General Manager
E. W. WOOLCOTT........................Business Manager
F. WHITIKER........................Superintendent
JULE KEEN........................Treasurer

HON. W. F. CODY, Buffalo Bill. DR. W. F. CARVER, Evil Spirit.

THE WILD WEST

Programme of the Entertainment.

—1—

Grand Introductory March of the "WILD WEST," introducing the Deadwood Coach, Indians, Squaws, Papposes, Cow-Boys, Mexicans, Bufaloe, Elk, Deer, Texas Steers; also introducing the following notables of the "Far West;"
BUFFALO BILL, DR. W. F. CARVER, Maj. FRANK NORTH, Col. TOM WILSON, GEORGE CLOTHER, and others.

—2—

AN EXCITING BAREBACK PONY RACE!
Between Omahas, Sioux and Pawnee Indians.

—3—

THE WONDERFUL PONY EXPRESS,
Showing the method of carrying dispatches previous to the introduction of the telegraph.

—4—

The startling and soul-stirring
Attack upon the "Deadwood Mail Coach,"
By the Indians; its rescue by the Scouts and Cow-boys, led by Hon. W. F. CODY (Buffalo Bill) and Dr. W. F. CARVER (Evil Spirit).

—5—

100 YARDS RACE!
Indian on foot vs. Indian on Pony, turning stake at 50 yards.

—6—

CAPT. A. H. BOGARDUS,
Champion Pigeon Shot of America, will give his great exhibition, using the LIGOWSKY CLAY PIGEON.

—7—

Novel and Extraordinary Shooting by
HON. W. F. CODY, *Buffalo Bill.* On foot and on horseback.
DR. W. F. CARVER, *Evil Spirit.* An exhibition never before given in America.

—8—

A SPIRITED AND LIVELY DASH,
By mounted Cow-boys.

—9—

COW-BOYS' FUN!
Introducing Bucking and Kicking Ponies.

—10—

ROPING, TIEING AND RIDING THE WILD TEXAS STEERS

—11—

LASSOING AND RIDING THE WILD BISON OF THE PLAINS

—12—

The entertainment to conclude with an effective illustration of

A Grand Hunt on the Plains!

The pursuit — Method of Shooting, Capture, etc., of Buffalo, Elk, Deer, Wild Horses and Cattle, giving a condensed view (so far as practical) of the exciting scenes of the chase in the "Wild West," joined in by the combined races of white and red men, with a grand realistic battle scene, depicting the capture, torture and death of a Scout by the savages. The revenge, recapture of the dead body and victory of the Cow-Boys and Government Scouts.

FINALE.

Plate 28 *New York Public Library*

Show Program, Boston, 1883

Plate 29 *Brown Bros.*

Buffalo Bill's Wild West Show Troupe

The grief-stricken father sat down at his desk and wrote letters to all the members of the family telling them the heartbreaking news. The following is the letter he sent to his sister Julia.

Rochester, New York
April 22, 1876

To my eldest sister Julia:

You are the first to write to after our sad, sad loss. Julia, God has taken from us our only little boy. He was too good for this world. We loved him too dearly, he could not stay.

God wanted him where he could live in a better world, so he sent the angel of death to take the treasure that he had given us five years and five months ago. And how dear he had grown, so dear to us in that time, and when we saw that there was danger of him leaving us, how we all clung to him and prayed God not to take him from us, our little boy Kit. When he sent that hasty messenger, the scarlet fever, there was no hope from the start. Death claimed him as its own at once and only gave us two short days to say farewell and bid him good-by, then he was gone. And now his place is vacant and can never, never be filled, for he has gone to be a beautiful angel in that better world where he will wait for us. Every one will know him there, as they did here. (For everyone knows our little Kitty.)

So if we only live good, that we may be permitted to go where he has gone we will have no trouble in finding him when we are there for everyone will know our Kitty. The messenger seems not to have been satisfied by plucking the brightest flower and is still hovering nearby, thinking whether he shall take the others or not, for the same fever has taken hold of our little girls, but so far only lightly. But with Kitty it claimed him from the first.

Lulu is worn out and sick. It is three o'clock in the morning. I am sitting by the bedside of our sick babies.

I was hundreds of miles away when Lulu telegraphed me and I only got home a few hours before Kitty died. He could not speak, but put his little arms around my neck as much as to say "papa has come."

I must now write to Lida, Nellie and May.

Goodby,

From Brother Will.[11]

The other Cody children soon recovered from the fever. Bill remained with them until he was sure they were completely well. Then he returned to his theatrical troupe. Wherever he went, crowds gathered to greet him at the station, to follow him to his hotel and to fill the theatre to capacity. On stage he was dashing, fearless and most effective. But the thrill of trouping was gone. The words he mouthed and the actions he simulated fired the imagination of his audience but were meaningless to him. Instead of upturned smiling faces, he looked out across the footlights and saw only one face, that of Kit Carson Cody.

CHAPTER 10

The Birth of Buffalo Bill's Wild West

EVENTS IN THE West jolted Buffalo Bill out of his grief. The Sioux Nation and the Northern Cheyennes—smarting under the treachery of the white men who had promised by solemn treaty in 1868 not to permit settlers to enter the Black Hills, only to break this pact in 1874 during the time of an abortive gold rush—were on the warpath. Sitting Bull was the instigator of the Indian uprising.

Cody received communications from Colonel Mills advising that he was needed at once in the field. Bill immediately cancelled the few remaining theatrical engagements and started for the West. At Cheyenne he was met by Lieutenant Charles King who accompanied him to the fort. As the two men rode into the post, one of the officers of the old Fifth Cavalry, which had come back from five years in the desert of Arizona to join in the fighting, recognized the scout and shouted, "Here's Buffalo Bill." Three mighty cheers went up from the soldiers.

General Carr at once appointed Bill to his old position of chief of scouts. The next day the entire command marched to Fort Laramie, from which they proceeded to scout the country between the Indian agencies and the

Black Hills. After two weeks in the territory, the regiment returned to Laramie, convinced that all hostile red men had been driven away. Once back at the fort, General Merritt (who had replaced General Carr) and the soldiers of the Fifth were horrified to hear that General Custer and his whole force had been massacred on June 25, 1876, on the Little Big Horn.

It was in the days that followed that Merritt and 500 picked soldiers made their forced march to War Bonnet Creek and intercepted a force of 800 Cheyennes attempting to reach Sitting Bull. It was during this campaign, on July 17, 1876, that Buffalo Bill met Chief Yellow Hand in a duel to the death and killed his famous adversary.[1] And it was during this engagement that the Fifth Cavalry drove the Cheyennes into the Red Cloud Agency, thereby smashing the entire Indian rebellion by one masterful stroke.

Subsequent to this action, the Fifth Cavalry joined General Crook's command in the Big Horn mountains and engaged in mopping-up operations against the red men. The troops reached the Powder River, where Buffalo Bill accompanied General Mills on an unusual scouting expedition down the Yellowstone on the steamer *Far West*. The steamer arrived at its destination, Glendive Creek, without the scout and the general having seen any Indians, although they had sighted some fresh Indian graves.

The *Far West* was to remain in Glendive overnight. Yet messages had to be taken immediately to General Crook and General Terry. Buffalo Bill volunteered to go and rode seventy-five miles through the badlands of the Yellowstone that night, arriving at General Terry's camp the next morning.

After Cody had a nap and something to eat, General

Terry requested him to carry some dispatches to General Whistler on the *Far West*. Cody agreed and set out at midnight on a fresh horse. He covered the forty-mile distance in four hours. Whistler read the messages and then asked Bill if he would take dispatches back to Terry, telling of Indian skirmishes in the vicinity. Cody mounted his horse immediately and rode to Terry's base.

The general insisted that Buffalo Bill accompany him to Dry Fork, on the Missouri, for a scout of the territory. When the command reached its goal, signs were found that the Indians had been killing buffaloes on the range. Terry called upon Bill to deliver dispatches to Colonel Rice, encamped at Glendive Creek on the Yellowstone, informing him of the situation.

Under cover of darkness Bill set out on his eighty-mile journey. Through drizzling rain and over unfamiliar terrain he rode, making thirty-five miles by daylight. Then he dismounted, intent upon hiding until nightfall. He breakfasted on hardtack and bacon and then lay back on his saddle to take a snooze.

A roaring, rumbling sound woke him. Bill seized his gun and jumped on his horse. He cautiously climbed a steep hill toward the direction of the noise. He peered over the summit and saw twenty Indians galloping at full speed after a huge herd of buffaloes. For two hours he watched the hunt and the butchering of the killed animals. At last the redskins rode off with their fresh meat—in the very direction that Cody would have to travel.

When night came, Buffalo Bill resumed his journey, taking a wide semicircular detour to avoid the Indian camp. He reached Colonel Rice's headquarters just before dawn.

Rice was in desperate straits. He had been fighting

against redskin bands daily and was in need of reinforcements. After a day's rest Bill was back in the saddle and on his way to General Terry. On the third day out Bill found the general at Deer Creek. Terry and his troops were heading for Rice to relieve the hard pressed command. Cody pointed out that General Terry was bearing too far east and would by-pass his objective. The scout joined up with the relief column and led Terry and his troopers directly to Colonel Rice's camp.

Buffalo Bill bade good-by to the officers and men and booked passage on the steamer *Far West* which was heading down the Missouri River. He disembarked at Bismarck and went on by rail to Rochester, New York, where he joined his family.

An actor, J. V. Arlington, had written a new five-act drama for Bill Cody, based on the war with the Sioux and including the duel with Yellow Hand. Custer's last stand, and the subsequent counteroffensive against the Sioux and Cheyenne forces by the Fifth Cavalry, had been given extensive coverage by the newspapers of the country. The public had been deeply stirred by these events and was eager to see one of the great heroes of the conflict, Buffalo Bill, re-create his real life triumph on the stage.

The Rochester run was a sellout. The New York City engagement at the Grand Opera House broke the attendance record. Throughout the land, wherever he toured, Buffalo Bill played to overflow audiences.

Bill looked for new worlds to conquer, and against the advice of friends took the show to the Pacific Coast. The initial engagement in the Far West was at the Bush Theatre in San Francisco for two weeks. All seats for the initial performance were sold out ten days before the opening; the receipts for the first show alone amounted to $1,400; throughout the run the "Standing Room Only" sign was always up. So steady was the demand for seats that the show remained in San Francisco an additional five weeks.

The play visited many other Far Western cities. This most successful season was closed at Virginia City, Nevada, where the townsfolk all shut up their shops on the last day of the run, in honor of Buffalo Bill.

In 1877 Bill Cody, in conjunction with his old army friend, Major Frank North, formed a partnership in the cattle business. They bought two ranches on the south fork of the Dismal River, sixty-five miles north of North Platte in Nebraska. While Cody was out on the road, Major North remained at the ranch site, supervising the construction of the buildings.

With the show season over, Cody and North met at Ogalla, headquarters of the Texas drivers, and bought, branded with the mark CN, and drove to the ranches a large herd of cattle. Bill helped with the work of tending the cattle and still found time to make preliminary notes for his autobiography which was eventually published by Frank Bliss at Hartford, Connecticut, in 1879. The scout made a special trip to Kansas in 1878 to secure the help of his sister Julia in regard to dates and details.

Buffalo Bill scheduled a new theatrical tour for the 1877-78 season, leaving Major North in charge of the work at the ranches. This time Bill hired a group of Sioux Indians at the Red Cloud Agency to play themselves in the show. Rehearsals were held at Rochester. Then Buffalo Bill, Mrs. Cody and the younger daughter traveled to New

York City for the opening. Arta, the older daughter, was left at a girls' seminary at Rochester.

May Cody, or *Lost and Won*, by Major A. S. Burk of the United States Army, was the name of the touring attraction. It was based on Mormon outrages leading up to and including the Mountain Meadow Massacre, all of which had transpired twenty years earlier but which were still fresh in the public mind because of the long delay in bringing the chief culprit, John D. Lee, to justice. Lee was finally tried and executed in March, 1877, just previous to the start of the pre-publicity for the new drama. Again crowds flocked to see Buffalo Bill, and the touring troupe broke all its own previous attendance records.

Tired of living out of a suitcase, Mrs. Cody left the troupe in February, 1878, and personally supervised the erection of a dwelling place for the family at Bill's Nebraska ranch. Built according to Buffalo Bill's own specifications, the residence was a rambling clapboard house topped by a tower with eight windows. The huge barn also carried out the tower motif, on a lesser scale, with three striking domes rising from the roof. The name of the establishment, SCOUT'S REST RANCH, appeared in huge block letters on top of the house. When Bill Cody came home in May, he was most pleased with the results.

Before he could enjoy the pleasures of home, however, he joined Major North in a six-week roundup of CN cattle. Only when all his stock were back at the ranch was Buffalo Bill able to rest. His sisters Nellie (Helen) and May visited him that summer, and he in turn went to their homes in Denver for a few days—stopping at Ogalla on route to buy a fresh herd from a Texas cattleman.

It was time to make plans for the 1878-79 dramatic

season. During the previous year his Indian actors had scored a terrific hit, especially with their wild war dances. Bill hired additional redskins at one of the Indian agencies and added C. A. Burgess, a Government interpreter, and Ed Burgess, known as the "Boy Chief of the Pawnees," to the cast.

This time the show headed south, opening the season at the Baltimore Opera House and then pushing on to Washington, D. C., Richmond, Virginia, and Savannah, Georgia. At this point it became impossible to go deeper into Dixie. Yellow Fever was raging in the area so the tour was rerouted, and the players doubled back in their tracks. Despite this apparent setback the season proved to be the best ever.

Buffalo Bill returned to his 7,000-acre ranch at North Platte. Julia Cody Goodman, who in later years was to be the hostess at Scout's Rest Ranch—in which capacity she entertained royalty, army officers, Government officials, cowboys, frontiersmen, scouts and Indians—maintains that the happiest periods of Bill Cody's life were spent among his old friends and trailmates at the ranch. Every summer, until the season of 1882-83, he returned to Nebraska after closing the show.

As the years went by, both his theatrical enterprise and his cattle business prospered and Buffalo Bill found himself a wealthy and very famous man. Yet he had become dissatisfied with presenting and appearing in plays. Something more spectacular would be more to his taste, something bigger and better which could more accurately represent the adventure, the excitement and the frontier flavor of the real West. Bill Cody had acquired an active dislike for the tameness of touring theatre and was nursing a vague dream of a type of spectacle that might replace it. But the actual birth of the Wild West show, the extravaganza which was to leave William F. Cody's indelible mark on the history of show business, came about completely by accident.

Buffalo Bill returned to Scout's Rest Ranch in the early summer of 1882 to find his North Platte neighbors planning a bang-up Fourth of July celebration. The businessmen wanted something unusual for the ceremonies, something that would attract people from miles around. They asked Bill Cody, the master showman, to devise something special for the occasion.

Cody accepted the challenge. He arranged a kind of rodeo, replete with ropin', ridin' and shootin'. He plastered the ranches for hundreds of miles around with handbills, and advertised the rules and prizes in the newspapers. The business leaders of the community footed the bill.

Ranchers, cowboys, frontiersmen, soldiers and scouts sent in entries. The great day came, and it seemed that all Nebraska had squeezed itself into North Platte. The events ran off like clockwork; the contestants gave the audience a grand show and the audience roared its approval. Thus, on that sun-drenched July afternoon in the small town of North Platte, Nebraska, was originated the spectacle that was the progenitor of all the rodeos and Frontier Day tournaments that were to follow. And this Independence Day fete was the embryo of Buffalo Bill's Wild West show.

Bill had tried the show on his neighbors and they had liked it. Now he decided to bring it to all America.

During the fall and winter he made careful plans. With the coming of spring he put these plans into action. He borrowed trained horses and buffaloes, hired Indians from the Pine Ridge Agency and recruited cowboys from neighboring ranches. The show was organized at Columbus, Nebraska in April, 1883.

The opening performance of "The Wild West, Rocky Mountain and Prairie Exhibition" was held at the fairgrounds in Omaha on May 17. With the sky as a roof and the hard earth as a huge stage, the performers brought the tumult of the West almost into the laps of the spectators. Indians, riding bareback, participated in elimination races. Cowboys competed in bronco busting, trick-riding, fancy roping, foot racing, bison riding, shooting on foot and on horseback and knife throwing. Mock battles were waged between the red men and the scouts. At the climax of the show a pony express rider dashed through the grounds, followed shortly by the Deadwood Mail Coach. A band of "hostile" Indians attacked the coach. And the scouts, led by Buffalo Bill on a magnificent white charger, galloped to the rescue, completely routing the attackers.

Audience response to the first performance exceeded even Bill Cody's fondest expectations. Overnight, it seemed, word of the success of the exhibition spread throughout the nation. Major John M. Burke, who served as press agent, told Cody that the exhibition publicized itself and really required no ballyhoo.

The Omaha crowds were so numerous that it appeared that the exhibition could remain there forever and still make money. But there were commitments in other cities all along the line. Eastward the show journeyed, playing to overflow audiences in all the large cities. The season was finished at Coney Island in a blaze of glory, with newsmen, spectators and celebrities vying to find laudatory adjectives for the sensational spectacle.

Back at Scout's Rest Ranch, Cody was deluged with

offers from circus owners and managers, requesting him to join their enterprises. But Buffalo Bill was convinced that a Wild West show would be strangled in the confines of a tent and resolved to keep his outfit intact and separate.

A business manager was needed—that Cody realized. The double burden of being chief performer and impresario was just too much for one man. During his stage career Bill had become acquainted with the actor-comedian, Nate Salsbury, who had his own touring musical company, "Salsbury's Troubadours." Not only was Salsbury an exacting showman, but he also possessed unusual business acumen. The comedian was intrigued with the Wild West show and easily was persuaded to accept a partnership in the exhibition. In the year 1884 the show went on the road under the aegis of Cody and Salsbury.

Buffalo Bill was not only willing to share the management responsibilities but also was willing to let other Western heroes share the performing limelight. Among these legendary characters who demonstrated their specialties before gaping men, women and children in all parts of the United States were: Buck Taylor, King of the Cowboys; Con Groner, the cowboy sheriff of the Platte; Captain David C. Payne, the Oklahoma Raider; John Y. Nelson, the Squaw Man; Bill Bullock, the Handsome Half-breed; Mustang Jack; Bill Halstead, the Steer Thrower; Jim Hathaway, the Aristocrat; White Beaver; Johnnie Baker, the Cowboy Kid; and a number of other plainsmen, including Utah Frank, Bronco Pete, Montana Joe, Blue Hall, Bridle Bill and Jim Lawson. Nearly 100 additional Indians were added to the company, warriors who had distinguished themselves in the Sioux War and the Custer Massacre.

This top-flight line-up of famous performers opened the new season at St. Louis. Two weeks later, at the driving park in Chicago, 41,448 people saw the exhibition in one day, despite threatening weather.[2] So well was the presentation accepted that Buffalo Bill forsook his usual summer vacation at Scout's Rest Ranch and toured all the large cities with the exhibition instead.

With fall and winter coming on, Cody and Salsbury decided to take a calculated risk. The World's Industrial and Cotton Exposition, celebrating the 100th anniversary of the export of Louisiana cotton, was to be held in New Orleans that winter. The partners decided to take the show south to cash in on the centennial celebration.

Even while final plans were being made for the trip to Louisiana, tragedy visited the Cody family once again. Little Orra died, and Bill journeyed to Rochester for the funeral. She was buried next to her brother, Kit Carson Cody. The only partial compensation for this tragic event was the presence in the Cody household of another infant daughter, Irma, born the previous year. Reluctantly the grieving father left his family and returned to the exhibition.

A river boat was hired at Cincinnati to transport the Wild West show to New Orleans. On the way down the river, stops were made at several towns, where the exhibition gave successful performances. Everything pointed to Buffalo Bill taking New Orleans by storm.

Then suddenly disaster struck. At Rodney Landing, Mississippi, the steamer collided with another craft. The captain ran the steamer ashore, patched up the hole in the hull and headed out into the river again—only to sink in thirty-feet of water in the middle of the stream. The wagons, camp equipment, arms and ammunition, donkeys, sheep, buffaloes and one elk went to the bottom. All the human beings were saved: the cowboys swam the horses to shore; the Indians were picked up by a passing barge; the Deadwood Coach and the bandwagon were towed to the river bank.

Buffalo Bill wired Salsbury, who was in Denver at the time, "Outfit at bottom of river, what shall I do? Cody."

Nate telegraphed back, "Go to New Orleans and open on your date. Have wired you funds. Salsbury."

Bill proceeded to the delta of the Mississippi and somehow rounded up a new outfit. Buffaloes came from Nebraska, recruited by one of the stars of the show, Major Frank North, commander of the Pawnee Scouts. Steers were purchased from the New Orleans stockyards. Two weeks after the sinking of the steamer, Cody had secured enough animals, wagons, arms, equipment and additional personnel to open on schedule.

But the winter season was doomed to failure. For forty-four straight days and nights it rained. The Race Track oval, where the show was set up, was a sea of quagmire. Losses were heavy and the future looked even darker than the present. Captain A. H. Bogardus, the featured marksman of the exhibition, and his four sons, Eugene, Edward, Henry and Peter, relieved the monotony by shooting holes in the fence that circled the raceway.

Just before New Year, word was received from the West that Frank North, who had been injured in Hartford, Connecticut when he fell from his horse during a performance, as the result of a saddle girth breaking, was dead. This seemed the last straw: a daughter dead; a capsized steamer; unrelenting rain for a month and a half—and now the untimely death of an old and trusted friend who was one of the stars of the show. The Sioux Indians in the company performed a solemn memorial dance for Major North—an extraordinary occurrence indeed, for the man whom they were spontaneously honoring had sparked the campaigns of their hated enemies, the Pawnee Scouts, in the years when the Sioux were a great red nation.

Things took a turn for the better as Buffalo Bill's Wild West (Major Burke had renamed the exhibition) headed north. The retreat from New Orleans soon became a victory. Harbinger of better times was Annie Oakley, "Little Sureshot," a nineteen-year old, pretty, five-foot, 100-pound wisp of a girl, who with her husband, Frank Butler, joined the show at Louisville on April 24. This frail lass, affectionately called Missie by everyone who traveled with the Wild West, instantly became a stellar attraction. Her trick shooting and unerring marksmanship with rifle, shotgun and pistol always brought the crowds roaring to their feet.

Through trial and error, and constant experimentation, the essential character of the Wild West had now been molded into shape. Occasionally the personnel would change; an act would be added or the program would be shuffled, but the basic format was set.

In each new city the show would be unloaded at the train station, and the parade to the exhibition grounds would begin. At the head of the line on a white horse rode Buffalo Bill, raising his hat to the cheering multitude that thronged the sidewalks. Next came the band wagon, pulled by six white horses almost dancing to the tunes played by the musicians. Then came the Indians, feathered and painted, shrieking war whoops—Pawnees, Sioux and Wichitas riding their barebacked, painted ponies—warriors and chiefs together. Following the red men came a contingent of Mexican vaquerros in bright serapes—oversized sombreros almost hiding their dark faces. Annie Oakley, straight and regal, looking like a frontier queen, rode by herself in a special carriage. Suddenly the streets were filled with cowboys and scouts, on horse and afoot, herding along steers, buffaloes, mules and horses—filling the air with a cacophony of yells, whip lashes, neighs, brays, bellows, creaks of saddle leather and beat of hoofs on the pavement. Bringing up the rear was the Deadwood Mail Coach (bullet riddled by Black Hills bandits) pulled by six mules and driven by bearded John Nelson.

The exhibition itself went off at a fast, furious pace. No sooner had the band serenaded the spectators into their seats than the sweet show tunes changed to a loud fanfare. Buffalo Bill and the other featured performers galloped into the arena and pulled up their mounts in front of the packed stands. Some of the steeds bowed, others reared and still others pranced back and forth. As quickly as they came, just as quickly did they disappear into the dark recesses of the arena, leaving Annie Oakley alone in the spotlight. With pistol, with rifle, with shotgun, she shot at standing targets and moving targets and flying targets, from every possible position. So fast did she shoot and so accurate were her shots that her whole performance blurred into one magnificent fusion of cracking bullets and exploding objects.

Then the scouts, cowboys and vaquerros took over. Trick riders leaped from horse to horse, from horse to ground and from ground to horse. Lassos whirled through the air and encircled charging buffaloes, swift moving steers and untamed horses. The riders and ropers joined forces in simulating a real Western roundup; steers were cut out of the herd, roped and branded. The Indians and the scouts put on a buffalo hunt, using blank cartridges and rubber tipped arrows to "kill" their quarry. The redskins demonstrated their tribal dances, climaxing the demonstration with a war dance. The Deadwood Stage lumbered into the lights. Four volunteers, usually newspapermen, climbed into the coach and set out on a journey into Indian territory. A band of braves swooped down on the stage, but Cody and his scouts intercepted the charge and drove the foe into the hills. The broncobusters took over. At each show the epic battle between riders and wild horses ensued. Sometimes the riders won, sometimes the horses, but always the crowd yelled and stamped and called for more. The cowboys, scouts and vaquerros gave them more: steer riding, buffalo riding—even elk riding.

Then the highpoint of the exhibition—the reënactment of the duel with Yellow Hand. First swiftly, then slowly, Buffalo Bill and an Indian brave, drafted to portray Yellow Hand, rode toward one another from opposite ends of the arena. When in range, they emptied their revolvers at each other. Dismounting, they chose new weapons—Yellow Hand a spear, Buffalo Bill a bowie knife. Then skillfully they acted out a ballet of death—parrying, thrusting, shifting, whirling, falling only to rise again—until Cody grabbed the spear with one hand and drove home the knife with the other. The great scout bent over the "dead" warrior and shattered the hush of the arena by hollering, "The first scalp for Custer." As applause crashed down upon him from every seat, Buffalo Bill climbed back on his horse Charlie, cantered to the very center of the grounds, where man and horse, as if fused together into a centaur, bowed in every direction. The band struck up a lively tune; the horseman rode off into the darkness. The show was over.

This, with some variations and occasional additions, was

the formula that brought men, women and children thronging to the box office. New Orleans was shortly just a bad dream in the reality of success. In rapid succession Chicago, key cities and towns in Indiana and Ohio, and Buffalo, New York put out the welcome mat for the Wild West. At Chicago, 40,000 people poured into the show grounds for one exhibit alone. In a small Ohio town all business establishments were closed down for the day and everyone, from the mayor to the single inmate of the jail, went out to see the exhibition. On Friday, June 12, at Buffalo, the famous chief Sitting Bull and five Sioux braves, three squaws and an interpreter joined the company. This was Major Burke's grand coup; the Wild West had heroes aplenty, but with the coming of Sitting Bull it would have even a greater attraction—a real, live villain.

The crowds came to hiss Sitting Bull and cheer Buffalo Bill during one-day stands in Pennsylvania and New York state. But it was in Boston that Sitting Bull came into his own as a drawing card. The Wild West had been booked into Beacon Park for a week. Immediately it seemed as if all the proper Bostonians wanted to see Custer's killer. The small city within a city that constituted the tents, stables and sleeping quarters of the exhibition troupe had always been a magnet for sightseers who flocked to it before and after each show. This proved to be especially true in Boston. The largest gathering was always in front of the Sioux chief's tent. There the spectators gaped at him in fear and loathing while he gazed blankly back, changing expression only when some brave soul pressed forward to request his picture or ask for his photograph, both of which he gladly gave—for a price.

So popular was the Wild West that Cody, Salsbury, and

Burke introduced an innovation: two shows daily, afternoon and evening, with the night performance illuminated by the light from calcium flares. And the cash and the customers flowed in.

The exhibition finally left Boston and headed northward for the first invasion of a foreign country, Canada. The first stop was Montreal; then in order, Ottawa, Kingston, Toronto, Hamilton and London. The Canadians were as enthusiastic about the Wild West as were their American cousins. Cody and Salsbury were sitting on top of the world. The fiasco of New Orleans was no longer even a bad dream; it was completely forgotten, buried under a whole series of smash successes. Even before the start of the Canadian tour the Wild West entrepreneurs had recouped their losses and made a handsome profit besides. The books showed that in the first five months of 1885 over 1,000,000 Americans had seen the show, giving Cody and Salsbury a clear profit of $100,000. And as Major Burke put it, "The Canadian tour is pure gravy."

Having conquered Canada, Cody and his co-players headed back to the States, making their first stand at Detroit. Then they moved on to Saginaw and Columbus. The season closed at Sportsman's Park in St. Louis, and the members of the company scattered to all corners of the United States.

Buffalo Bill hurried back to Scout's Rest Ranch where his sister Julia and her husband, Al Goodman, paid him a visit. He persuaded his sister to accept the position of hostess, and his brother-in-law to act as foreman of the entire establishment.

In mid-April the Wild West assembled again at St. Louis. The show was larger than ever before: 240 people were in the company, including three more women—two cowgirls and another shooting star—a bunch of new cowboys, the notorious bandit Doc Middleton, the superpatriot Sergeant Bates, the fugitive from Canadian justice, half-breed Gabriel Dumont, and many others. Twenty-six railroad cars were required to transport the company, the animals, and the new accoutrements—a complicated lighting system, painted backdrops and thousands of folding seats. A full-blown spectacle, "Custer's Massacre," had been scheduled to climax the production. Ironically enough, the natural star for this feature, Sitting Bull, had not rejoined the troupe but had remained on the reservation. To take his place there were now two featured villains, the Sioux chiefs American Horse and Rocky Bear.

At the opening performance at St. Louis, 40,000 people viewed the show, prominent among whom were Buffalo Bill's old commanders, General Sheridan and General Carr. Eastward the Wild West pushed: to Terre Haute, Dayton, Wheeling, Cumberland, Hagerstown, Fredrick City, Washington, D. C. for a week, where the performers were greeted by the personal representative of President Cleveland, Philadelphia where 200,000 spectators saw the show in two weeks, and finally New York.

All summer long, twice-a-day all week except Sundays, Buffalo Bill's exhibition held forth at Erastina Woods on Staten Island. Daily, 17 steamboats brought crowds from as far away as the upper Hudson to see the show. And the 20,000 seats were always filled. Newspapermen made the Wild West their regular assignment. It appeared as if all America was beating a path to Buffalo Bill's tent.

Many of the visitors made repeated visits. One of these repeaters was Mark Twain who wrote a letter to the show's star:

Dear Mr. Cody:

I have now seen your Wild West Show two days in succession, and have enjoyed it thoroughly. It brought vividly back the breezy wild life of the plains and the Rocky Mountains. Down to its smallest details the Show is genuine—cowboys, vaquerros, Indians, stagecoach, costumes and all; it is wholly free from sham and insincerity and the effects it produced upon me by its spectacles were identical with those wrought upon me a long time ago by the same spectacles on the frontier. Your pony express-man was as tremendous an interest to me yesterday as he was twenty-three years ago when he used to come whizzing by from over the desert with his war news; and your bucking horses were even painfully real to me as I rode one of those outrages once for nearly a quarter of a minute. It is often said on the other side of the water that none of the exhibitions which we send to England are purely and distinctively American. If you will take the Wild West Show over there you can remove that reproach.

Yours truly,
Mark Twain[3]

Authors brought their notebooks, and artists set up their easels on the camp grounds. Journalists were feted by Major Burke in a special press tent. Their stories, drawings and articles were seen by millions of Americans.

At the end of summer Ned Buntline, the man who had done most to bring Buffalo Bill to the attention of the public, died.

With the coming of fall Cody and his associates decided to transfer their exhibition from Staten Island to Madison Square Garden. Steele MacKaye, the noted playwright and producer, with the assistance of the scenic artist, Matt Morgan, was hired to stage the Wild West show at the Garden for the winter season. For the production Morgan painted a gigantic backdrop, covering 15,000 square feet of canvas.

Against this background MacKaye arranged for the members of the company to perform a pageant which he titled "The Drama of Civilization." Essentially this drama was the tried and true fare of Buffalo Bill's Wild West, with pastoral trimmings. Opening with a peaceful scene of animals and Indians in the forest, it quickly erupted into a fight between rival tribes; Annie Oakley's sharpshooting act; an attack on a wagon train by hostile braves and the rescue of the attacked ones by Buffalo Bill and the valiant scouts; a blazing prairie fire, for which MacKaye's technical crew used special effects brilliantly; Custer's Last Stand; the dangerous gallop of a pony express rider; and a bandit attack on the Deadwood Stage. For the grand finale a cyclone was produced with a "two-hundred horse-power wind machine which blew down mining shacks and hurled passengers off the coach."[4] After the storm was over, peace —the pastoral peace of the opening scene—descended on the plains.

From the opening of the show on Thanksgiving evening in 1886, when 9,000 people packed the Garden to the roof, to the closing performance on February 22, 1887, New Yorkers made the Wild West their own show. They mobbed performers in the street, gaped at the Indians strolling in Central Park on Sundays and swamped the Garden box office for tickets. A successful season; a gala season; a triumphant season: was it any wonder that Cody, Salsbury, and Burke agreed to put Mark Twain's suggestion into practice and take the Wild West to Europe?

CHAPTER 11

Rough Riders of the World

ON MARCH 31, 1887 the Wild West—men, women, animals and equipment—was loaded aboard the steamship *State of Nebraska*. With thousands waving good-by from the pier, and the cowboy band playing "The Girl I Left Behind Me," the ship nosed its way down the Hudson and out to open sea. On deck Red Shirt, Sitting Bull's successor, and the other chieftains—Cut Meat, Little Bull and Poor Dog—appeared pale and wan. They, like almost everyone else aboard, were seasick—as sick as cows with hollow horns; but in addition they were sick with fear, believing in the old tribal legend that a red man who crossed the ocean would be afflicted by a cancerous disease which would cause his death.

On the seventh day out, when they had almost forgotten their fright in the face of the fact that instead of wasting away they were actually gaining weight from the fine food being served, another danger confronted them. A violent North Atlantic storm beat against the *State of Nebraska* and mountainous seas lashed over the decks. The engines broke down and the ship spun like a tiny top in a foaming kettle. The chiefs and the braves crouched in the hold, praying to the Great Spirit for salvation. In a few hours the motors started up again, the steamer pushed ahead and rode out the storm.

After an eleven-day voyage, the ship docked at Gravesend. Major Burke, who had gone ahead to make preliminary arrangements, led Lord Gower and a contingent of British newspapermen up the gangway. The cowboy band played "The Star-Spangled Banner" while the welcoming committee greeted and interviewed the Wild West company. Burke introduced Red Shirt to the members of the press as the "monarch of the Sioux nation," adding that it was only proper that an American ruler should come to London to pay his respects to the members of the British Royal House on the occasion of Queen Victoria's Jubilee. Then the press agent presented Buffalo Bill to the assemblage, introducing him as Colonel William F. Cody—a title Buffalo Bill had received shortly before making the trip, when Governor John M. Thayer of Nebraska had appointed him to his staff. The London newspapers gave considerable play to the arrival of the Wild West, and taking their cue from Burke, emphasized that the exhibition constituted a semiofficial cultural representation from the United States.

Crowds jammed the docks, and cries of "Welcome to England" and "Hurray for Buffalo Bill" rent the air as Colonel Cody and the others stepped ashore. The entire party was taken to Victoria Station in carriages. There, everyone descended into the underground railway and journeyed to the west-end of London to Earl's Court Exhibition Grounds, where the shows were to be held. Then the members of the cast of the Wild West were given an official welcome and formal dinner.

During the weeks when the exhibition grounds were being readied, Buffalo Bill became the lion of the London social season. Alone, or with members of his company, he attended breakfasts, luncheons, dinners, garden parties, athletic meets, midnight socials, soirees, festivals, theatrical events, excursions and dedications. Soon the tall, handsome plainsman and the featured players of his cast became as familiar to the average Londoner as his political leaders or favorite cricketeer. The ubiquitous Major Burke plastered all of London with posters bearing Colonel Cody's picture. Commenting on the omnipresence of these placards, a reporter for the *Globe* wrote in rhyme:

I may walk it, or bus it, or hansom it; still
I am faced by the features of Buffalo Bill;
Every boarding is plastered, from East-end to West
With his hat, coat and countenance, lovelocks and vest.[1]

Just like their American counterparts, small boys were unable to wait until the Wild West officially opened to investigate its wonders. They, and their fathers, and then entire families, visited the exhibition camp. Prime Minister Gladstone took time off from affairs of state and called at the camp on April 28. Then a week later, without preliminary formalities, Their Royal Highnesses, the Prince and Princess of Wales, their three daughters and a group of lords and ladies pulled up in front of the unfinished show buildings. Royalty had come to the Wild West.

Buffalo Bill escorted the vistors around the grounds. Then he led the regal party to a special box draped with bunting of both the British and American colors. In the meantime Major Burke and Nate Salsbury had scurried about alerting the cast that a spur of the moment dress rehearsal was to be given for the Crown Prince and his associates. Burke also sent messages to all the London newspapers informing them that the royal party was present.

The show ran smoothly. The Prince leaned forward in the box and followed every action with delight. At the close of the performance His Royal Highness requested Buffalo Bill to present the featured actors, which the plainsman did. Annie Oakley was introduced to Princess Alexandra. "Little Sureshot" smiled, bowed slightly and then extended her hand to the Princess. Charmed by the naturalness of this gesture, Alexandra put out her own hand and grasped Annie's in a firm handshake. The Prince, in the company of Red Shirt, now made a more leisurely and thorough tour of the camp. Colonel Cody served as guide and interpreter—reverting to the roles that had first brought him fame on the frontier—and by the end of the inspection the Sioux chief and the British chief had a genuine respect for one another. At seven o'clock in the evening the visit came to an end with the Prince promising to come again in the near future.

On the following day the London newspapers carried a complete account of the royal visit to the Wild West, including a laudatory endorsement of the exhibition by the Prince himself. Burke, Salsbury and Cody were overjoyed; the success of the show was assured.

The spectacle officially opened on May 9. Following the lead of their beloved Prince, court figures and political leaders, celebrated entertainers and writers, society notables and financial magnates roved through the camp and saw the show. Within a few days Buffalo Bill was packing 20,000, 30,000 and 40,000 persons into the huge amphitheatre, three-quarters of a mile in circumference.

Shortly after the opening Queen Victoria sent a special messenger to Colonel Cody requesting a special showing for herself and her retinue. Since the death of her beloved husband, Prince Albert, the Queen had rarely appeared in public, although occasionally gifted entertainers went to her courtyard, by Her Majesty's invitation. But now it was different. As Buffalo Bill said, "The Wild West was too big a thing to be taken to Windsor Castle, and it became necessary for the Queen to go to the Wild West."

On the appointed day Queen Victoria and her royal entourage, including Grand Duke Michael of Russia, the Crown Prince of Austria, Prince Louis of Baden, the King and Queen of Belgium, the King of Denmark, the Crown Prince and Princess of Germany, the King of Greece, the King of Saxony and assorted other members of the nobility, arrived at the arena promptly at five o'clock. Buffalo Bill met Her Majesty at the door, his sombrero in hand, and welcomed her to "the Wild West of America."[2] Prince Edward walked slightly behind the Queen. As the royal party entered the grounds, the Prince waved a greeting to his "old friend," Red Shirt.

As soon as the Queen and her party were seated in the royal box, Buffalo Bill gave a signal and Sergeant Bates marched around the arena, carrying the American flag. He stopped in front of the Queen and dipped the colors three times in salute.

The Queen's reaction to this gesture can best be described in Colonel Cody's own words:

> Absolute silence fell over the great throng. Then the Queen rose and saluted the flag with a bow, her suite following her example. There was a wild cheer from everyone in the show, Indians included, and soon all the audience

was on its feet, cheering and waving flags and handkerchiefs.[3]

After this auspicious beginning the performance itself was letter perfect. When the show was over, there was another presentation. One by one the featured players advanced to the royal box and bowed to Her Majesty. Graciously she had a word of praise and commendation for each of them. Red Shirt alone did not make obeisance to the Queen. Resplendent in war paint and full headdress, he stood straight and proudly before her, a ruler in his own right. Through an interpreter he said that he had come a long way to bring the greetings of the great Sioux people to Her Majesty. The Queen smiled. With dignity the chief turned away to make place for the next performer.

Like the Prince of Wales, Queen Victoria returned to the Wild West, this time on the 20th of June. The second command performance was attended by 300 members of the court. All of the royal personages who had seen the show previously came back, including the Prince of Wales for his third go round. With them appeared the Prince and Princess of Saxe-Meiningen, the Crown Prince of Sweden and Norway, Princess Victoria of Prussia and the Duke of Sparta. Buffalo Bill induced three kings and a prince to climb into the Deadwood Coach, and then gave them the ride of their lives, climaxed by an Indian attack. The Prince of Wales, who had begged off from the ride, knowing what was in store for the royal passengers, sent Colonel Cody a precious souvenir after the show in appreciation of the three special royal performances—a feathered crest outlined in diamonds, with the words *Ich Dien* lettered in contrasting jewels underneath.

For every king who saw the show hundreds of thousands

of commoners packed the amphitheatre. By summer's end two and a half million people had visited the Wild West. By October it was time to move on for a tour of the English provinces. Buffalo Bill, exhausted at having played all 300 London performances and making innumerable personal appearances besides, slipped off to Italy with his daughter Arta for a vacation.

The Wild West moved on to the Midlands as soon as Buffalo Bill returned. The show played the principal cities, setting up shop for the longest run in a gigantic hall in Manchester.

In the spring of 1888 Cody and his co-performers went back to London. Again England's first city welcomed the American troupe, filling the arena to capacity show after show. The final English performance was given at Hull on Saturday, May 5, 1888. Then the players packed their bags and boarded the steamer *Persian Monarch*. Happy as they had been in Europe, everyone was glad to be going home.

The New York *World* summed up America's feeling about the homecoming of the Wild West:

> The harbor probably has never witnessed a more picturesque scene than that of yesterday, when the *Persian Monarch* steamed up from Quarantine. Buffalo Bill stood on the captain's bridge, his tall and striking figure clearly outlined, and his long hair waving in the wind; the gaily painted and blanketed Indians leaned over the ship's rail; the flags of all nations fluttered from the masts and connecting cables. The cowboy band played "Yankee Doodle" with a vim and enthusiasm which faintly indicated the joy felt by everybody connected with the "Wild West" over the sight of home.[4]

Buffalo Bill hurried out to North Platte to see his friends and family. His two nephews, Henry and Finley Goodman, were not in awe of their famous uncle. To the contrary, he had not been in the house a day when they conspired to play a practical joke on him. They came running into the front yard, hollering, "Uncle, get your gun . . . quickly . . . there's a lot of ducks on the lake." Buffalo Bill grabbed his rifle and ran to the water. Sure enough, five or six ducks were floating on the lake. Colonel Cody fired once, twice, three times. Each shot had the same effect: a duck bobbed for a moment but continued to float, unperturbed. The boys, who had followed their uncle to the shore, couldn't contain themselves any longer and burst out laughing. Bill had really been fooled. He had been shooting at decoy ducks which the youngsters had carefully placed in midstream.

Back East, Salsbury and Burke had set up the exposition on the old stamping grounds, Erastina Woods on Staten Island. Colonel Cody joined them there in time for the Memorial Day opening show, when 30,000 persons turned out. This was the average daily attendance until the end of August; then the Wild West pulled up stakes to fulfill touring commitments which took it to Philadelphia, Washington, Baltimore and Richmond. At the Virginia city the cast disbanded for a long, much needed rest.

In the spring, less than a year after the exhibition had returned from England, the Wild West set sail again for Europe, this time for France, and set up camp directly opposite the vast 200-acre exhibition grounds where the French Government was sponsoring the industrial and artistic *Exposition Universel* of 1889. Salsbury had leased thirty acres of land on which to erect the arena that would house the show.

On May 18 a crowd of 20,000 people attended the opening performance. The French were not too familiar with the American frontier; they had come out of curiosity, they demanded to be "sold." Sell them, Buffalo Bill and his troupe did. By the end of the afternoon the whole crowd joined with Monsieur Carnot, president of the Republic, American ambassador Whitelaw Reid, and Queen Isabella of Spain in shouting, *Vive! Vive! Vive!*

The 20,000 viewers went home to tell their friends, their families and their customers that the Wild West was *tres magnifique*. And 20,000 Frenchmen couldn't be wrong. Parisians, visitors from the French provinces, international vacationers and leaders in the arts and sciences descended upon the exhibition in droves. Rosa Bonheur, nearing seventy, found new youth at the Wild West. She virtually lived at the camp, painting Indians, cowboys, horses, bulls and buffaloes. Colonel Cody posed for her. He shipped the finished life-size painting to Mrs. Cody at North Platte.

In the autumn the show pushed on to Marseilles; in December it moved to Barcelona. In the Spanish city triumph turned to tragedy. Poverty stalked the metropolis. The pestilence of influenza and smallpox attacked the people of Barcelona—soon the entire city was in quarantine—and laid low half the company of the Wild West. The show grounds were empty. In a short time ten Indians and three helpers were dead. On the day before Christmas death claimed Frank Richmond, the dynamic master of ceremonies.

Late in January Salsbury, Cody and Burke finally arranged for the Wild West to get through quarantine. The company set sail for Italy.

The first stand on the Italian peninsula was at Naples.

The City of Hills presented a problem to the Wild West management: in order to provide level ground for the exhibition it was necessary to fill in an area of two city blocks, sometimes plugging up holes fifteen-feet deep. But it was worth it. The Neapolitans loved the show and gave it enthusiastic support.

Rome was the next stop. On March 4, 1890 the Prince of Sermoneta issued a challenge to the cowboys of the Wild West which they eagerly accepted. The Prince owned some wild horses and he declared that no one in the world could ride them. The broncobusters retorted that not only would they be able to ride the wild animals, but also insisted that it would be easy.

Roman authorities erected special booths around the riding area to protect the crowd from the charging broncos. More than 20,000 people pressed up against the barriers to watch the contest. The fractious horses were let loose. Twisting, kicking, darting and jumping they sped around the field. The huge crowd gasped; it seemed impossible that the brutes could be tamed. Then Buffalo Bill gave the signal. The cowboys rushed forward and in five minutes' time by the Prince's own reckoning had roped, subdued, mounted and tamed every recalcitrant animal. Each rider guided his mount over to where the Prince was standing. Meekly and quietly the horses ringed him in a half circle. A roar of laughter and thunder of applause arose from the multitude. The Prince walked across the arena and shook Colonel Cody's hand.

Having conquered Rome, the Wild West pressed on to Florence, Pisa, Bologna and Milan. In April the show played in Munich, and then three weeks in Venice. The beginning of summer found the exhibition in Berlin.

Plate 30 *Brown Bros.*

Nate Salsbury

Plate 31 *Bettmann Archive*

Annie Oakley
photographed about 1890

Plate 32 *Brown Bros.*

Major Gordon Lillie (Pawnee Bill)
and Buffalo Bill

Plate 33

Chief Short Bull

Plate 34

King Edward VII and Queen Alexandria visit the Wild West Show after a special performance, London, 1903. Buffalo Bill is at left, with hat in hand.

Plate 35 *Wonderland Museum*

Letters from Buffalo Bill to his family, showing varied and picturesque stationery he used

Then followed Dresden, Magdeburg, Braunschweig, Leipzig, Hannover, Hamburg, Bremen and Stuttgart. By autumn Cody and his troupe were touring the cities along the Rhine—Duisburg, Düsseldorf, Cologne and Frankfurt. The season ended at Strasbourg where the Wild West bedded down for the long winter.

Unrest broke out in the camp, discontent that had little to do with internal conditions at the Wild West. The trouble originated in the United States—two sources of dissension, each independent of the other, but both having a deleterious effect on the exhibition company.

Stories had begun to seep into American newspapers—unfounded and untrue accounts inspired by political considerations—that Colonel Cody's Indian performers had been mistreated during the eighteen-month European jaunt of the Wild West. United States consuls in Germany investigated these reports and found them to be false, but back home the criticisms continued.

News of another sort had filtered through to the red men at Strasbourg; strange and disturbing news that made them want to return to the States. For a few years the American Indians had remained docilely on their reservations while the white men were gobbling up more and more of their territory. This was bad enough, but now food rations to the Indians were being curtailed. The situation was strained to the breaking point.

Out in Nevada and Utah an Indian Messiah had appeared who spoke of the resurrection of Indian glory, and of revenge against the whites. This new spokesman was Wovoka, a medicine man of the Paiutes, who announced that all dead Indians would be brought back to life if living red men participated in certain ritual dances, ceremonies and rites. Wovoka's simple doctrine had an amazing effect on the Western tribes. Emissaries traveled to the Messiah, learned from him the weird rites that would assure a red renaissance and returned to their own tribesmen with the magic formula. Night and day the braves stamped out the dance that was to bring them new birth. Wily old Sitting Bull, smarting under a thousand indignities, counseled the Sioux to support the messianic movement.

Colonel Cody's Indians longed to join their embattled brothers on the plains.

Leaving Salsbury in charge of the Strasbourg setup, Cody, Burke and the Indians set sail for home. Once back in the United States the entire party went to Washington, where the braves told their story to the Indian Bureau after which the Wild West was fully freed from the charge of mistreating the tribesmen.

In the West the Ghost Dancers were reaching a fierce frenzy of anti-white feeling. Sitting Bull called for the Sioux and their neighbors to fulfill Wovoka's prophecy by driving out all intruders and reclaiming all hunting grounds. U.S. cavalrymen poured into Indian territory and the tribesmen bolted for the badlands. The Government feared that at any moment Sitting Bull would spearhead a concerted massing of all the tribes.

Colonel Cody's old commander, General Nelson A. Miles, later in charge of the Department of the Missouri, wired the scout for help. Buffalo Bill made contact with Miles at Chicago and was temporarily appointed to the post of Brigadier General. Then Miles issued an order for Brigadier General Cody to personally arrest Sitting Bull.

Buffalo Bill went to Bismarck by train, then on to Fort

Yates by horse. On the morning of November 28, General Cody, alone in a wagon drawn by a team of horses, set out to bring in Sitting Bull. Unarmed, carrying merely blankets and trinkets to indicate his good will, Bill was certain that he could persuade Sitting Bull to return with him to the fort.

Indian agent James McLaughlin resented Cody's presence on the scene. McLaughlin believed that only a display of power would break the back of the incipient rebellion. He had wired Washington the night before, asking President Harrison to rescind General Miles' order. In midmorning the cancellation came. Troopers were sent to head off Cody. By nightfall the disgruntled scout was back at Yates.

Now that McLaughlin had thwarted Cody's attempts at peaceful persuasion, the Indian agent instigated his own bloody and senseless course of action. A band of forty-three Indian policemen was sent to Grand River to arrest *Tatanka Iyotake,* Sitting Bull. The indoctrinated red men surprised the Sioux chief before dawn on December 15 as he lay asleep in his cabin. Without objection he submitted to arrest, insisting only that he be allowed to wear his store clothes and that his favorite horse—a gift from Buffalo Bill—be saddled for him.

When the police led their captive out of the cabin, 160 Ghost Dancers surrounded them. Inside Sitting Bull's dwelling his two wives began to cry and his deaf-mute son to blubber. The captors tried to shove Sitting Bull through the angry crowd. Crow Foot, the chief's eldest son, shouted to his father, "You call yourself a brave man. And now you give yourself up—to Indians in blue uniforms."[5]

Tatanka Iyotake yelled an order and broke away from

his captors. Two of the Sioux fired, killing two officers. The police returned the fire and Sitting Bull fell dead, two bullets lodged near his heart. As the gunfire continued the great chief's horse bowed, kneeled and tossed his mane in the air; rifle shots were an old cue from the Wild West, a signal to go into his act. When the shooting was over, eight Ghost Dancers and six policemen lay dead. The rest of Sitting Bull's band fled to the south and joined Big Foot and his 400 braves, and Kicking Bear and Short Bull with their 3,000 fanatical followers, at a redskin rendezvous in the Badlands.

Troops of the Seventh Cavalry surrounded the warriors at Wounded Knee Creek, South Dakota, on December 29. The Indians agreed to surrender. In the hills above the creek soldiers stood behind four Hotchkiss cannon which were aimed at the Indian tents. Slowly the red men walked between rows of troopers, giving up their guns. One young medicine man refused to hand over his rifle. An officer grabbed the gun and it went off.

On the summits the artillerymen—acting without orders from an officer—sent a stream of explosive shells into the Indian camp, mowing down braves, squaws and papooses. The two-pound shells poured down at the rate of fifty a minute, driving the redskins across the creek into an unexposed stronghold. Behind them, 200 red warriors and 43 cavalrymen lay lifeless.

On January 16 the messianic movement ended. Braves surrendered in droves and their leaders were taken as hostages. Thus in the beginning of 1891 America no longer had a frontier.[6]

General Miles gave Buffalo Bill permission to hire 100 of the Ghost Dancers, including Chiefs Short Bull and Kicking Bear, for the Wild West. Sitting Bull's performing horse was also added to the outfit. On April 1, 1891 Cody, Burke and the recent additions to the cast sailed for Europe on the S.S. *Switzerland*, rejoining the show at Strasbourg.

The Wild West reopened on April 19 and then embarked on a continental tour covering cities of the upper Rhine, as well as Brussels, Antwerp and the English provinces. Old friends of the exhibition found the nature of the show changing; more and more it was becoming an exhibition of comparative horsemanship—the styles and techniques of riders from Arabia, Britain, France, Germany and Mexico were contrasted with those of the American cowboys and Indians.

During the winter the Wild West was housed in the Exposition Building at Glasgow, Scotland. A contingent of 100 Zulu warriors joined the troupe while it was in winter quarters, and the newcomers were soon shivering in the large drafty hall.

In April, 1892 Buffalo Bill and his performers made a quick trip through the provinces and then set up camp at their old hangout, Earl's Court. A new feature was a march around the arena by survivors of the Charge of the Light Brigade. But the main emphasis was on horsemanship; Major Burke, in a flash of publicity genius, subtitled Buffalo Bill's Wild West, "Congress of Rough Riders of the World." Cossacks from Russia and gauchos from South America were added to the show. A rider representing each country participating in the exhibition competed with the others in a daily international hurdle race. The English horseman always won. With the race over he shed his fox-hunting costume and changed to his cowpunching duds; the Britisher was actually cowpoke Harry Stanton from Kansas.

Once again Queen Victoria requested that the Wild

West give a command performance for the members of her court. Now that the exhibition had become a congress of rough riders it was relatively easy to bring the Wild West directly to the Queen. On the morning of May 7, 1892 the show was held on the tennis grounds at Windsor Castle. Afterwards, Victoria presented jeweled medallions to the performers and a magnificent signet ring to Buffalo Bill.

On October 12, after a five-month run in the British capital and three and a half years abroad, the exhibition gave its final European presentation. Three days later the Wild West headed home.

The New York welcome for Buffalo Bill's company was tumultuous. When the festivities were over, the performers scattered to their home communities, and the animals were sent to Bridgeport, Connecticut. Only Nate Salsbury was unable to visit friends and loved ones. Instead he went immediately to Chicago where he tried to secure a concession for the Wild West at the World's Columbian Exposition, scheduled to begin in the Spring of 1893. Turned down by the Exposition officials, he leased fifteen acres of ground directly opposite the Fair entrance and set to work supervising the building of grandstands that would seat 18,000 people.

On April 3, 1893 the Wild West, with over 500 men and women in the company, opened for business four weeks before the World's Fair. When the two spectacles were finally running simultaneously, many visitors thought that the Wild West was *the* Fair. During July and August, although Buffalo Bill was holding two performances a day, thousands had to be turned away at every show. By September more than six million spectators had seen the Wild

West; Bill Cody and Nate Salsbury had cleaned up a clear profit of more than one million dollars.

In October the show disbanded for the winter.

The 1894 season rolled around; on May 12 the first performance of the year was held at Ambrose Park, Brooklyn, where Cody and his partner had spent a large fortune to improve the grounds.

A steady flow of customers visited the Wild West, but nothing like the crowds of previous years. The United States was in the throes of a depression; the Cody exhibition suffered less than other entertainments, but it suffered just the same.

Major Burke dreamed up a number of publicity stunts to stimulate attendance: the marriage at Ambrose Park of Miss Holy Blanket to Mr. High Bear, with a frontier missionary officiating; special press conferences for featured performers; invitations to the artist, Frederic Remington, and to General Guy Vernor Henry, veteran of the war against the Sioux, to visit the Wild West—with the newspapers tipped off, of course.

On September 24, Burke arranged the best publicity break of all, but it was a little late in the season to help. Buffalo Bill, Annie Oakley, five Indians and the press agent traveled over to Orange, New Jersey. There, in the studio of Thomas A. Edison, a few simple activities of the Wild West were recorded on motion pictures—the forerunner of all the Western movies to come.

On October 6, Cody, Salsbury and Burke struck their Brooklyn camp for the year. Buffalo Bill went home to North Platte, and then took an extended trip through the Big Horn country in Wyoming. He bought a huge tract of land, and hired a crew of men to dig an irrigation canal.

In the years that followed Colonel Cody was to invest millions of dollars in making Big Horn Basin—a valley bounded on the south by the Shoshone Mountains, on the east by the Big Horn Mountains and on the west by the Rockies—into a fertile paradise. In October of 1894, however, he was merely engaged in the first stage of this project, supervising the canal digging of a crew of 2,000 men on the 3,000 acres of land he had purchased from the Government under the Carey Act.

The 1895 show season brought a significant change: Nate Salsbury was no longer at the helm; he was replaced as business manager by James A. Bailey, a veteran circus man, though Nate still retained a partnership in the exhibition. Bailey's influence was soon felt; the revised schedule was backbreaking—131 stands in 190 days—with the two show trains and their 700 passengers covering a 9,000 mile route from April to October. But the tour was very successful, with profits totaling upwards of $500,000.

In 1896 the Wild West followed the Barnum and Bailey Circus into the Garden to open its season. After a two weeks' stand the big show trains headed west on a tour that was to hit 132 cities and towns over a 10,000 mile circuit. In June the exhibition moved into Chicago, the first attraction to use the new Coliseum, largest indoor arena in the world. For the initial occasion in its history the Wild West crossed the Mississippi River; then in October the company pushed beyond the Missouri River.

This marked the first time since its formation thirteen years before that the people of North Platte had had an opportunity to see the world famous show of their favorite son. Once again it appeared as if all the citizens of Nebraska had descended upon the little town which usually held less than 4,000 persons. Buffalo Bill and his performers went all-out to give the scout's friends and neighbors a crackerjack show. And the audience ate it up, cheering and stomping on the bleacher benches until Colonel Cody, with tears streaming down his cheeks, made a short speech thanking them for their faith in him, a trust that had been responsible for the original Fourth of July rodeo that had led to the birth of the Wild West.

On the day following his homecoming, Buffalo Bill rode out to Scout's Rest Ranch and took part in a reunion of the entire Cody clan. But there could be no real rest for the old scout; the schedule called for additional stands at Lincoln, St. Joseph, Leavenworth and Kansas City—and Colonel Cody rejoined the show.

An upsurge of sympathy for the oppressed people of Cuba gripped the American public in 1897. Buffalo Bill capitalized on the spirit of the time by adding a battery of light artillery to the equipment of the show. Opening in Madison Square Garden, the Wild West made 147 separate stops, including a return to Canada. The tour also played the Chicago Coliseum again. In both Canada and the United States crowds were large and enthusiastic.

Major Burke corralled a group of Cuban campaigners for the 1898 tour of the Wild West. Although war between the United States and Spain had not yet been declared, Buffalo Bill featured drills by members of the Sixth U.S. Cavalry and the Fifth U.S. Artillery, as a dramatic demonstration of America's feeling of solidarity for Cuba.

Congress declared war on April 19. Two weeks later the Wild West paraded past General Miles in the nation's capital, where the general reviewed the march of the performers. Wherever Colonel Cody's show went—New

Jersey, New England, New York, Pennsylvania, Michigan, Minnesota, Iowa—the spectators went wild when Cuban troopers and American cavalrymen rode across the dusty arena together, holding the United States and Cuban flags aloft. Field pieces and caissons, to implement the martial motif, were purchased. This added equipment bulged over the sides of the already overloaded show trains; eight sleeping coaches transported the cast, fifteen flat cars hauled the Deadwood Stage, two prairie schooners, two electric lighting engines, two water tanks, four buggies, thirty-five baggage wagons and innumerable props, scenic effects and assorted gear.

The long show trains pulled into Omaha, Nebraska late in the summer. The Wild West was the major attraction at the Trans-Mississippi Exposition, celebrating the passing of the pioneer and the winning of the West. This was the very spot where the first official show had been given fifteen years before. In honor of Buffalo Bill, Governor Holcomb designated August 31 as "Cody Day" throughout the state, and officiated in special ceremonies at the fair grounds.

While 24,000 people watched and listened, Bill's first boss, Alexander Majors, and Senator Thurston delivered addresses of praise for the scout. Colonel Cody responded briefly. Then the showman demonstrated his appreciation by the method he knew best: he climbed on his horse, rode out to the center of the arena and gave a memorable performance as the super-star of the show that bore his name.

The show trains chugged slowly across the Nebraskan plains, halting at whistle-stops for one-night stands, so that Colonel Cody's friends all over the state might be able to see the Wild West.

Next, Kansas—flat, uninteresting country—the long pull across the wheat belt, with stops at cities, towns and hamlets. At Kansas City, during an afternoon show, Buffalo Bill fell from his horse three times. Burke hastily summoned a physician; the diagnosis—pneumonia.

For the first time since the start of the Wild West, Buffalo Bill was not in the cast. The gloomy troupers went on without him while he lay in a hospital bed. Against doctors' orders he rejoined the exhibition in a week, at Joplin, Missouri. Wan and white he played out the season.

Colonel Cody needed rest, lots of it. He journeyed out to his holdings in Wyoming, resolved to do nothing but hunt and sleep. But once there he was busier than ever. All around him he saw rich farm and pasture land, valuable mineral deposits and magnificent scenery. Big Horn Basin, he estimated, was large enough to be divided into 65,000 separate farms, each of eighty acres. Only one thing was lacking: easy, convenient transportation to the valley. There was one entrance to Yellowstone Park; a visitor had to travel to Livingston, Montana on the Northern Pacific Railway, and then 100 miles by stage over a twisting route to reach the valley from the north—and this was the only way.

Colonel Cody knew that if Big Horn Basin was to become anything other than a rich man's hideaway, if men with limited means were to be attracted to the valley, it would be necessary to find another entrance. In the winter of 1899, still weak from his siege of pneumonia, he used his energy, influence and money to make the Park and the valley more accessible.

CHAPTER 12

Trail's End...the Last Camp

THE BATTLE OF San Juan Hill was substituted for Custer's Last Stand at the climax of the Wild West show during the 1899 season. More than 500 men, among them sixteen of Theodore Roosevelt's own Rough Riders, took part in the finale. As usual the Indians were cast as villains—Spanish villains instead of Sioux villains. This time the red men, instead of carving to shreds Custer's circle of soldiers, were themselves attacked, as defenders of the Spanish fort atop San Juan Hill, and put to rout by Roosevelt's Riders, U.S. troopers and infantrymen, Garcia's scouts and Grimes's artillery. Governor Roosevelt himself shook hands with his old comrades-at-arms in a formal ceremony on opening night at Madison Square Garden; then he and other political dignitaries, military leaders and war heroes sat back and enjoyed the show.

The warlike exhibition packed people in from Maine to Texas. Riders representing Hawaii, the Philippines and the West Indies were among the new recruits to the show. All along the way the overflow crowds responded enthusiastically to old favorites and recent innovations alike.

The year 1900 found the show on the road again, playing

throughout the East and the Midwest. People everywhere were still flushed with the United States victory in the Spanish-American War; the Battle of San Juan Hill—Buffalo Bill style—was a show-stopper.

The Mysterious East fused with the Wild West in 1901. In reënacting the storming of Tientsin by foreign troops during the recent Boxer Rebellion, Colonel Cody cast the Indians as the Chinese defenders of the walled city. Chiefs Flat Iron, Iron Tail, No Horse, and Sammy Lone Bear and their braves changed from Spanish uniforms to pigtails, coolie hats and tunics for this spectacle.

Buffalo Bill did not slight the Boer War. A detachment of Afrikaners—and some Canadians who had fought them in South Africa—now did battle under the spotlights.

A regiment of Royal Northwest Mounted Police gave an exhibition of precision riding; the "Maze of Nations" featured 200 riders going through an intricate ballet on horseback; a U.S. Coast Guard crew fired a life line to a foundering ship on the other side of the arena, and the passengers of the sinking vessel made their way to safety, one by one, over the taut rope. In the entire extravaganza of the Wild West the hard core, cowboys and Indians, was still to be found, but contemporary history and changing public tastes were forcing Cody, Salsbury and Burke to drastically revise the basic formula.

East, west, south the show went—pushing forward, doubling back and then going ahead again until the Wild West route, when viewed on a map, looked more like the tracks of a mouse trapped in a maze than the schedule-stops of a traveling exhibition. One city on this map was circled in red, Buffalo, New York, for it was there that the show played on the Pan-American Exposition Grounds, as General Miles and the Apache chief, Geronimo, watched from the stands.

As winter approached, Colonel Cody returned to his 3,000-acre holdings in Wyoming. Buffalo Bill had finally arranged for another entrance to the Big Horn Basin, and for transportation to the spot. An Associated Press dispatch, date-lined Cody, Wyoming, November 12, 1901, told the story:

> The Burlington Railroad ran its first train into the metropolis of the Big Horn Basin, the town of Cody, Wyoming, at ten A.M. today. Hundreds greeted the arrival of this, the first train in the valley of the Shoshone, and celebrated the occasion with a grand barbecue and speech-making during the day and with fireworks at night.

The 1,000 inhabitants of Cody went wild when the engine pulled into the newly painted depot. They knew that other settlers would shortly swell their numbers, now that a railway line ran to the outer world.

Colonel Cody presently accomplished the second step in his efforts to make it easy for newcomers to reach the valley. He enlisted the support of Frank Mondell, a Wyoming congressman, in convincing county authorities and state officials that a road was needed to connect the town of Cody to Yellowstone National Park. The linking road, seventy miles in length, was soon completed. The valley and the Park now had two entrances and a transportation system, which not only brought people to and through the mountainous walls that enclosed the 15,000 square miles of the Big Horn Basin, but also permitted them to conveniently inspect the natural wonders and scenic beauties of the land that stretched below. The road that bisected the face of the valley was officially named the Cody Trail.

In preparation for the influx of visitors Colonel Cody supervised the building of a large, modern hotel at the town site, calling it the Irma Hotel in honor of his youngest daughter. Buffalo Bill participated in the ground-breaking ceremonies in the winter of 1901. The builders—taking into consideration the elaborateness of the plans and the projected size of the structure—estimated that it would take two years before the hotel could be opened to the public.

Permission was received from the Government to build two additional hotels in the Forest Preserve. These way-side inns—Pahaska's Tepee (close to Sylvan Pass, 10,000 feet above sea level) and Elephant Head Lodge (42 miles from Cody on the trail leading to the Park)—were built in record time.

In this way—by providing irrigation, an additional entrance, railroad transportation, a road, inns and a hotel —Colonel Cody transformed a hidden paradise twice the size of the state of Massachusetts into a living-farming area, a thriving mining center and a vacation wonderland.

Sadness settled over the Wild West during the 1902 season. Annie Oakley, "Little Sureshot," was no longer with the company. On the next to last day of the season the year before, she had been seriously injured in an accident when the locomotive pulling the second section of the show train, in which she was riding, crashed into another engine. Partially paralyzed and slightly crippled, she remained behind in her home at Nutley, New Jersey.

The tour itself was long and harrowing. One-night stands and split-weeks were the rule, not the exception. From coast to coast the show trains went, until every town and city blurred into every other in a weary pattern of unbroken monotony. The Wild West was growing old.

As winter neared, there was no postseason break for rest and revitalization. The exhibition returned to New York and was loaded aboard a steamer bound for England. Before leaving, Buffalo Bill made sure that the Irma Hotel would be capably managed. His sister Julia Cody Goodman—who had moved to Cody, Wyoming after the death of her husband in 1901—agreed to take charge of furnishing the hotel, hiring the staff and supervising the running of the establishment once it was officially open.

In London the Wild West set up camp at Earl's Court. The show still had its old pull and thousands of Londoners visited the exhibition grounds, watching the roustabouts preparing the tents and the arena area for the December 26 opening performance. All signs pointed to a banner stay.

On Christmas Day a cablegram arrived from the United States, informing Colonel Cody that his partner, Nate Salsbury, had died at his home in Long Branch, New Jersey on Christmas Eve. The entire company of 800 performers joined the boss in mourning Salsbury's death. But as Nate would have wanted it, the show went on. On the day after Christmas the Wild West opened to packed stands. In the center of the grounds the American flag hung limply at half-mast. Members of the U.S. Cavalry attachments with the show guided their crepe-covered horses solemnly across the arena, their regimental banners dipped in salute. In a spontaneous gesture the huge crowd stood up; Britishers and Americans alike watched bareheaded as the cavalrymen said their symbolic good-by to Nate Salsbury.

The New Year brought a change in luck for the Wild West. Buffalo Bill's old friend, the Prince of Wales, had now ascended to the throne. Though he was now King Edward VII, weighed down by affairs of state, he managed to sneak away and see several performances. The King presented a diamond pin to Colonel Cody, as a token of his affection. After the presentation, which took place at the end of a show, the King toured the grounds. One little Sioux boy was fascinated by His Majesty's jeweled cane and tried to grab it out of the King's hand. A tug of war ensued; the monarch and the Indian boy, each holding a different end of the cane, pulled vigorously. Suddenly the youngster let go and the King reeled backwards, almost losing his balance. Righting himself, His Majesty patted the boy's head and saw to it that he was given another, less valuable souvenir.

Back home at Cody, Wyoming, the Irma Hotel opened its doors to the public. Julia Cody Goodman was hostess at a pre-opening party on the evening of November 13, 1903, when more than 1,000 of Colonel Cody's friends and neighbors celebrated until dawn. On November 19, the first paying guest signed the register and the Irma Hotel was in business.

The 1903 London season ended in the fall. After a few months' vacation, the exhibition reopened in the same city during the Christmas season. Colonel Cody wrote a letter to his sister telling of the show's success:

Olympia, London.
Dec. 29, 1903.

Dear Julia:

Your letter to New York received here found me quite well for the amount of work and responsibility, and the nervous excitement of getting opened; and what an opening and what a success. The people of England have gone wild over the show. The King sent his sister and brother-in-law, the Duke of Argyil, to open the show, the King is not in London himself. Am sending the papers, have them posted in the office. We have turned people away at every performance since we opened.

Mr. Salsbury's death gives me more work and responsibility, and I won't be able to come over to Irma's wedding, or to attend to business, or to get a day's rest. I hope Mr. Ridgeley will get the books started and get daily reports from hotel and stable, and be able to send me monthly reports of all departments.

Hope Nellie is well by this time. How are Mr. Town, Josie and the rest?

Tell Mr. Peake about my great success here, also Mr. Calkins.

Love and health to all,
Brother.[1]

After the London stand the Wild West toured England, Scotland and Wales, closing the 1904 year with a three months' run at the town of West Brompton. London papers pointed out that it was no mere coincidence that representatives of Great Britain and the United States had selected the same town in which to spearhead the movement to establish an International Court of Arbitration for settling disputes between the governments of the United States and England. The Wild West and Buffalo Bill, these journals stated, had made an inestimable contribution to understanding and good will between the two nations.

In 1905 and 1906 Buffalo Bill and his troupe made a farewell trip through Western Europe. In Germany, Emperor William, who had visited the Wild West on the occasion of Queen Victoria's Jubilee in 1887 when he was still the Crown Prince, welcomed Colonel Cody to Berlin. The Emperor requested the scout to select a representative cowboy and a typical Indian to sit as models for the royal portrait painter, Carl Hinkle. Buffalo Bill chose his own nephew, Henry Goodman, as the symbol of the American cowpuncher. The red man and the white man posed daily at the royal studio until their portraits were finished. Emperor William was delighted with the results and added the paintings to his private collection.

In Rome the Wild West held forth at the Colosseum itself. When the Rough Riders of the World rode into the amphitheatre, the spectators cheered madly. They were intrigued by every aspect of the show, but more like Missourians than Romans they doubted that the bucking horses were genuine outlaws, and demanded to be shown.

Colonel Cody ordered that two of the buckers, Skyrocket and Shooting Star, be let loose in the stadium. The two horses ran wildly around, battering heavy posts, trampling fences and charging headlong into brick walls. The Romans, all but one of them, were convinced.

A Florentine Count was the exception. It was his theory that the outlaws had been trained to buck, batter and trample; he claimed that he could ride either Skyrocket or Shooting Star.

Buffalo Bill arranged for the Count to try his luck at an evening performance. Colonel Cody stated he was willing to wager that the Count would not be able to stay sixty seconds on either horse. The showman also magnanimously offered to pay all hospital expenses.

On the appointed date the Count attended an afternoon show, saw Shooting Star and Skyrocket splinter a fence and then watched two cowboys barely remain on the bucking broncos' backs for a one-minute period. When evening came the horses were ready, the crowd was waiting but the Count did not appear. Buffalo Bill, now sixty years old, mounted Skyrocket and stuck to the bucking outlaw for two minutes, slipping to the ground just as the horse dashed into a wall.

With the Italian triumph behind them, the exhibition performers thrilled thousands in Galicia, Croatia, Slavonia, Bohemia, Belgium and Austria. At the close of this third brilliant European tour the Wild West returned to America.

After four years away from his own country, Buffalo Bill was very happy to be back in the United States. No time for rest or for visits to North Platte or the Big Horn Basin; the show came first—and the people of America wanted to see the Wild West again. The 1907 season began at the traditional stamping ground, Madison Square Garden, to turn-away crowds. Then the show trains pushed across the nation. At every stop Colonel Cody was given the welcome of a returning hero. Young boys, their fathers and their grandfathers visited Buffalo Bill's Wild West and Congress of Rough Riders of the World. The transcontinental tour broke all the exhibition's own previous records.

So great was the response to the show, and so insistent was the public demand in community after community for the appearance of Buffalo Bill, that no break was taken between the 1907 and 1908 seasons. It was only in the autumn of 1908 that Colonel Cody was at last able to take a much needed rest in Wyoming.

He was delighted to discover that the Cody Trail was jammed with travelers. Although the building up of the

Big Horn Basin had cost him millions of dollars, the heartfelt greeting he was given by the citizens of Cody—thrifty, enterprising, prosperous people—made him believe it had all been worth-while.

His sister Julia had found managing the Irma Hotel too strenuous in 1906 and had handed over the reins to Mr. and Mrs. Louis Decker. (Buffalo Bill's sister, May Cody Bradford, had married Louis Decker, a son of Sophia Billings Decker, in 1906. Her first husband had died a few years before.) Now, Julia brought her brother up-to-date regarding events that had occurred in the family since last he had been home. His eldest daughter, Arta Cody Boal, had died and been buried beside the other Cody children in Rochester, New York. Her husband, Horton Boal, had died five years before she did. Two children survived Arta—a daughter Clara and a son Cody.

Colonel Cody, happy among his family and friends, decided to quit the sawdust trail. For a year and a half he invested money in a variety of enterprises. Old comrades and scheming strangers beat a path to his door and were seldom turned away. He had a childlike faith in the honesty of others and little understanding of the world of business and finance. Most of his money was poured into improving the Big Horn Basin, the climactic embellishment being a huge irrigation dam which its builders maintained was an engineering marvel that was years ahead of the time.

Soon most of Buffalo Bill's capital disappeared down the deep drain of pet projects and unwise investments. There was only one way to get money—return to the touring circuit.

Before he revived the Wild West for the 1910 season, Colonel Cody, accompanied by his sister Julia and his nephew Walter, visited old friends in Kansas. The famous scout and his devoted sister relived the days of their youth, as they walked across the parade grounds at Fort Leavenworth and rode through Salt Creek Valley.

Bill and Julia were saddened to hear of the death of their sister, Mrs. Helen Wetmore, in California. Mrs. Wetmore's first husband had died many years before. She had married her second husband, a magazine editor from Duluth, Minnesota, in 1898.

But now it was show time once again. Colonel Cody's youngest daughter, Irma, widowed by the death of her husband, Lieutenant Scott, accompanied him on his comeback tours until she met and married Fred Garlow, at North Platte. Bill had a new partner for his venture, his old crony Major Gordon W. Lillie, popularly known as "Pawnee Bill." The show was called "Buffalo Bill's Wild West and Pawnee Bill's Far East."

The people of Illinois, Iowa, Nebraska, Colorado and Wyoming, where the exhibition concentrated its activities for three years, had missed Buffalo Bill and his extravaganza. They showed their feelings for the sixty-four-year-old scout by flocking to every performance. Once again the master showman was packing them in and turning them away. In 1910 alone the new partners made a profit of over $400,000.

The program for the Wild West and Far East featured a contribution from Buffalo Bill's old supporter, Mark Twain, entitled "A Horse Tale," under the by-line of the great writer himself. The article read:

> I am Buffalo Bill's horse. I have spent my life under his saddle—with him in it, too, and he is good for two hundred pounds, without his clothes; and there is no telling how much he does weigh when he is out on the war-path and

has his batteries belted on. He is over six feet, is young, hasn't an ounce of waste flesh, is straight, graceful, springy in his motions, quick as a cat, and has a handsome face, and brown hair dangling down on his shoulders, and is beautiful to look at; and nobody is braver than he is, and nobody is stronger, except myself. Yes, a person that doubts that he is fine to see should see him in his beaded buckskins, on my back and his rifle peeping above his shoulder, chasing a hostile trail, with me going like the wind and his hair streaming out behind from the shelter of his broad slouch. Yes, he is a sight to look at then—and I'm part of it myself.

I am his favorite horse, out of dozens. Big as he is, I have carried him eighty-one miles between nightfall and sunrise on the scout; I am good for fifty, day in and day out, and all the time. I am not large, but I am built on a business basis. I have carried him thousands and thousands of miles on scout duty for the army, and there's not a gorge, nor a pass, nor a valley, nor a fort, nor a trading post, nor a buffalo-range in the whole sweep of the Rocky Mountains and the Great Plains that we don't know as well as we know the bugle-calls. He is Chief of Scouts to the Army of the Frontier and it makes us very important.[2]

With a most successful first season behind them, Colonel Cody and Major Lillie hit the circuit again in 1911. Crowds were thinner but the partners still managed to earn a profit of $200,000.

The handwriting was on the wall in 1912. Sparse audiences, a never ending tour, profits reduced to $123,000; after the farewell performance at Rawlins, Wyoming on July 26, 1913, Buffalo Bill and Pawnee Bill paid all debts and then dissolved their partnership. The Wild West and Far East was sold at auction in Denver on August 21.

In a letter to Elizabeth Jane Leonard, co-author of this present biography, Major Lillie said in part:

> I am interested in the fact that you are writing the real and authentic history of my old friend, Colonel Cody and the Cody family.
>
> I presume that I knew Colonel Cody more intimately than any man living outside of his own family. I was with Colonel Cody's show two years, 1883 and 1885, and was his partner the last five years of his show career. He and I occupied a private railroad car for seven months each year for the five years. In that way, naturally, we would become very intimately acquainted. In fact Colonel Cody has told me a great many things of his early life, which I have never seen in print.[3]

The Colonel and the Major went their separate ways. The Wild West and the Far East was dead.

Before the year was out Buffalo Bill had signed on with the Sells Floto Circus as its stellar attraction. The manager of the outfit, a publicity-wise Denver newspaperman, cashed in on Cody's popularity by advertising the show as Buffalo Bill's Wild West.

For two seasons the white-haired scout toured with Sells Floto. Then in 1916 the 101 Ranch-Real Wild West Show made him a better offer. He liked George Arlington, the exhibition manager. Though ill and exhausted Colonel Cody had high hopes for the forthcoming season. Some of the old campaigner's enthusiasm can be found in a letter he wrote to his sister:

> Miller Bros. & Arlington
> 101 Ranch, Wild West
> Cleveland, Ohio
> May 12, 1916
>
> Dear Julia:
>
> I have been to Okla., saw Will and Henry at Tulsa . . . , got another treatment from Will [William A. Goodman, chiropractor].

It's really wonderful what he can do. I have never met a doctor his equal . . . and he gives no poisonous medicine.
So glad you keep your health.
I am going to make good money with this show.
Love, and God ever bless you, my Christian sister.
Brother.
P.S. Took lunch today with Darwin Cody and relations. Lots of Codys here.

Previous tours that Buffalo Bill had made had been billed as his "final appearances" or as his "farewell performances." But the need for money or the lure of the sawdust trail had invariably brought him back. Now as he looked out of the windows of his private railroad car or sat by himself in the darkness of his tent, the realization came to him that this was indeed his last tour.

The elements seemed to conspire against the show. Driving rain and unbearable heat alternated in keeping crowds away. Only the magic of Buffalo Bill's name kept the exhibition going.

The old plainsman, now almost seventy, suffered terribly from arthritis. Everything possible was done to make him comfortable, for without him the show was nothing at all. A valet attended to his every need; a groom cared for his three horses; and his old friend, Major Burke, ever faithful, stood by to help in any way that he could.

It was Burke who, seeing war clouds gathering over Europe, had sold manager Arlington on the idea of featuring a "Pageant for Preparedness." And it was Burke who nursed and coddled and inspired Colonel Cody in playing the starring part in this drama.

Buffalo Bill would be carried from his tent to the side of the arena. There, behind a huge drape that cut him off from the view of the crowd, he would be lifted on to his horse. Slumped in the saddle, he would wait for Burke's cue.

"Ready, Colonel,"[4] the words would ring out.

Automatically, like an old war horse responding to a bugle call, the scout would sit erect, straight as a ramrod, hold his head up proudly and prepare to enter the ring. Burke snapped his fingers; the curtains parted; and Buffalo Bill rode forward. Three times around the cinder track he would ride, leading the grand march. Strung out behind him were the cowboys and Indians. All eyes were on Cody. Every movement of the old scout was noticed and etched forever in the mind of the viewer. For this silver-haired old man, smiling gaily as he passed, was the conjurer of a grand illusion. He was not old, he was young. He was not an embittered performer leading the parade in a third-rate, broken-down show. No, he was youth eternal: the adventurer, the pioneer, the plainsman, the pony express rider, the buffalo hunter, the Indian fighter, the Chief of Scouts, the star of the Wild West.

Now Colonel Cody stood alone in the middle of the ring. Into the air went glass balls, one after another. As each flashed overhead Buffalo Bill raised his rifle and shattered it. His hands were unsteady but his eyes were still keen and his will strong. Zing! Crash! Zing! Crash! Zing! Crash! Ball after ball after ball. Then a crescendo of applause.

The Colonel's horse reared into the air and then came down. Cody flourished his sombrero to the crowd and slowly rode to where Burke was waiting behind the scene. The drape was closed. The old scout slumped forward in pain. Carefully, tenderly, Burke lifted him out of the saddle and helped him to the ground.

"Magnificent, Colonel!" the old press agent would say.

"Better than ever." And then the attendants would step forward and carry the failing star to his quarters.

Try as he might, it was impossible for Colonel Cody to sit upright in the saddle during the last two weeks of the tour. He refused to quit until the final engagement was played, and was driven around the ring in a carriage. His last public appearance was at Portsmouth, Virginia on November 11, 1916. Major Burke walked to the center of the arena, and with tears pouring down his cheeks made the announcement that this marked Buffalo Bill's closing performance. The members of the audience climbed to their feet and gave Colonel Cody a ten-minute ovation. Buffalo Bill had reached the end of the trail.

His sister Julia knew that he was coming home, although at the time she did not realize just how ill he was. In a letter to her from Greensboro, North Carolina, dated October 31, 1916, he had written:

Dear Julia:

Your letter came. Yes, it does seem wrong that you have had to work so hard all your life. Sometimes one might think God was unjust but we don't do we? Here I've worked all my life and am a poor man. But I thank our Heavenly Father for all his blessings to me.

I'll soon see you and we must have a long visit.

I am so thankful my health is better.

God bless you,
Brother

P.S. I'll be with May, November 17-18-19 & 20.

Winter was approaching when Buffalo Bill arrived at Cody, Wyoming. He ducked the welcoming committee that had gathered to greet him, and went directly to his home and to bed. In the days that followed he would walk over to his sister's house, sit on a porch chair and talk to her for hours. His investments had failed, his holdings crumbled, his money disappeared. Finally, he had lost both Scout's Rest Ranch and his holdings in Wyoming. Most crushing of all, he told Julia, was the loss of old friends—fair-weather friends who had turned against him when things went bad. "I'm tired, Julia," he would say, "very tired." Then Julia would make up the bed in the spare room for him and he would escape his troubles in sleep.

One day he informed her that he was going east on business. Before leaving he kissed her and said, "Julia, I'm sick at heart, I'm sick in the body, I can't stand it much longer. When I come back, I want you to have your preacher come over here. I want to talk to him about the next world for I feel that my time is coming soon. I know that your church suits me."[5]

Julia promised to arrange for W. O. Harper, minister of the First Presbyterian Church of Cody, to see him. Buffalo Bill's generous contributions had helped build the church.

On the way east on his business trip Colonel Cody stopped off at the Denver home of his sister, May Decker, and took suddenly ill. A message was sent to the family in Wyoming, saying, "Come on first train, William very ill." Colonel Cody's wife, his daughter Irma and her husband, and Mrs. Goodman came at once.

In a few days the sick man rallied. His improvement was so apparent that the members of the family returned to Wyoming. At her brother's request, Julia remained in Denver.

Helplessly, Julia watched Colonel Cody pace back and forth, back and forth, as if his room were a prison cell.

Once he stopped for a moment, turned to her and said, "To think that in my old age I should be treated like this, shunned and forgotten by the very men I thought were my best friends, Julia, I can't bear it."

The physician attending the Colonel diagnosed his illness as acute cardiac trouble and hypertension. In private he told the two sisters, "Mr. Cody is dying from a breaking heart."

Wire services kept an anxious world informed of the contents of late medical bulletins. Boy Scouts kept a constant vigil on the porch, eager and ready to be of service to the greatest scout America had ever known. Telegrams, letters and phone calls bringing mesages of cheer arrived from the great, the near-great and the man-in-the-street.

On January 6, 1917 word went out that Colonel Cody was sinking rapidly. On the following day his entire family gathered at his bedside. He lapsed into a coma on January 9. At one o'clock in the morning on Wednesday, January 10, Buffalo Bill died.

The members of the family who were present—Mrs. Louisa Frederici Cody, Mrs. Irma Cody Garlow, Mr. Fred Garlow, Mrs. May Cody Decker, Mr. Louis Decker and Mrs. Julia Cody Goodman—released the sad news to waiting reporters. In a few hours the entire world knew that Buffalo Bill was dead.

Messages of sympathy poured in to the bereaved family from individuals and organizations. King George V of England and President Woodrow Wilson of the United States were among the first to send condolences. Wires came from General Nelson A. Miles, Major General H. L. Scott, United States Army Chief of Staff, and from the governors of many states.

Funeral services were held on Sunday, January 14.

At 9:30 in the morning the body of Bill was taken from Mrs. Decker's house on Lafayette Street and transported in the bronze, glass-topped coffin to the Colorado capitol. Officers of Denver Lodge 17 of the Elks were the immediate escorts. A garrison of United States troops from Fort Logan marched with the cortege. A band of seventy cowboys walked behind the coffin. Two of them led a riderless horse, saddle empty, reins loose, pistols hanging from the saddle horn. The steed was McKinley, Colonel Cody's mount, from whose back he had recently given his last salute to an exhibition audience.

At the State House four members of the Elks, four members of the Grand Army of the Republic, and four members of the Colorado National Guard took their places around the flag-draped casket as the guard of honor. Infantrymen formed two lines in the corridors of the capitol building. For three hours thousands of people filed past the coffin to say farewell to the great frontiersman.

Final services were held in the large auditorium of the Elks' club. With the family sat Johnnie Baker, the orphan cowboy kid, to whom Colonel Cody had been like a father.

Mrs. Fannie D. Hardin, of the Ladies of the G.A.R., Albert U. Mayfield, leader of the National Order of Cowboy Rangers, and Dr. Charles H. Marshall, of Saint Barnabas Episcopal Church, all paid tribute to the great scout. A bugle sounded taps. The eulogy was delivered by John W. Springer, of the Elks. He said, in part:

> His life typified Dr. Johnson's truism—It is better to live rich, than to die rich. His friends were legion from presidents, kings, czars, and royalty to the millions of the common people. His life was for the latter class—and this man with the courage of a lion had the heart of a child, and the

> sweetness of a woman. He was an international educator of men. Millions have personally seen his superb figure as he traveled in the states and all over Europe, bringing home to the effeminate East the strength of the heroes out of the plains.
>
> It is fitting that his tomb should be hewn out of the eternal granite of the Rockies—where millions of pilgrims may pay their devotions at the last resting place of the first—the last—and the chiefest of all American Pioneers.

At the close of the services a military band in the balcony played Colonel Cody's favorite song, "Tenting on the Old Camp Ground."

On June 3, 1917 a procession of cars wound their way up the fifteen-mile road that led from Denver to the summit of Lookout Mountain, 2,000 feet above the city. There Buffalo Bill was buried in a rock-bound grave. A simple granite slab marks the spot, while an American flag flutters high above it.

The last man to interview Buffalo Bill before he died was Chauncey Thomas.[6] The words which the writer set down near the close of this interview constitute an appropriate closing:

The voice was tired now, and the doctor came.

"Brother Will, it is now time for him to go," said Mrs. Goodman gently, and I arose. The Old Scout was in pajamas and slippers, and had drawn over them a house coat. Instantly Buffalo Bill was on his feet, straight as an Indian, head up as in days of old. The man recalled the Spanish cavalier, courtly as the prince he was in his kindly grace, all unaided by gorgeous trappings or picturesque surroundings, just the Man Himself standing

there, waxen pale, his silver hair flowing down over his straight, square shoulders, his hand out in the last farewell. He asked for me afterwards, but the doctor said "No." But as we all stood up in the little room a silence fell. It was the last time. I knew it, he knew it, we all knew it. But on the surface not a sign.

"Goodbye."

I took his hand, looked into those clear, calm eyes for a moment—I must not keep him standing—said "Goodbye" and turned from one of the finest, truest, grandest men on this earth. That was the last time I ever talked with Buffalo Bill.

A few days later I saw him again, but he was asleep, never to wake. He lay like a statue, magnificent in the majesty of death. I stood alone beside his bier, save for the presence of his sister-mother, Mrs. Goodman, and silently looked at the Man.

"The friend of kings and the king of friends," I said. Tears started, but with the same calm irony that made Cody what he was, she stopped them quietly, nodded, and I turned away, never to see the Grand Old American again.

I never knew a more kingly man. Put the four words, knight, gentleman, superman, and cavalier, all into one word, and that word is Cody. Women on the plains have prayed for him, have called that name as the one thing between them and suicide; the silent Indians have used that name as one they could trust; the rulers of half the millions of Europe have used that name in the familiar friendship of man to man—for they received him as the equal he was—but the dashing hero of the children has but one name—"Buffalo Bill."[7]

Plate 36 *Bettmann Archive*

Buffalo Bill saves a lady from the Indians—scene from Wild West Show

Plate 37 *Phillips St. Claire*

Col. William F. Cody (Buffalo Bill)
(The last of the Great Scouts)
From the painting by Rosa Bonheur
Courtesy Coe Collection

Plate 38

Rosa Bonheur (from photograph taken while painting the portrait of Buffalo Bill, Paris, 1889)

Culver Service

Plate 39

Chief Sitting Bull and Buffalo Bill

Plate 40

Buffalo Bill with "Little Iron Tail" and "The Idaho Kid"

Plate 41

Buffalo Bill's favorite photograph, showing his famous saddle lariat, and his gun, "Lucretia Borgia"

Notes and Appendix

Chapter 1

1. F. M. Fryxell, "The Green Tree," *American Forests and Forest Life,* Vol. 33, No. 402 (June, 1927), pp. 357-360.
2. J. G. Masters, *Blazing the Trail.*
3. *Ibid.*
4. *Ibid.*
5. In 1924 Julia Cody Goodman received the following letter to which was attached a copy of the deed signed by her parents when they sold their land at Le Claire before leaving for Kansas. Julia was living in Cody, Wyoming at the time she received this communication.

Princeton, Iowa.
May, 9, 1924.

Mrs. Julia Cody Goodman,
Cody, Wyoming.
Dear Mrs. Goodman:

I send you with this letter a true copy of the deed signed by your parents, Isaac Cody and Mary Cody transferring land to Adrian H. Davenport, R. H. Rogers, and James Jack of Le Claire, Iowa.

This deed is dated March the 8th, 1852. There is a movement being made to place a monument on the birth place of W. F.

Cody, known the world over as "Buffalo Bill." In 1849 my grandfather, Captain John Culbertson, came from Cumberland County, Pennsylvania to Scott County, Iowa, and moved into the stone house built by your father. My parents and grandparents were neighbors of Isaac Cody's family.

Yours very truly,
John Knox. M.D.

DEED

THIS INDENTURE. made the 8th day of March A. D. 1852 between Isaac Cody and Mary Cody, his wife, of the first part and Adrian H. Davenport, R. H. Rogers and James Jack of Le Claire, Iowa, of the second part Witnesseth: That the said parties of the first part for the consideration of Two Thousand Dollars, the receipt whereof is hereby acknowledged, do, by these presents, grant, bargain, sell and convey unto the parties of the second part their heirs and assigns forever, the following described tract of real estate lying and being situated in the county of Scott and State of Iowa. To-wit: The North West quarter of the South East quarter of section twenty-eight, township seventy-nine, North of Range five of the 5th P.M., also the North East quarter of the South East quarter of section twenty-eight in township seventy-nine North of Range five East of the 5th P.M. each containing forty acres, and also a certain parcel of land commencing at a post in the creek at the North West corner of the South East quarter of section twenty-seven and thence South seventeen chains and eighty links, thence West twenty chains to the place of beginning containing Thirty-five acres and sixty-two one hundreths of an acre situated in the above mentioned township and range.

To have and to hold said premises above described unto the said parties of the second part, their heirs and assigns forever. And the said Isaac Cody and Mary Cody, his wife, will forever warrant and defend the title against all persons whomsoever.

In testimony whereof, the said parties of the first part have hereunto set their hand and seal the date first above written. Executed and Delivered in the presence of ——————

Isaac Cody
Mary B. Cody.

State of Iowa, Scott County. ss.

Be it remembered that on the 9th day of March A.D. 1852. before the undersigned P. Wm. Gish, a justice of the peace in and for said County, personally appeared Isaac Cody and Mary Cody his wife, to be personally known to be the identical persons whose names are affixed to the foregoing deed as grantors and acknowledged the instrument to be their voluntary act and deed.

P. W. Gish.
Justice.

Chapter 2

1. Richard J. Walsh, *The Making of Buffalo Bill: A Study in Heroics,* p. 26.
2. Colonel W. F. Cody, *An Autobiography of Buffalo Bill,* p. 5.
3. William F. Cody, *The Life of Hon. William F. Cody, "Buffalo Bill,"* p. 27.
4. Richard J. Walsh, *op. cit.,* p. 28.
5. Colonel W. F. Cody, *op. cit.,* p. 8.
6. William F. Cody, *op. cit.,* p. 34.
7. *Ibid.*
8. Richard J. Walsh, *op. cit.,* pp. 30-33.
9. *Ibid.*
10. William F. Cody, *op. cit.,* p. 39.
11. Colonel W. F. Cody, *op. cit.,* p. 11.
12. Helen Cody Wetmore, *Last of the Great Scouts,* pp. 18, 19.
13. Colonel W. F. Cody, *op. cit.,* p. 13.
14. *Ibid.*
15. Mrs. Ruth Irish Preston, of Davenport, Iowa, at the suggestion of Louise C. Rogers, of Le Claire, Iowa, made a copy of this letter available to Julia Cody Goodman in July, 1927. The accuracy of the copy was attested to at Davenport by W. E. Whittlesey, a Notary Public, on July 1, 1927. The original copy of Isaac Cody's letter is part of the collection in The Academy of Sciences, Davenport, Iowa.

16. In 1931, the Kansas State Historical Society at Topeka was queried regarding the Lecompton Constitution, and the following communication, dated July 15, 1931 was received:

Concerning your question about the Lecompton bribe: The Lecompton constitution was submitted to Congress and was returned to Kansas unaccepted with the "English Bill" added to it. The following notes from *Some Aspects of the English Bill for the Admission of Kansas,* by F. H. Hodder, in the *Kansas State Historical Collections,* Vol. 10, p. 225, will explain why it was called the Lecompton bribe: "The so-called 'English Bill' submitted the question of admission under the Lecompton constitution to the people of Kansas in conjunction with the acceptance by them of a specific land grant from the United States, viz, two sections in every township for the use of schools, two townships for a state university, ten sections for public buildings, salt springs not exceeding twelve in number with six sections adjoining each, and five per cent of the proceeds of the sales of public lands within the state.

"The ballots were to read 'For proposition of Congress and admission' and 'Against proposition of Congress and admission.'

"It was further provided that, should this proposition be rejected the people of Kansas were authorized to frame a new constitution whenever but not before 'the population of said territory equals the ratio of representation required for a member of the house of representatives,' which at that time was 93,560.*

"In discussions at the time, both in and out of Congress, and in the accounts given by historians ever since, the English Bill has been denounced as an attempt to bribe the people of Kansas into acceptance of the Lecompton constitution . . ."

* 11 *U.S. Statutes at Large,* p. 269. "The possible postponement of admission until the population should equal the basis of representation was derived from the original Douglas enabling act of the first session of the Thirty-fourth Congress. The submission of the Lecompton constitution and land grant together was the logical result of the claim of Douglas that the ordinance was a part of the constitution and could not be changed without the consent of the people." (*Globe,* 35-1, p. 1258.)

17. Colonel W. F. Cody, *op. cit.,* p. 13.

CHAPTER 3

1. Colonel W. F. Cody, *op. cit.*, p. 15.
2. Alexander Majors, *Seventy Years on the Frontier,* p. 243. Colonel Alexander Majors was toastmaster at a "Cody Day" banquet at the Omaha Trans-Mississippi Fair in 1900. In his toast to Colonel William F. Cody, the guest of honor, Colonel Majors said:

> One day, away back in the late '50's in our Kansas camp, came to me a handsome, wiry lad who said he had his mother's permission to take a place with us as a messenger. He seemed to think that his mother's permission entirely settled the matter. I told him that I thought he was rather young for such strenuous and hazardous work, but he made light of that, and there was about him such an air of self-confidence and such diffidence and modesty in other ways, that he captured me at once and I gave him the place, which was one of peril, requiring caution, coolness and endurance. Little did I think then that I was starting out in life one who was destined to win fame and fortune throughout the world.

3. Richard J. Walsh, *op. cit.*, p. 42; Colonel W. F. Cody, *op. cit.*, p. 17; and Helen Cody Wetmore, *op. cit.*, pp. 33, 34. There is a slight disagreement among these authors as to the exact wording of the oath.
4. Frank A. Root and William E. Connelley, *The Overland Stage to California,* p. 308.
5. Stanley Vestal, *Dodge City: Queen of Cowtowns,* p. 55.
6. Alexander Majors, *op. cit.*, p. 141.
7. Colonel W. F. Cody, *op. cit.*, p. 19.
8. William F. Cody, *op. cit.*, p. 63.
9. Stanley Vestal, *op. cit.*, Chapter V, and *passim.*
10. Richard J. Walsh, *op. cit.*, p. 49.
11. Alexander Majors, *op. cit.*, p. 142.
12. William F. Cody, *op. cit.*, p. 78.
13. *Ibid.*
14. *Ibid.*, p. 79.

Chapter 4

1. General George A. Custer, *Life on the Plains,* pp. 33, 34.
2. This is another letter made available to Julia Cody Goodman through the kindness of Mrs. Ruth Irish Preston. The information to be found in footnote 15 to Chapter 2 also applies in full to Mary Cody's letter.
3. Colonel W. F. Cody, *op. cit.,* pp. 33, 34.
4. Alexander Majors has the following to say about the initial period of the pony express, in *Seventy Years on the Frontier,* p. 164:

> W. H. Russell and John S. Jones bought mules and coaches on credit giving their notes payable in ninety days; sent men out to establish a station every ten or fifteen miles from Leavenworth due West going up the Smoky Hill fork and direct to Denver. The line was organized, stations built and put in running shape in remarkably quick time. They made their daily trips in six days, traveling about one hundred miles every twenty-four hours. The first stage ran into Denver on May 17, 1859. Jones and Russell were unable to meet their notes and the institution became the property of Russell, Majors and Waddell. A few months after that we bought out the semi-monthly line of Hockaday and Liggett, that was running from St. Joseph to Salt Lake City, thinking that by blending the two lines we might bring the business up to where it would pay expenses, if nothing else. This we failed in for they did not nearly meet expenses.

5. Richard J. Walsh, *op. cit.,* p. 67.
6. Colonel W. F. Cody, *op. cit.,* p. 45.
7. William F. Cody, *op. cit.,* p. 99.

Chapter 5

1. William F. Cody, *op. cit.,* pp. 112, 115-118.
2. In a letter from The Adjutant General's Office, Washington,

D. C. dated June 23, 1930, Elizabeth Jane Leonard received the following communication, signed by I. H. Bridges, The Adjutant General. The section pertaining to William F. Cody's Civil War service is quoted in full:

Dear Madam:

I have your letter of June 16, 1930, in which you request information regarding William F. Cody, "Buffalo Bill."

The official records show that William F. Cody enrolled and mustered into service at Fort Leavenworth, Kansas, February 19, 1864, as a private of COMPANY H. 7th Kansas Cavalry, and that he was mustered out with the company and honorably discharged the service September 29, 1865 at Fort Leavenworth, Kansas, a private.

During his period of service he is reported as present with the company or is otherwise satisfactorily accounted for.

The personal description of this soldier is reported as follows: age 18 years, born in Scott County, Iowa; occupation teamster; eyes and hair brown; complexion fair; height 5 feet 10 inches.

3. William F. Cody, *op. cit.*, p. 140.

Chapter 6

1. Richard J. Walsh, *op. cit.*, p. 95.
2. William F. Cody, *op. cit.*, pp. 141, 142.
3. Colonel W. F. Cody, *op. cit.*, p. 96.
4. William F. Cody, *op. cit.*, p. 152.
5. *Ibid.*, p. 157.
6. Colonel W. F. Cody, *op. cit.*, pp. 113, 114.
7. Richard J. Walsh, *op. cit.*, p. 106.
8. Paul Radin, *The Story of the American Indian, passim.*
9. Richard J. Walsh, *op. cit.*, p. 111.
10. William F. Cody, *op. cit.*, p. 167.
11. Stanley Vestal, *op. cit.*, p. 40.
12. William F. Cody, *op. cit.*, p. 173.

Chapter 7

1. Colonel W. F. Cody, *op. cit.,* p. 135.
2. *Ibid.,* p. 136.
3. *Ibid.,* p. 139.
4. William F. Cody, *op. cit.,* p. 207.
5. In a special statement written for the *Rough Rider,* an illustrated periodical published in New York in 1907, which served as a program for Buffalo Bill's Wild West show, General Carr wrote:

> On my first expedition we soon learned to understand each other. He saw that I knew the direction I wanted to go, and I saw that he knew how to take me there. He was treated by the officers as one of themselves, in fact he was offered a commission by General Philip Sheridan.
>
> Some scouts have failed in several instances, Cody never. Once Cody scouted for me on the almost level prairies in drifting snow, that obstructed all signs to follow General Penrose. Bill had to find high ground, where the snow had been blown off to find the trail; luckily for us he found it and we saved five days marching by going straight, and arrived in time to save Penrose's command, which was in a most pitiable condition.

6. Richard J. Walsh, *op. cit.,* p. 137.
7. William F. Cody, *op. cit.,* p. 238.

Chapter 8

1. Published in Buffalo Bill's publication, *Rough Rider,* New York, 1907.
2. *Ibid.*
3. *Ibid.*
4. *Ibid.*
5. *Ibid.* This was the considered judgment of Brigadier General E. M. Hays.

6. In 1906 Brigadier General W. P. Hall wrote the following letter to William F. Cody:

War Department
National Board for Promotion
and Rifle Practice
Washington, D. C.
Dec. 22, 1906.

Hon. W. F. Cody,
"Buffalo Bill"
New York City.
My Dear Cody:

I understand that you are going to present in your great arena, the battle of "Summit Springs," Nebraska, which was fought in 1869 between the fifth U.S. Cavalry, General E. A. Carr commanding, and the "dog soldiers" including Sioux, Cheyennes, and Arapahoes, under the celebrated chief, Tall Bull. You as chief of scouts, for General Carr, did great work in that engagement. I recall that you shot Tall Bull, and captured his celebrated race horse which you named Tall Bull.

It was a lively engagement and, as before intimated, you deserve great credit for the part you took in that and many other Indian fights. I wish you much luck in this production.

Sincerely yours,
W. P. Hall. Brig-General. U.S.A.

In 1885, General Carr sent the following letter to Buffalo Bill's friend and associate, Major John Burke:

St. Louis, Missouri,
May 7, 1885.

Major John M. Burke,
Dear Sir:

I take pleasure in saying that in an experience of about thirty years on the plains and in the mountains, I have seen a great many guides, scouts, trailers, and hunters, and Buffalo Bill, (W. F. Cody) is king of them all. He has been with me in seven Indian fights and his services have been invaluable.

Very respectfully yours,
Eugene A. Carr.
Brevet Major-General, U.S.A.

7. *Ibid.*
8. This letter also appeared in Buffalo Bill's publication, *Rough Rider.*
9. This interview with W. H. McDonald appeared in the *Omaha World-Herald* on April 26, 1953, under the by-line of Doris Minney. McDonald was the first white child born on the site of old Fort McPherson. As a youngster, Indian papooses were his playmates and often he would go to the Indian camp to play with redskin children.

   Further on in the interview, McDonald said:

> After Buffalo Bill took his famous troupe to Europe to present command appearances before royalty, he did not forget North Platte friends . . . the bankers McDonald. He'd write or cable asking for loans from five thousand to fifteen thousand dollars. But he always paid us back.
>
> There's one thing folks should know about Buffalo Bill [says Mr. McDonald]. Bill didn't drink hard liquor the last nine years of his life. One fourth of July I was in Omaha. I met three of my friends including Cody. We decided to go into a bar to wet our whistles. "What'll you have, Colonel?" the bartender asked.
>
> "Lemonade," Buffalo Bill said quietly.
>
> Everyone wanted to know "how come?"
>
> "Gentlemen, I haven't drunk hard liquor for three years. Oh, in my time I've drunk enough to float a battleship. Yes, two battleships. But since I've quit drinking I feel better."

10. Jay Monaghan, *The Great Rascal,* p. 4.
11. Elizabeth Jane Leonard has in her possession a letter from Nelson's daughter, Mrs. Julia Nelson Goings, which reads:

> I first met colonel W. F. Cody in 1883. Myself, and father, John Y. Nelson, my mother Jennie, and brothers John, Jim and Tom, also my sister Rosa were members of his show from 1883 up to 1889 . . . when I left the show and went to school at Philadelphia, Pennsylvania for five years.
>
> I knew his daughters and Mrs. Cody. I knew him to be a good wholesome man.

Chapter 9

1. Stanley Vestal, *op. cit.,* p. 38.
2. Colonel W. F. Cody, *op. cit.,* p. 223.
3. Richard J. Walsh, *op. cit.,* p. 167.
4. Colonel W. F. Cody, *op. cit.,* p. 229.
5. Captain Meinhold's report was transmitted to Elizabeth Jane Leonard in a letter from The Adjutant General's Office of the War Department, Washington, D. C., dated June 23, 1930. This letter was signed by Major General I. H. Bridges, The Adjutant General.
6. J. Sterling Morton and Albert Watkins, *History of Nebraska,* p. 558.
7. Richard J. Walsh, *op. cit.,* p. 178.
8. *Ibid.,* p. 180.
9. Stanley Vestal, *op. cit.,* p. 23.
10. *Ibid.*
11. This is a complete and exact copy of the letter received by Julia Cody Goodman from her brother.

Chapter 10

1. See introductory chapter, *The Duel With Yellow Hand.*
2. Richard J. Walsh, *op. cit.,* p. 230.
3. Walter Havighurst, *Annie Oakley of the Wild West,* p. 79.
4. Richard J. Walsh, *op. cit.,* p. 262.

Chapter 11

1. Walter Havighurst, *op. cit.,* p. 112.
2. Colonel W. F. Cody, *op. cit.,* p. 320.

3. *Ibid.,* p. 321.
4. *Ibid.,* pp. 323-324.
5. Stanley Vestal, *op. cit.,* p. 281.
6. Walter Havighurst, *op. cit.,* p. 152.

Chapter 12

1. This letter is essentially a true copy of the original, except that a few minor business references are deleted.
2. The program, nine inches high by seven inches wide, was the official sixty-page magazine of the Wild West and Far East. It was printed by the I. M. Southern Co., N. Y. & Cincinnati, with no publication date given, although it would seem that 1910 would be the most likely year. Mark Twain's piece appears on pp. 36 and 37.
3. These reminiscences of Pawnee Bill have been integrated into this book.
4. Richard J. Walsh, *op. cit.,* p. 358.
5. Elizabeth Jane Leonard received the following letter from the Reverend Harper, telling of William F. Cody's religious belief:

Presbyterian Church
W. O. Harper, Pastor
Keota, Iowa.

Dear Mrs. Leonard:

Your letter of September 29, came Saturday evening. I am glad to reply promptly. The best I can do is to tell you about my association and talk with him. (William Cody.)

I went to Cody in the fall of 1905 to be the first pastor of the newly organized Presbyterian church there. Col. Cody's three sisters, Mrs. Wetmore, Mrs. Goodman, and Mrs. Bradford were members of my church there, though Mrs. Bradford technically had not transferred her membership from the church in Denver.

I was at Cody until the last of January 1907. Both those winters I was at Cody, Colonel Cody was there. He came to church with his sisters a number of times, and I had a good many talks with him.

January 27, 1907 was my last Sunday there. He was up at the T. E. Ranch during the week and happened to think of Sunday being my last. So he came down, and, with his three sisters, occupied a front seat at church that morning. He dropped an envelope in the plate. It was sealed and directed to me. In it was a generous bill and the following note:

"Cody, Wyoming,
January 27, 1907.

Dear Mr. Harper:

Thanks for your letter. And it touches me deeply. And I will give it deep thought, and see if I can't do as well as my old friend, Charley White, is doing. I am glad that I know where you are. I like you and believe in you, for you are sincere.

Ever with hope for life eternal, I am yours,

W. F. Cody."

In explanation of the reference in this letter, I would say that I had written in my letter considerable on the subject of religion. Among other things I had mentioned that Charley White, one of the old scouts of the plains, and whose home had been in Aurora, Nebraska, where I was then living, had been converted and was a very earnest Christian. He had, a few years before my coming to Aurora, joined the Presbyterian church there.

Of course I have the originals of these letters in my mementos or I would be unable to give them as above.

Colonel Cody as I positively know, believed in the existence of a God, that religion was a reality, and that a future life was a certainty. He told me once that when he was alone, out in the woods, often the thought of God came to him with great force. And he added, that he worshipped there.

A few years later than the above, he sent me an invitation to be a guest of the show when it was in Nebraska. I accepted the invitation and visited the show at York, Nebraska. He entertained me and introduced me as the "Sky Pilot." I had and still have a high regard for the Codys.

Yours truly,
W. O. Harper.

6. This interview was published in *Outdoor Life,* in the May 1917 issue, under the title "Buffalo Bill's Last Interview," beginning on p. 487.
7. During the flu epidemic of 1918 Mr. and Mrs. Fred Garlow died and were buried at Cody, Wyoming. Irma Cody Garlow was the last member of William F. and Louisa Cody's family.

   Mrs. William F. Cody took charge of the Garlow children for a few years. She spent the winter of 1920-21 with her sister Elizabeth in Los Angeles, California. Upon her return to Cody, Wyoming she contracted a heavy cold from which she never fully recovered. She died on October 21, 1921 and was buried in the same plot beside her husband, Colonel William F. Cody, on Lookout Mountain near Denver.

   Of Buffalo Bill's direct line there are five surviving grandchildren, namely: the children of Horton and Arta Cody Boal—Clara Boal (Benn), of London, England, and Cody Boal, of North Platte, Nebraska; and the children of Fred and Irma Cody Garlow—Jane Cody Garlow, Frederick Garlow and William Cody Garlow—all of Cody, Wyoming. Surviving first cousins of William F. Cody are: John Odell, of Pasadena, California, and Charlotte Mexigold Clemenhagen, of Ontario, Canada.

Cody Genealogy

DIRECT LINE TO WILLIAM FREDRICK CODY (BUFFALO BILL)

Note [by Julia Melvina Cody]: In order to establish the genealogy of my beloved brother, William Fredrick Cody, beyond a question of a doubt, careful research has been made. As a result I am privileged to present the absolute facts, founded upon the authority of reliable historical evidence.

Philip Le Cody was born about 1672. Place of birth is unknown. His wife's name was Martha. Philip and Martha Le Cody lived at Wenham and Beverly, Massachusetts, and were members of the First Congregational Church of Beverly. They moved to Hopkinton, Massachusetts on November 19, 1724.

Philip Le Cody died in 1743. His will is dated August 10, 1739 and was presented for probate on February 3, 1743. It is recorded at East Cambridge, Middlesex County, Massachusetts.

The first record of Philip and Martha Le Cody is the following entry in the Massachusetts Vital Statistics: "John, son of Philip and Martha Le Cody, born January 1, 1695-6."

Sidney Perley, historian and author of the history of Salem, Massachusetts, makes the following statement: "Prefix 'Le' found only in French. Philip Le Cody was undoubtedly a

French Huguenot." We find the family strongly Protestant from first to last.

Records show that Philip Le Cody and his eldest son, John, used the prefix "Le" as long as they lived in Beverly—a period of 25 years.

Philip and Martha Le Cody had children as follows:

John	born	Beverly, Massachusetts	January 1, 1695-6
Joseph*	"	" "	August 12, 1700
Abraham	"	" "	September 21, 1701
Isaac	"	" "	January 17, 1703-4
Thomas	"	" "	June 19, 1707
Mary	"	" "	May 2, 1710

Joseph, second son of Philip and Martha Le Cody, was executor of his father's will, and also of his brother Thomas'. By purchase and inheritance Joseph became sole owner of his father's old farm at Hopkinton, Massachusetts. His wife's name was Mary Martin.

Joseph and Mary Martin Cody had children as follows:

Joseph
Mary
Philip,* baptized on April 20, 1729, at Ipswich, Massachusetts.
Jerusha, a daughter
Johnathan
Isaac

Note: Joseph, son of Isaac Cody, and grandson of Joseph and Mary Martin Cody, served in the French and Indian War at Crown Point and in the American Revolution at the battle of Lexington. Among his descendants were: Rev. H. J. Cody, D.D., LL.D., canon of the Episcopal Cathedral, Toronto, Ontario, Canada, prominent leader in religion, education and politics; also, Charles Paxton Cody, architect, of Erie, Pennsylvania, member of the American Institute of Architects, and past-president of the Pennsylvania State Association of the American Institute of Architects (1926).

Philip, third child of Joseph and Mary Martin Cody, married Abigail Emerson of Uxbridge, Massachusetts, on November 12, 1754. He died at Oxford, Massachusetts, in 1808.

Philip and Abigail Emerson Cody had children as follows:

John	born	August 17, 1755
Joseph	"	December 10, 1757
Abigail	baptized	January 27, 1760
David	born	May 28, 1766
Philip*	"	September 30, 1770
Isaac	"	March 21, 1773
Martha		
Mary		

Note: Isaac was the ancestor of the eminent Judge Hiram Cody, and his grandson, Hiram S. Cody, of the Cody Trust Company, Chicago, Illinois.

Philip, fifth child of Philip and Abigail Emerson Cody, went to New York state as a young man, married Lydia Martin there, and moved to Canada (where Toronto now stands) in 1799.

Philip and Lydia Martin Cody had children as follows:

Elizabeth	born	Probably at Niagara Falls, New York; she married a Mr. Custead.	January 5, 1798

Alice	"	Canada; she married a Mr. Markli.	June 27, 1800
Sophia	"	Canada; she married a Mr. Billings, and a Mr. Decker.	September 14, 1801
Elias	"	Port Credit, Ontario, Canada.	August 12, 1804
Nancy	"	Canada; she married a Mr. Mexigold.	March 30, 1805
Elijah	"	Canada.	1807
Martha	"	Canada; she married a Mr. Barnhart.	December 17, 1809
Isaac*	"	Near Toronto, Ontario, Canada.	1811
Joseph	"		January 12, 1813
Lydia	"	She married a Mr. Odell.	June 27, 1814
Philip	"		November 10, 1816

Note: Philip Cody and his family moved to Cleveland, Ohio, in 1829-30. He died there in 1850 at the age of 80. He was one of the first seven settlers at Port Credit (now Toronto), Ontario, Canada. The corner lot on Dundas Street, which he presented to the community in 1816, is a landmark today with its ancient Protestant church, burial ground, stone arch and iron fence.

Isaac Cody, eighth child of Philip and Lydia Martin Cody, was married three times:

He first married Miranda O'Connor, of Cleveland, Ohio (exact date unknown). Miranda O'Connor Cody died six months after marriage.

A Miss Somers, of Medina County, Ohio, became his second

wife (exact date unknown). A daughter, Martha, was born in 1835. Mrs. Somers Cody died shortly after Martha's birth.

He married his third wife, Mary Bunting Laycock, of Cincinnati, Ohio, in 1840, and went to the Iowa Territory that same year.

Isaac and Mary Bunting Cody had children as follows:

Samuel Cody	born	Le Claire, Iowa T.	February 22, 1841
Julia Melvina	"	Homestead Le Claire, Iowa T.	March 28, 1843
William Fredrick*	"	Homestead Le Claire, Iowa T.	February 26, 1846
Eliza Alice	"	Breckenridge Farm, Iowa†	March 20, 1848
Helen (Laura Ella)	"	Le Claire, Iowa	June 27, 1850
Mary Hanna (May)	"	Walnut Grove Farm, Iowa	October 12, 1852
Charles Whitney	"	Salt Creek Valley, Kansas T.	May 10, 1855

†*Note*: Iowa Territory was admitted to the Union as a state in 1846.

William Fredrick Cody, son of Isaac and Mary Bunting Cody, was married to Louisa Frederici, of St. Louis, Missouri, on March 6, 1866.

William Fredrick and Louisa Frederici Cody had children as follows:

Arta Lucile	born	Leavenworth, Kansas	December, 1866
Kit Carson	"	Maxwell, Nebraska	December, 1870
Orra	"	Maxwell, Nebraska	August 13, 1872
Irma Louisa	"	North Platte, Nebraska	February 9, 1883

The nearest relatives of William Fredrick Cody to bear the Cody name are the descendants of Philip Cody V, brother of Isaac Cody V, second cousins.

Philip Cody V had three sons, namely:

Darwin D. Cody	He had one son: Lewis P. Cody
Lindus Cody	He had three sons: Harry B. Cody, Frank L. Cody, Arthur P. Cody
Aldus Cody	He had three sons: Sherwin Cody, Luther M. Cody, Richard A. Cody

Signed by
JULIA MELVINA CODY
and
LUTHER M. CODY, secretary Cody Family Organization, and compiler of Cody Family Directory

Frederici Genealogy

John Frederici was born in Alsace-Lorraine, and was of French descent. He came to America as a young man with his parents, several brothers and two sisters. He was married in September, 1841.

Mrs. Frederici, his wife, was born in Pennsylvania, of German parentage.

Mr. and Mrs. John Frederici had children as follows:

Christopher Columbus	born	June, 1842
Louisa	" St. Louis, Mo.	May 27, 1844
Elizabeth	" " " "	March 17, 1846
Frank	" " " "	October 28, 1856

At the time of the marriage of his daughter, Louisa, to William F. Cody, Mr. Frederici was a policeman in St. Louis, Missouri.

In 1878 the family came to Nebraska and Mr. Frederici engaged in farming in the North Platte Valley. He raised the first crop of grain in that vicinity; basically it was a stock-raising region.

Mrs. John Frederici died at the age of 56. Mr. Frederici spent his last years with his daughter, Mrs. William F. Cody, in her North Platte residence. He died there at the age of 88.

Mr. and Mrs. Frederici are both buried in North Platte, Nebraska.

The only survivor of this family as of 1927 was Elizabeth Frederici Flint, who resided then in Los Angeles, California.

The above dates are nearly correct, if not exactly so.

Signed by
IRMA FREDERICI WIENBARG,
daughter of Frank and Mary
Buck Frederici

Bibliography

BLAKE, HERBERT CODY. *Blake's Western Stories.* Brooklyn, 1929.

BRADLEY, GLENN DANFORD. *The Story of the Pony Express.* Chicago, 1913.

BRADY, MITZI ZOSKE and DELAND, C. E. "Michael R. Russell and Some Notes on His Associations with William F. Cody ('Buffalo Bill')," *South Dakota State Historical Society . . . Historical Collections.* 1928, Vol. 14.

BUEL, JAMES WILLIAM. *Heroes of the Plains.* Philadelphia, 1883.

"Buffalo Bill Birthday Edition," *The Cody Enterprise.* February 22, 1932.

Buffalo Bill's Wild West Combined With Pawnee Bill's Great Far East (program). New York & Cincinnati, n.d. (1910).

BURKE, JOHN M. *"Buffalo Bill" From Prairie to Palace.* Chicago, 1893.

CATTERMOLE, E.G. *Famous Frontiersmen, Pioneers and Scouts.* Chicago, 1883.

CODY, LOUISA FREDERICI (in collaboration with COOPER, COURTNEY RYLEY). *Memories of Buffalo Bill.* New York, 1919.

CODY, LUTHER MORRILL, ed. *The Cody Family Directory.* Frostproof, Fla., 1927.

CODY, WILLIAM F. *The Adventures of Buffalo Bill.* New York, 1904.

CODY, COLONEL W. F. *An Autobiography of Buffalo Bill.* New York, 1920.

CODY, WILLIAM F. *Buffalo Bill's Life Story.* New York, 1920.

CODY, WILLIAM F. *Life and Adventures of Buffalo Bill.* Chicago, 1917.

CODY, WILLIAM F. *The Life of Hon. William F. Cody, "Buffalo Bill"* (Original autobiography). Hartford, 1879.

CODY, WILLIAM F. *Story of the Wild West and Campfire Chats.* Chicago, 1888.

CODY, WILLIAM F. *True Tales of the Plains.* New York, 1908.

COOPER, COURTNEY RYLEY. *Annie Oakley.* New York, 1927.

CROFT-COOKE, RUPERT, and MEADMORE, W. S. *Buffalo Bill: The Legend, The Man of Action, The Showman.* London, 1952.

COURSEY, OSCAR WILLIAM. *"Wild Bill."* Mitchell, South Dakota, 1924.

CUSTER, MRS. ELIZABETH BACON. *Tenting on the Plains.* New York, 1887.

CUSTER, GENERAL GEORGE A. *My Life on the Plains.* New York, 1874.

DAVIES, GENERAL H. E. *Ten Days on the Plains.* New York, 1871.

FINERTY, JOHN FREDERIC. *Warpath and Bivouac.* Chicago, 1890.

Fourteenth Annual Report of the U.S. Bureau of American Ethnology. Government Printing Office, Washington, D.C., 1893.

FRYXELL, F. M. "The Green Trees," *American Forests and Forest Life,* June, 1927, Vol. 33, No. 402, pp. 357-360.

GARST, SHANNON. *The Story of Buffalo Bill.* Indianapolis, 1938.

GRIFFIN, CHARLES ELDRIDGE. *Four Years in Europe with Buffalo Bill.* Albia, Iowa, 1908.

HAVIGHURST, WALTER. *Annie Oakley of the Wild West.* New York, 1954.

HAWKEYE, HARRY. *Buffalo Bill, King of Scouts.* Baltimore, 1908.

HEITMAN, FRANCES B. *Historical Register and Dictionary of the U.S. Army.* (57th Cong., 2nd Session, H. doc. No. 466). Government Printing Office, Washington, D.C., 1903.

INGRAHAM, PRENTISS. *The Pony-Express Rider.* New York, 1891.

INMAN, COLONEL HENRY and CODY, WILLIAM F. *The Great Salt Lake Trail.* Topeka, 1898.

INMAN, COLONEL HENRY and CODY, WILLIAM F. *The Old Santa Fe Trail.* Kansas, 1897.

JOHNSTON, WINIFRED. "Passing of the 'Wild West': A Chapter in History of American Entertainment," *Southwest Review.* 1935, Vol. 21, pp. 35-51.

KING, CHARLES. *Campaigning with Crook.* New York, 1890.

MAJORS, ALEXANDER. *Seventy Years on the Frontier.* Chicago, 1893.

MASTERS, J.G. *Blazing the Trail.*

MCLAUGHLIN, JAMES. *My Friend the Indian.* Boston, 1926.

MILES, GENERAL NELSON APPLETON. *Personal Recollections and Observations.* Chicago, 1896.

MINNEY, DORIS. (Interview with W. H. McDonald), *Omaha World-Herald* (Sunday Magazine). April 26, 1953.

MONAGHAN, JAY. *The Great Rascal.* New York, 1953.

MONAGHAN, JAY. "The Stage Career of Buffalo Bill," *Journal of the Illinois State Historical Society.* December, 1938, XXXI, No. 4, pp. 411-423.

MORTON, J. STERLING and WATKINS, ALBERT. *History of Nebraska.* Lincoln, Nebraska, 1918.

MULLER, DAN. *My Life With Buffalo Bill.* Chicago, 1948.

NEBRASKA NED (pseud.). *Buffalo Bill and His Daring Adventures in the Romantic Wild West.* Baltimore, 1913.

PAXSON, FREDERIC L. *The Last American Frontier.* New York, 1910.

PEACOCK, THOMAS B. *Buffalo Bill: Thrilling Adventures of Colonel W. F. Cody.* Denver, 1921.

PRICE, GEORGE FREDERIC. *Across the Coninent With the Fifth Cavalry.* New York, 1883.

RADIN, PAUL. *The Story of the American Indian.* New York, 1944.

ROOT, FRANK A. and CONNELLEY, WILLIAM E. *The Overland Stage to California.* Topeka, 1901.

Rough Rider (Wild West program). New York, 1907.

SABIN, EDWIN L. *Buffalo Bill and the Overland Trail.* Philadelphia & London, 1914.

SANDOZ, MARI. *The Buffalo Hunters: The Story of the Hide Men.* New York, 1954.

SHACKLEFORD, WILLIAM YANCEY. *Buffalo Bill Cody, Scout and Showman.* Girard, Kansas, 1944.

SHERIDAN, BRIGADIER-GENERAL MICHAEL V. *Personal Memoirs of Philip Henry Sheridan.* (2 Vols.) New York, 1902.

THOMAS, CHAUNCEY. "Buffalo Bill's Last Interview," *Outdoor Life.* May 1917, p. 487.

VESTAL, STANLEY. *Dodge City: Queen of Cowtowns.* New York, 1951.

VISSCHER, WILLIAM LIGHTFOOT. *The Thrilling and Truthful History of the Pony Express.* Chicago, 1908.

WAGNER, DOROTHY. "Buffalo Bill, Showman," *Palimpsest.* 1930, Vol. 11, p. 522-540.

WALSH, RICHARD JOHN (in collaboration with SALSBURY, MILTON S.) *The Making of Buffalo Bill: A Study in Heroics.* Indianapolis, 1928.

WETMORE, HELEN CODY. *Last of the Great Scouts.* New York, 1899.

WILLSON, WINGROVE. *Buffalo Bill, Chief of Scouts.* London, 1925.

INDEX

(Since the name and activities of William F. Cody—Buffalo Bill—occur on practically every page of this chronologically arranged biography, a detailed breakdown is not furnished in this index.)

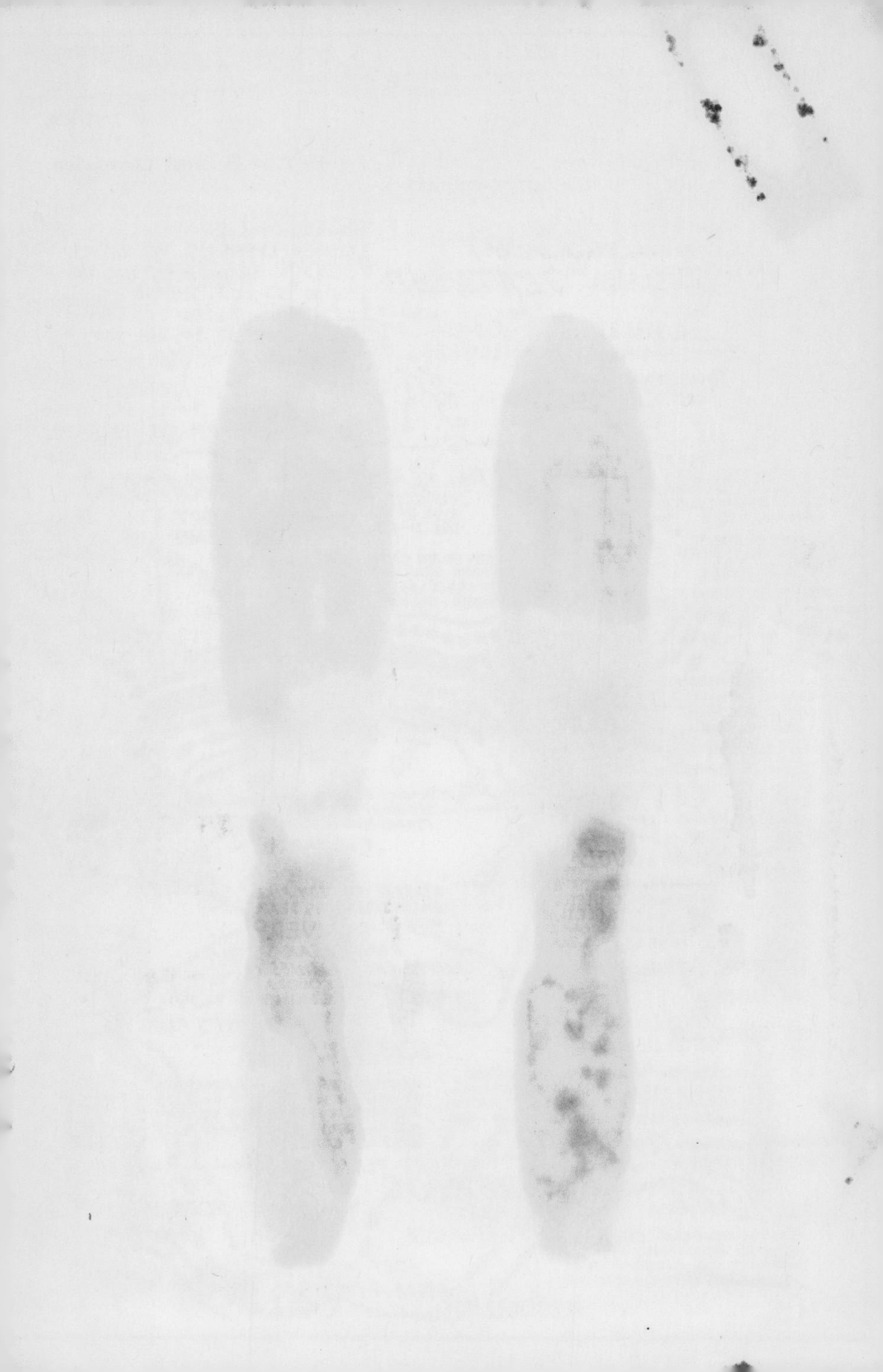

2/7/56

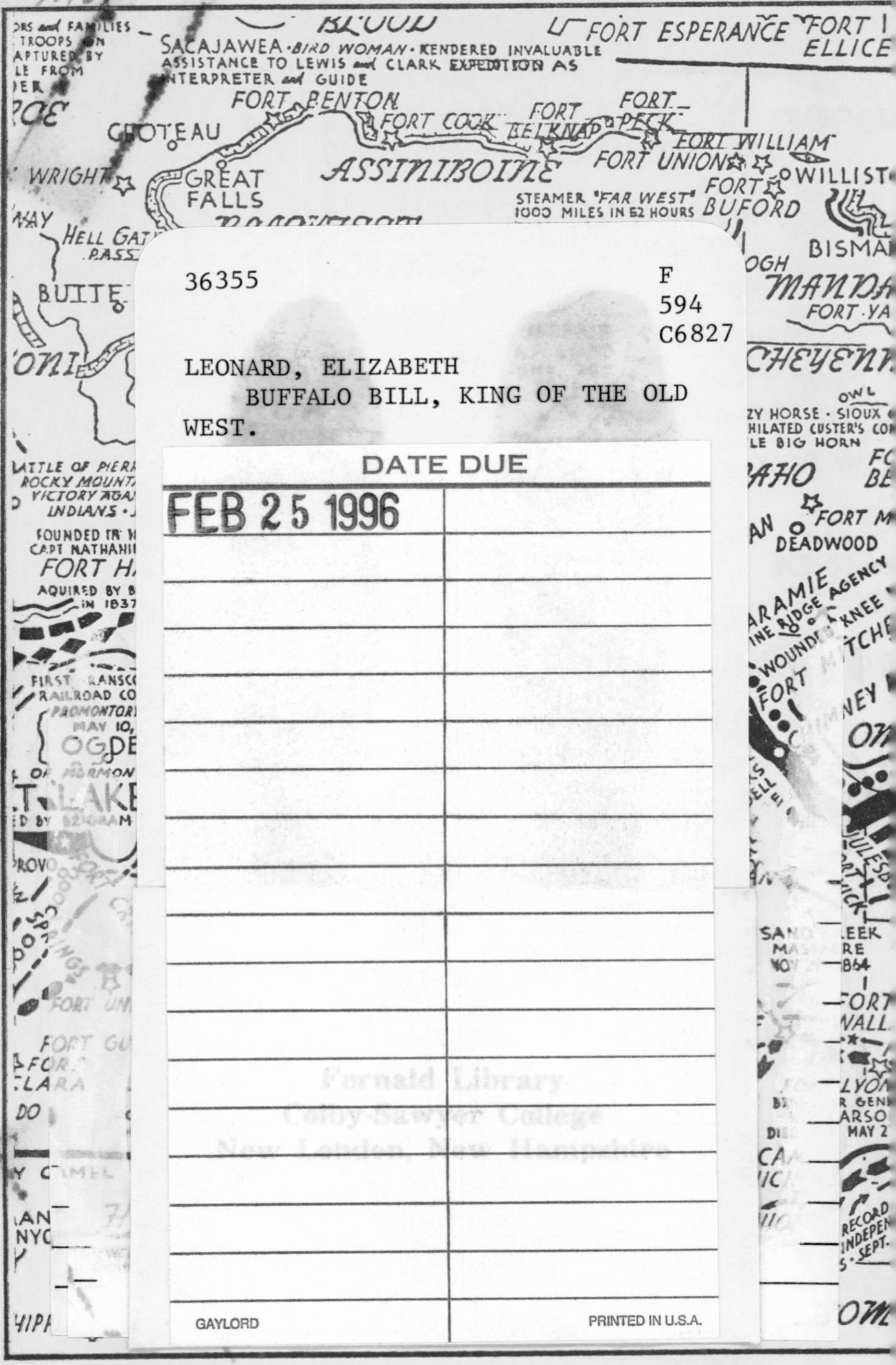

SACAJAWEA · BIRD WOMAN · RENDERED INVALUABLE ASSISTANCE TO LEWIS and CLARK EXPEDITION AS INTERPRETER and GUIDE
FORT ESPERANCE
FORT BENTON
FORT COOK
FORT BELKNAP
FORT PECK
FORT WILLIAM
CHOTEAU
ASSINIBOINE
FORT UNION
GREAT FALLS
STEAMER "FAR WEST" 1000 MILES IN 52 HOURS
FORT BUFORD
DEADWOOD